The MCSE Windows 2000 Network Infrastructure Cram Sheet

This cram sheet provides you with the distilled facts about Exam 70-216, "Implementing and Administering a Microsoft Windows 2000 Network Infrastructure." Review these important points as the last thing you do before entering the test center. Pay close attention to those you feel you need to review. A good exam strategy is to transfer all the facts you can recall from this cram sheet onto a piece of paper.

DNS/DHCP/WINS

1. DNS is a distributed database that maps domain names to IP addresses.
2. Caching-only servers do not maintain any zone information. They resolve names on behalf of clients and cache the results. Caching-only servers are useful when network traffic needs to be reduced.
3. Primary DNS servers maintain the working copy of the zone database file; the secondary DNS servers maintain a replica.
4. BIND 4.9.6 supports SRV records. BIND 8.1.3 supports dynamic updates.
5. Three zone types are supported: standard primary, standard secondary, and Active Directory–integrated.
6. When configuring zones, use the Name Servers tab and Zone Transfers tab to limit which servers can receive DNS updates and transfers.
7. DNS supports dynamic updates so clients can dynamically register and update their own resource records. By default, Windows 2000 clients register the A record and the DHCP server registers the PTR record. Secure updates can also be configured so only those clients with permission to the zone file can perform updates.
8. Using delegation, administrators can divide a namespace among multiple zones.
9. Dynamic Host Configuration Protocol (DHCP) is used to dynamically assign IP addresses and other parameters to DHCP clients.
10. Every DHCP server requires a scope. For fault tolerance, use the 80/20 rule with multiple DHCP servers. Scopes must not overlap because DHCP servers do not share scope information.
11. Superscopes enable a DHCP server to assign IP addresses from multiple scopes to DHCP clients on one physical network. Multicast scopes enable messages to be sent to a group of computers.
12. DHCP can be integrated with DNS. DHCP can update the resource records on behalf of DHCP clients and those clients that do not support dynamic update.
13. DHCP server must be authorized within Active Directory before it can lease IP addresses to DHCP clients. To authorize a DHCP server, you must be a member of the Enterprise Admins group.

CERTIFICATE SERVICES

1. Digital certificates bind a public key to a specific identity. Certificate authorities are responsible for issuing digital certificates.
2. There are four types of CAs: Enterprise Root CA, Enterprise Subordinate CA, Standalone Root CA, and Standalone Subordinate CA.
3. If Active Directory is not available, use a Standalone CA.
4. CAs can be organized into a hierarchical structure. This distributes the load of issuing certificates so that CAs can be implemented for different tasks.
5. If you are providing services to Internet clients, use a third-party CA.
6. Certificates that are revoked will appear on the certificate revocation list. The CRL is published once a week by default.
7. The capability to encrypt files can be removed by deleting the Encrypting Data Recovery Agent container and initializing the empty policy.

6. Windows 2000 supports two types of encryption: MPPE and IPSec.
7. VPNs are created using a tunneling protocol. A tunnel can be established using either PPTP or L2TP.

IP ROUTING

1. Routing can be configured within the Routing and Remote Access snap-in.
2. Static routing is good for small networks in which the topology does not often change.
3. Use the `Route` command to add static entries to the routing table. To add persistent routes use the `-p` parameter with the command.
4. RIP routers periodically send their entire routing table to other routers. RIP causes an increase in network traffic. Routing is based on hop counts.
5. OSPF routers only transmit updates. Routing is based on metrics.

ICS/NAT

1. NAT allows you to use a private IP addressing scheme on the local area network while still providing Internet access. A single connection is shared between multiple hosts.
2. The server running NAT will receive Internet requests, replace the header info, store the information in a mapping table, and forward the request to the Internet. The request is returned to the appropriate client using the information in the mapping table.
3. ICS is similar to NAT and is designed for small office or home networks. It assigns a client on the internal network an IP address from a preconfigured range.

14. WINS is used to map NetBIOS names to IP addresses.
15. Static mappings can be created for those clients that are unable to register with a WINS server.
16. A WINS proxy enables name resolution in a routed network. A WINS proxy listens for name resolution broadcasts and forwards the messages to a WINS server. You can enable the WINS proxy through the Registry.
17. WINS replication should be configured to facilitate browsing between subnets and for fault tolerance. WINS server can be configured as push and/or pull replication partners. Pull partners should be configured for WINS servers connected by slow links. Push partners should be configured when the WINS servers are connected by fast links.
18. The default resolution type for Windows 2000 DHCP clients is H-node.
19. Resolution occurs in the following order for WINS clients:
    - NetBIOS Name Cache
    - WINS
    - Broadcast
    - LMHOSTS
    - HOSTS
    - DNS
20. Using the LMHOSTS file is an alternative to using a WINS server, but the file must be configured on each client.

PROTOCOLS

1. TCP/IP is automatically installed with Windows 2000 when a network adapter is detected.
2. IP addresses can be assigned dynamically using a DHCP server or assigned statically.
3. Clients use automatic private IP addressing if they are enabled for DHCP but no DHCP server is available. DHCP clients will assign themselves an IP address in the range of 169.254.0.1–169.254.255.254.
4. Windows 2000 supports the NWLink protocol, which is Microsoft's version of Novell's IPX/SPX protocol. NWLink is not installed by default, but can be added through the Network and Dial-up connections applet.
5. The frame type defines how data is formatted. If only multiple frame types are detected on the network, autodetect defaults to 802.2. Netware servers 3.3 and later use 802.2. Netware servers earlier than 3.3 use the 802.3 frame type.
6. Network bindings determine the protocols and services available for a network adapter as well as the order in which they are used.
7. IP packet filters control the type of inbound traffic that is allowed to enter a computer and/or network. IP traffic can be filtered by protocol and by destination port number.
8. Network Monitor can be used to capture and analyze network traffic.
9. IPSec is used to protect data sent between two hosts on a network.
10. IPSec supports two modes: tunneling mode and transport mode. In tunneling mode, only the IP header is encrypted.

REMOTE ACCESS

1. Remote access allows users to dial into a server and access the network as though they were physically connected to it.
2. DCHP relay agent enables DHCP clients to obtain an IP address from a DHCP server on the network when they dial in. A DHCP relay agent can also be used to assign IP addresses to Unix clients and clients on other subnets.
3. Remote Access Policies determine who has permissions to dial in and the characteristics of the connection. Remote Access Policies consist of conditions, permissions, and profiles.
4. Multilink enables multiple phone lines to be combined into a single logical connection to increase available bandwidth.
5. The following protocols can be used for authentication: PAP, SPAP, CHAP, MSCHAP, and EAP.

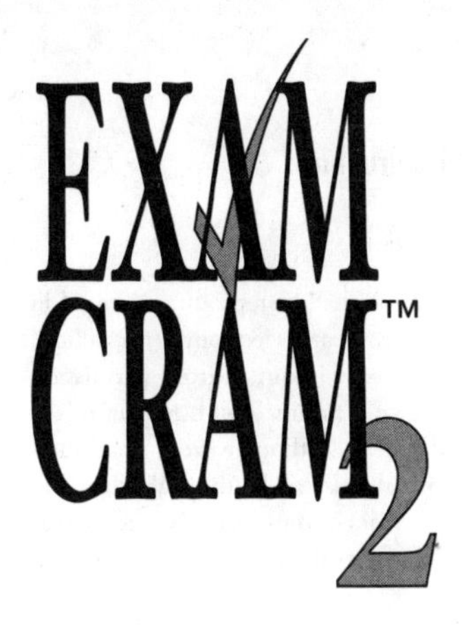

Windows® 2000 Network Infrastructure

Diana Huggins

Windows® 2000 Network Infrastructure: Exam Cram 2 (Exam 70-216)

International Standard Book Number: 0-7897-2863-x

Library of Congress Catalog Card Number: 2003100813

Printed in the United States of America

First Printing: March 2003

06 05 04 03 4 3 2 1

Trademarks

All terms mentioned in this book that are known to be trademarks or service marks have been appropriately capitalized. Que Certification cannot attest to the accuracy of this information. Use of a term in this book should not be regarded as affecting the validity of any trademark or service mark.

Windows is a registered trademark of Microsoft Corporation.

Microsoft is a registered trademark of Microsoft Corporation.

Warning and Disclaimer

Every effort has been made to make this book as complete and as accurate as possible, but no warranty or fitness is implied. The information provided is on an "as is" basis. The author and the publisher shall have neither liability nor responsibility to any person or entity with respect to any loss or damages arising from the information contained in this book or from the use of the CD or programs accompanying it.

Publisher
Paul Boger

Executive Editor
Jeff Riley

Development Editor
Steve Rowe

Managing Editor
Charlotte Clapp

Project Editor
Tonya Simpson

Copy Editor
Kezia Endsley

Indexer
Mandie Frank

Proofreader
Linda Seifert

Technical Editors
Marc Savage
Jeff Dunkelberger

Team Coordinator
Pamalee Nelsen

Multimedia Developer
Dan Scherf

Interior Designer
Gary Adair

Que Certification • 201 West 103rd Street • Indianapolis, Indiana 46290

A Note from Series Editor Ed Tittel

You know better than to trust your certification preparation to just anybody. That's why you, and more than two million others, have purchased an Exam Cram book. As Series Editor for the new and improved Exam Cram 2 series, I have worked with the staff at Que Certification to ensure you won't be disappointed. That's why we've taken the world's best-selling certification product—a finalist for "Best Study Guide" in a CertCities reader poll in 2002—and made it even better.

As a "Favorite Study Guide Author" finalist in a 2002 poll of CertCities readers, I know the value of good books. You'll be impressed with Que Certification's stringent review process, which ensures the books are high-quality, relevant, and technically accurate. Rest assured that at least a dozen industry experts—including the panel of certification experts at CramSession—have reviewed this material, helping us deliver an excellent solution to your exam preparation needs.

We've also added a preview edition of PrepLogic's powerful, full-featured test engine, which is trusted by certification students throughout the world.

As a 20-year-plus veteran of the computing industry and the original creator and editor of the Exam Cram series, I've brought my IT experience to bear on these books. During my tenure at Novell from 1989 to 1994, I worked with and around its excellent education and certification department. This experience helped push my writing and teaching activities heavily in the certification direction. Since then, I've worked on more than 70 certification-related books, and I write about certification topics for numerous Web sites and for *Certification* magazine.

In 1996, while studying for various MCP exams, I became frustrated with the huge, unwieldy study guides that were the only preparation tools available. As an experienced IT professional and former instructor, I wanted "nothing but the facts" necessary to prepare for the exams. From this impetus, Exam Cram emerged in 1997. It quickly became the best-selling computer book series since "*...For Dummies*," and the best-selling certification book series ever. By maintaining an intense focus on subject matter, tracking errata and updates quickly, and following the certification market closely, Exam Cram was able to establish the dominant position in cert prep books.

You will not be disappointed in your decision to purchase this book. If you are, please contact me at etittel@jump.net. All suggestions, ideas, input, or constructive criticism are welcome!

Ed Tittel

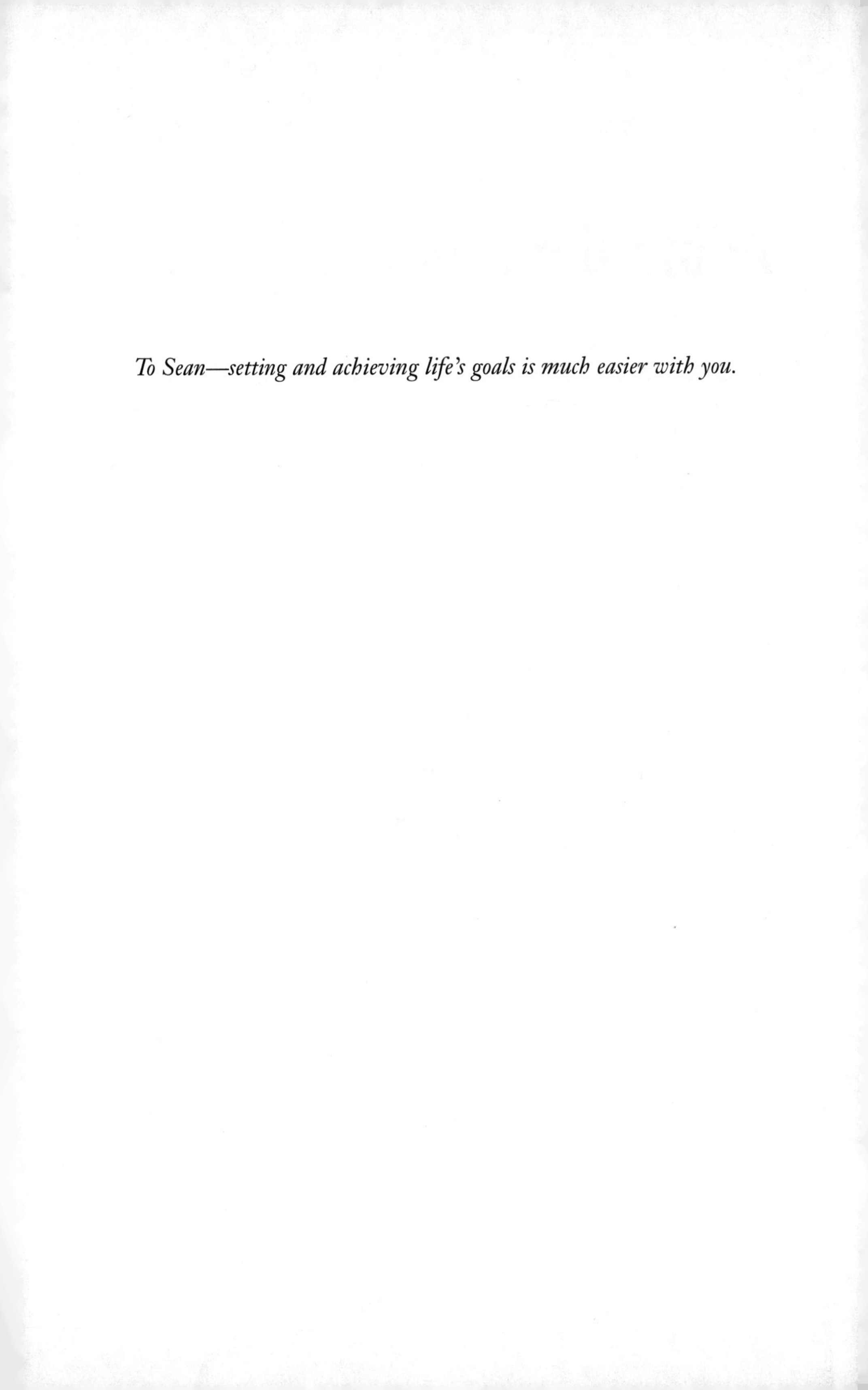

To Sean—setting and achieving life's goals is much easier with you.

About the Author

Diana Huggins is currently an independent contractor providing both technical writing and consulting services. Prior to this, she worked as a senior systems consultant. Some of the projects she worked on include a security review of Microsoft's official curriculum, content development for private companies, as well as network infrastructure design and implementation projects.

Diana's main focus over the past few years has been on writing certification study guides. To complement her efforts, she also spends a portion of her time consulting for small- to medium-sized companies in a variety of areas and continues to work as an independent technical trainer.

Diana currently has her Microsoft Certified Systems Engineer (MCSE) and Microsoft Certified Trainer (MCT), along with several other certifications from different vendors. Although her focus is on the Information Technology industry, she also holds a bachelor's degree in education. Diana runs her own company, DKB Consulting Services. The main focus of the company is on developing certification training courseware and online practice exams, as well as content delivery.

Acknowledgments

First and foremost, I'd like to thank my son for being so patient when "mommy" says she has a few more pages to go and thank my Dad for helping out while I do finish them.

Thanks to Dawn Rader, managing editor, for her assistance and dedication in keeping the project up-to-date and on track, as well as for her flexibility and understanding with the tight deadlines.

Last but not least, a big thanks to Que Publishing for recognizing the value of the *Exam Cram* series as an exam-preparation tool and allowing it to continue with the *Exam Cram 2* series.

We Want to Hear from You!

As the reader of this book, *you* are our most important critic and commentator. We value your opinion and want to know what we're doing right, what we could do better, what areas you'd like to see us publish in, and any other words of wisdom you're willing to pass our way.

As an executive editor for Que, I welcome your comments. You can email or write me directly to let me know what you did or didn't like about this book—as well as what we can do to make our books better.

Please note that I cannot help you with technical problems related to the *topic* of this book. We do have a User Services group, however, where I will forward specific technical questions related to the book.

When you write, please be sure to include this book's title and author as well as your name, email address, and phone number. I will carefully review your comments and share them with the author and editors who worked on the book.

Email: `feedback@quepublishing.com`

Mail: Jeff Riley
Que Certification
201 West 103rd Street
Indianapolis, IN 46290 USA

For more information about this book or another Que title, visit our Web site at `www.quepublishing.com`. Type the ISBN (excluding hyphens) or the title of a book in the Search field to find the page you're looking for.

Contents at a Glance

Table of Contents

Introduction

Welcome to the *Exam Cram 2* series. The purpose of this book is to prepare you to take Microsoft certification exam 70-216, "Implementing and Administering a Microsoft Windows 2000 Network Infrastructure."

Books in the *Exam Cram 2* series are designed to help you understand the material you will encounter on the exam. The purpose is to cover the topics you are likely to encounter on the exam; these books do not teach you everything you need to know about a topic. The book contains as much information as possible about the exam.

The book begins by providing useful information about how to prepare for the exam and what to expect on test day. To begin, we recommend that you take the self-assessment included in the book. It will help you to evaluate your current knowledge base against what is required for an MCSE candidate. This helps you determine where your training should begin, which might be some classroom training or reading one of the several study guides available.

It is also strongly recommended that you gain some hands-on experience with the technologies being covered on the exam. Again, this might be through some classroom training or by installing and configuring the software on a home system. In any case, nothing beats hands-on experience when it comes to learning essential exam topics.

When you pass 70-216, you receive the status of Microsoft Certified Professional and demonstrate your efficiency and knowledge on the exam topics. Passing this exam can also earn you credit toward the following certifications:

- *Microsoft Certified Systems Engineer (MCSE)*—This is one of the core exams required to obtain MCSE status.
- *Microsoft Certified Database Administrator (MCDBA)*—This exam can be used as one of the electives for the MCDBA certification.
- *Microsoft Certified Systems Administrator (MCSA)*—This exam can be used as one of the electives required to achieve MCSA status.

Taking a Certification Exam

After you've fully prepared for an exam and feel that you're ready for the next step, you need to register with a testing center to take the exam. To do so, contact either Prometric or Virtual University Enterprise using the following information:

- *Prometric*—You can register for an exam online at `www.prometric.com`. You also can register by phone at 1-800-775-3926 (within the United States and Canada). If you're outside these two countries, call 1-410-843-8000.
- *Virtual University Enterprise (VUE)*—You can register online at `www.vue.com` or call a local testing center. You can find a local testing center on the Web site.

You can register for an exam by contacting either of the parties just listed. You must register at least one day in advance and any cancellations must be made by 7 A.M. the day before you are scheduled to take the test.

To make the registration process go smoother, be sure you have the following information handy. You are required to provide the following during the registration process:

- Your name, organization, and mailing address.
- Microsoft Test I.D. In the United States, this is your Social Security number. For those in Canada, this is your Social Insurance number.
- The specific number of the exam you want to take.
- A method of payment. Credit card is usually the easiest method, although you can make other arrangements.

At this point, you will be given the date, time, and location of your exam.

Arriving at the Exam Site

It is generally a good idea to arrive at the exam site at least 15 minutes before you are scheduled to take the test. Be sure you bring two pieces of identification with you, one of which must be a photo I.D., such as a driver's license. You must show the identification when you sign in.

In the Exam Room

Granted, you cannot mimic the pressures and environment of actually being in the exam room with a live exam in front of you. However, this section tries to describe what being in the room is like.

After you've signed in for the exam, you're directed into a testing room. You aren't permitted to take anything into the testing room with you. You're given a few blank pieces of paper and a pen upon entering the room. This is where the facts on the Cram Sheet can be very handy. If you read over the distilled facts prior to the exam, this is a good time to write down as many of them as you can remember.

When you complete the exam, your score is tabulated and you will know immediately whether you passed or failed. If you need to retake the exam, you must contact VUE or Prometric to schedule a new test (and, unfortunately, this also means paying the price of another exam).

If you fail an exam, you can retake the test as soon as you are ready. If you fail the same exam a second time, you must wait at least 14 days before you can reschedule.

How to Prepare for an Exam

All Microsoft exams have a set of objectives outlining the topics you need to understand to achieve exam success. This is a good place to start to determine the topics covered. You can then determine which ones you need to obtain study material for.

An abundance of resources available both online and in print can be used to prepare for an exam. Microsoft's Web site is a good source of information pertaining to both the exam itself and for in-depth coverage of exam topics. Due to the popularity of the MCSE certification, there are also a number of printed study guides and online resources. Some of the resources you might find useful include

- The Windows 2000 product CD. One of the best resources you can use when preparing for an exam is the help included with the operating system. It usually covers different aspects of all the technologies included with the operating system.
- The Microsoft Training and Certification Web site at `http://www.microsoft.com/traincert/default.asp` provides links to exam resources and describes how an individual should prepare for an exam.

- The InformIT Web site at `http://www.informit.com/examcram2/index.asp` provides an abundance of information about certification exams and how to prepare for them.
- Microsoft training kits. Microsoft Press publishes study guides for the different certification exams, including exam 70-216. You can find more information about the training kit at `http://www.mspress.microsoft.com/findabook/list/series_ak.htm`.
- *Microsoft TechNet.* This monthly publication provides information on the latest technologies and topics, some of which pertain to the exam topics covered in 70-216.
- Classroom training. For those who can afford the price of classroom training, many companies offer courses designed for preparing students to pass the exam.
- The *Exam Cram 2* series. The *Exam Cram 2s* have always been a popular resource for exam preparation.

Notes on This Book's Organization

This section highlights all the different elements and pieces found in your *Exam Cram 2*. Items such as exam alerts, tips, notes, and practice questions are explained here:

- *Terms You'll Need to Know*—Each chapter begins with a list of terms you must learn and understand in order to fully grasp the content being covered; each of these terms is defined in the glossary.
- *Techniques You'll Need to Master*—Following the important terms is a list of concepts/tools/techniques you must understand before attempting to challenge the exam.
- *Chapter content*—The introductory paragraph alerts you to the topics covered throughout the chapter. Following this, a number of topics relating to the chapter title will be covered in detail.
- *Exam Alerts*—Concepts and topics that are likely to appear on the exam are highlighted in a special layout known as an Exam Alert. An Exam Alert appears within the chapter content like this:

Exam Alerts are included in each chapter to point your attention to a particular concept or topic that you are more than likely to encounter on the exam. So, as you are working through the chapter, be sure you pay close attention to the topics addressed in the alerts. Exam Alerts can also be a good way of refreshing yourself with important information right before taking the exam, although the information is usually included in the Cram Sheet.

This is not to say that the general content within a chapter is not important. The Exam Alerts are there to flag the information that is more certain to appear in some scenario format.

- *Tips and Notes*—Throughout a chapter you might also find side tips and notes. The layout and purpose of each is as follows:

Tips are designed to give you some added piece of information pertaining to a topic being covered, such as an alternative or more efficient way of performing a certain task.

Notes are designed to alert you to a piece of information related to the topic being discussed.

- *Practice questions and answers*—The end of each chapter has a series of 10 questions designed to test your understanding of the topics covered throughout the chapter. Detailed explanations are provided for each of the 10 questions explaining both the correct and incorrect answers.
- *Need to Know More?*—Each chapter ends with a listing of additional resources offering more details about the chapter topics.

Other elements of the book worth mentioning are the Sample Tests and Answer Keys found in Chapters 10 through 13. These questions cover all the topics covered throughout the book. The questions can be used for review purposes and to determine your exam readiness.

In addition to this, you'll also find a glossary of key terms used throughout the book and the appendixes listing additional resources that you might find valuable.

Last but not least, be sure to utilize the Cram Sheet included with the book. The Cram Sheet distills all the important facts and topics and summarizes them in a few short pages. These are the facts that we feel should be memorized for the test. The Cram Sheet is the last thing you should review before going into the test. And once you enter the test room, the first thing you should do is transfer all the facts to paper.

How This Book Helps You

The topics in this book have been structured around the objectives outlined by Microsoft for exam 70-216. This ensures you are familiar with the topics you'll encounter on the exam.

Some of the topics covered later in the book might require an understanding of topics covered in earlier chapters. Therefore, it's recommended that you initially read the book from start to finish. When it comes time to brushing up or reviewing certain topics, you can always use the index to go directly to specific sections while omitting others.

In preparing for exam 70-216, we think you'll find this book a very useful reference to some of the most important topics and concepts of network infrastructure. It prepares you for the test day by outlining what you can expect. It covers all the important topics you can expect to find on the exam. Also, it provides many sample test questions to help you evaluate exam readiness and understanding of the material as well as familiarize you with the Microsoft testing format.

Self-Assessment

Based on recent statistics from Microsoft, as many as 400,000 individuals are at some stage of the certification process but haven't yet received an MCP or other Microsoft certification. We also know that three or four times that number might be considering whether to obtain a Microsoft certification of some kind. That's a huge audience!

The reason we included a self-assessment in this *Exam Cram 2* book is to help you evaluate your readiness to tackle MCSE certification. It should also help you understand what you need to know to master the topic of this book—namely, Exam 70-216, "Implementing and Administering a Microsoft Windows 2000 Network Infrastructure." But before you tackle this self-assessment, let's talk about concerns you might face when pursuing an MCSE, and what an ideal MCSE candidate looks like.

MCSEs in the Real World

The next section describes an ideal MCSE candidate, although only a few real candidates will meet this ideal. In fact, the description of that ideal candidate might seem downright scary. But take heart: Although the requirements to obtain an MCSE might seem formidable, they are by no means impossible to meet. However, be keenly aware that it takes time, involves some expense, and requires real effort to get through the process.

More than 200,000 MCSEs are already certified, so it's obviously an attainable goal. You can get all the real-world motivation you need from knowing that many others have gone before, so you will be able to follow in their footsteps. If you're willing to tackle the process seriously and do what it takes to obtain the necessary experience and knowledge, you can take—and pass—all the certification tests involved in obtaining an MCSE. In fact, we've designed the *Exam Cram 2* series of books to make it as easy on you as possible to prepare for these exams. But prepare you must!

The same, of course, is true for other Microsoft certifications, including

- MCSD, which is aimed at software developers and requires one specific exam, two more exams on client and distributed topics, plus a fourth elective exam drawn from a different, but limited, pool of options.
- MCSA, which is aimed at network administrators and requires three core exams plus one elective.
- Other Microsoft certifications, whose requirements range from one test (MCP) to several tests (MCP+SB, MCDBA).

The Ideal MCSE Candidate

Just to give you some idea of an ideal MCSE candidate, here are some relevant statistics about the background and experience such an individual might have. Don't worry if you don't meet these qualifications or don't come that close—this is a far from ideal world, and where you fall short is simply where you'll have more work to do.

- Academic or professional training in network theory, concepts, and operations. This includes everything from networking media and transmission techniques through network operating systems, services, and applications.
- Three-plus years of professional networking experience, including experience with Ethernet, token ring, modems, and other networking media. This includes installation, configuration, upgrade, and troubleshooting experience.
- Two-plus years in a networked environment that includes hands-on experience with Windows 2000 Server, Windows 2000 Professional, Windows NT Server, Windows NT Workstation, and Windows 95 or Windows 98. A solid understanding of each system's architecture, installation, configuration, maintenance, and troubleshooting is also essential.
- Knowledge of the various methods for installing Windows 2000, including manual and unattended installations.
- A thorough understanding of key networking protocols, addressing, and name resolution, including TCP/IP, IPX/SPX, and NetBEUI.
- A thorough understanding of NetBIOS naming, browsing, and file and print services.

- Familiarity with key Windows 2000-based TCP/IP-based services, including HTTP (Web servers), DHCP, WINS, and DNS, plus familiarity with one or more of the following: Internet Information Server (IIS), Index Server, and Proxy Server.
- An understanding of how to implement different connectivity models, such as remote access, IP routing, Internet connection sharing and network address translation, and virtual private networks.
- An understanding of how to implement security for key network data in a Windows 2000 environment.
- Working knowledge of NetWare 3.x and 4.x, including IPX/SPX frame formats, NetWare file, print, and directory services, and both Novell and Microsoft client software. Working knowledge of Microsoft's Client Service for NetWare (CSNW), Gateway Service for NetWare (GSNW), the NetWare Migration Tool (NWCONV), and the NetWare Client for Windows (NT, 95, and 98) is essential.

Fundamentally, this boils down to a bachelor's degree in computer science, plus three years' experience working in a position involving network design, installation, configuration, and maintenance. We believe that well under half of all certification candidates meet these requirements, and that, in fact, most meet fewer than half of these requirements—at least when they begin the certification process. But because all 200,000 people who already have been certified have survived this ordeal, you can survive it too—especially if you heed what this self-assessment tells you.

Put Yourself to the Test

The following series of questions and observations is designed to help you determine how much work you must do to pursue Microsoft certification and what kinds of resources you may consult on your quest. Be absolutely honest in your answers, or you'll end up wasting money on exams you're not yet ready to take. There are no right or wrong answers, only steps along the path to certification. Only you can decide where you really belong in the broad spectrum of aspiring candidates.

Two things should be clear from the outset, however:

- Even a modest background in computer science is helpful.
- Hands-on experience with Microsoft products and technologies is an essential ingredient to certification success.

Educational Background

1. Have you ever taken any computer-related classes? [Yes or No]

   If Yes, proceed to question 2; if No, proceed to question 4.

2. Have you taken any classes on computer operating systems? [Yes or No]

   If Yes, you will probably be able to handle Microsoft's architecture and system component discussions. If you're rusty, brush up on basic operating system concepts, especially virtual memory, multitasking regimes, user mode versus kernel mode operation, and general computer security topics.

   If No, consider some basic reading in this area. We strongly recommend a good general operating systems book, such as *Operating System Concepts, 5th Edition*, by Abraham Silberschatz and Peter Baer Galvin (John Wiley & Sons, 1998, ISBN 0-471-36414-2). If this title doesn't appeal to you, check out reviews for other, similar titles at your favorite online bookstore.

3. Have you taken any networking concepts or technologies classes? [Yes or No]

   If Yes, you will probably be able to handle Microsoft's networking terminology, concepts, and technologies (brace yourself for frequent departures from normal use). If you're rusty, brush up on basic networking concepts and terminology, especially networking media, transmission types, the OSI reference model, and networking technologies such as Ethernet, token ring, FDDI, and WAN links.

   If No, you might want to read one or two books in this area. The two best books that we know of are *Computer Networks, 3rd Edition*, by Andrew S. Tanenbaum (Prentice-Hall, 1996, ISBN 0-13-349945-6) and *Computer Networks and Internets, 2nd Edition*, by Douglas E. Comer (Prentice-Hall, 1998, ISBN 0-130-83617-6).

   Skip to the next section, "Hands-On Experience."

4. Have you done any reading on operating systems or networks? [Yes or No]

   If Yes, review the requirements stated in the first paragraphs after questions 2 and 3. If you meet those requirements, move on to the next section. If No, consult the recommended reading for both topics. A strong background will help you prepare for the Microsoft exams better than just about anything else.

Hands-On Experience

The most important key to success on all the Microsoft tests is hands-on experience, especially with Windows 2000 Server and Professional, plus the many add-on services and BackOffice components around which so many of the Microsoft certification exams revolve. If we leave you with only one realization after taking this self-assessment, it should be that there's no substitute for time spent installing, configuring, and using the various Microsoft products upon which you'll be tested repeatedly and in-depth.

5. Have you installed, configured, and worked with

    - Windows 2000 Server? [Yes or No]

      If Yes, be sure you are familiar with not only installing and configuring the operating system but also with the different services included. When studying for exam 70-216, you should pay close attention to the TCP/IP interfaces, utilities, and services.

      Some of the other services you must be very familiar with are DNS, DHCP, WINS, RRAS, and Certificate Services. The exam requires in-depth knowledge and a fair amount of experience with each one.

You can download objectives, practice exams, and other data about Microsoft exams from the Training and Certification page at **www.microsoft.com/traincert/**. Use the "Exam Resources" link to obtain specific exam info.

If you haven't worked with Windows 2000 Server, TCP/IP, and IIS (or whatever product you choose for your final elective), you must obtain one or two machines and a copy of Windows 2000 Server. Then, learn the operating system and do the same for TCP/IP and whatever other software components on which you'll also be tested.

In fact, we recommend that you obtain two computers—each with a network interface—and set up a two-node network on which to practice. With decent Windows 2000-capable computers selling for about $500 to $600 apiece these days, this shouldn't be too much of a financial hardship. You might have to scrounge to come up with the necessary software, but if you scour the Microsoft Web site, you can usually find low-cost options to obtain evaluation copies of most of the software that you'll need.

➤ Windows 2000 Professional? [Yes or No]

If Yes, be sure you understand the concepts covered in Exam 70-210.

If No, you will want to obtain a copy of Windows 2000 Professional and learn how to install, configure, and maintain it. You can use *MCSE Windows 2000 Professional Exam Cram 2* to guide your activities and studies, or work straight from Microsoft's test objectives if you prefer.

For any and all of these Microsoft exams, the resource kits for the topics involved are a good study resource. You can purchase softcover resource kits from Microsoft Press (search for them at **http://www.microsoft.com/mspress/**), but they also appear on the TechNet CDs (**www.microsoft.com/technet**). We believe that resource kits are among the best preparation tools available, along with the *Exam Cram 2* series of books.

6. For any specific Microsoft product that is not itself an operating system (for example, FrontPage 2000, SQL Server, and so on), have you installed, configured, used, and upgraded this software? [Yes or No]

   If the answer is Yes, skip to the next section. If it's No, you must get some experience. Read on for suggestions on how to do this.

   Experience is a must with any Microsoft product exam, be it something as simple as FrontPage 2000 or as challenging as Exchange Server 2000 or SQL Server 7.0. For trial copies of other software, search Microsoft's Web site using the name of the product as your search term. Also, search for bundles like "BackOffice" or "Small Business Server."

If you have the funds, or your employer will pay your way, consider taking a class at a Certified Training and Education Center (CTEC) or at an Authorized Academic Training Partner (AATP). In addition to classroom exposure to the topic of your choice, you get a copy of the software that is the focus of your course, along with a trial version of whatever operating system it needs (usually Windows 2000 Server).

Before you even think about taking any Microsoft exam, be sure you've spent enough time with the related software to understand how it's installed and configured (depending on the exam, this may be an operating system or specific services and applications), how to maintain such an installation, and how to troubleshoot that software when things go wrong. This will help you in the exam, and in real life!

Testing Your Exam Readiness

Whether you attend a formal class on a specific topic to get ready for an exam or use written materials to study on your own, some preparation for the Microsoft certification exams is essential. At $100 a try, pass or fail, you want to do everything you can to pass on your first try. That's where studying comes in.

Each chapter includes 10 practice questions. We also have included 2 practice exams covering all topics in this book, so if you don't score well on the first test, you can study more and then tackle the second test. If you still don't hit a score of at least 70 percent after these tests, you'll want to investigate the other practice test resources we mention in this section.

For any given subject, consider taking a class if you've tackled self-study materials, taken the test, and failed anyway. The opportunity to interact with an instructor and fellow students can make all the difference in the world, if you can afford that privilege. For information about Microsoft classes, visit the Training and Certification page at `www.microsoft.com/traincert/` (use the "Training Resources" link).

If you can't afford to take a class, visit the Training and Certification page anyway, because it also includes pointers to free practice exams and to Microsoft Certified Professional Approved Study Guides and other self-study tools. And even if you can't afford to spend much at all, you should still invest in some low-cost practice exams from commercial vendors.

7. Have you taken a practice exam on your chosen test subject? [Yes or No]

   If Yes, and you scored 70 percent or better, you're probably ready to tackle the real thing. If your score isn't above that threshold, keep at it until you break that barrier.

   If No, several sites on the Internet provide free sample questions. Visit as many sites as possible so you become comfortable with Microsoft's testing format. It also will give you an idea on how prepared you are.

When it comes to assessing your test readiness, there is no better way than to take a good-quality practice exam and pass with a score of 70 percent or better. When we're preparing ourselves, we shoot for 80-plus percent, just to leave room for the "weirdness factor" that sometimes shows up on Microsoft exams.

Assessing Readiness for Exam 70-216

In addition to the general exam-readiness information in the previous section, there are several things you can do to prepare for the "Implementing and Administering a Windows 2000 Network Infrastructure" exam. As you're getting ready for Exam 70-216, visit the MCSE mailing list. Sign up at `www.sunbelt-software.com` (look for the "Subscribe to" button).

Microsoft exam mavens also recommend checking the Microsoft Knowledge Base (available on its own CD as part of the TechNet collection, or on the Microsoft Web site at `http://support.microsoft.com`) for "meaningful technical support issues" that relate to your exam's topics. Although we're not sure exactly what the quoted phrase means, we have also noticed some overlap between technical support questions on particular products and troubleshooting questions on the exams for those products.

Onward, Through the Fog!

When you've assessed your readiness, undertaken the right background studies, obtained the hands-on experience that will help you understand the products and technologies at work, and reviewed the many sources of information to help you prepare for a test, you'll be ready to take a round of practice tests. When your scores come back positive enough to get you through the exam, you're ready to go after the real thing. If you follow this assessment regime, you'll not only know what you need to study, but when you're ready to make a test date at Prometric or VUE. Good luck!

Microsoft Certification Exams

Terms you'll need to understand:

✓ Case study
✓ Multiple-choice question formats
✓ Build-list-and-reorder question format
✓ Create-a-tree question format
✓ Drag-and-connect question format
✓ Select-and-place question format
✓ Fixed-length tests
✓ Simulations
✓ Adaptive tests
✓ Short-form tests

Techniques you'll need to master:

✓ Assessing your exam-readiness
✓ Answering Microsoft's varying question types
✓ Altering your test strategy depending on the exam format
✓ Practicing (to make perfect)
✓ Making the best use of the testing software
✓ Budgeting your time
✓ Guessing (as a last resort)

Introduction

Exam-taking is not something that most people anticipate eagerly, no matter how well prepared they might be. In most cases, familiarity helps offset test anxiety. In plain English, this means you probably won't be as nervous when you take your fourth or fifth Microsoft certification exam as you'll be when you take your first one.

Whether it's your first exam or your tenth, understanding the details of taking the new exam (how much time to spend on questions, the environment you'll be in, and so on) and the new exam software will help you concentrate on the material rather than on the setting. Likewise, mastering a few basic exam-taking skills should help you recognize (and perhaps even outfox) some of the tricks and snares you're bound to find in some exam questions.

This chapter explains the exam environment and software and describes some proven exam-taking strategies that you can use to your advantage.

Assessing Exam Readiness

I strongly recommend that you read through and take the self-assessment included with this book (it appears just before this chapter). It can help you compare your knowledge base to the requirements for obtaining an MCSE or MCSA, and it also can help you identify parts of your background or experience that might need improvement, enhancement, or further learning. If you get the right set of basics under your belt, obtaining Microsoft certification will be that much easier.

After you've gone through the self-assessment, you can remedy those topical areas in which your background or experience might be lacking. You also can tackle subject matter for individual tests at the same time, so you can continue making progress while you're catching up in some areas.

After you've worked through an *Exam Cram 2*, have read the supplementary materials, and have taken the practice test, you'll have a pretty clear idea of when you should be ready to take the real exam. Although I strongly recommend that you keep practicing until your scores top the 75 percent mark, 80–85 percent is a better goal because it gives you some margin for error when you are in an actual, stressful exam situation. Keep taking practice tests and studying the materials until you attain that score. You'll find more pointers on how to study and prepare in the self-assessment. But now, on to the exam itself.

What to Expect at the Testing Center

When you arrive at the testing center where you scheduled your exam, you must sign in with an exam coordinator and show two forms of identification, one of which must be a photo ID. After you've signed in and your time slot arrives, you'll be asked to deposit any books, bags, cell phones, or other items you brought with you. Then, you'll be escorted into a closed room.

All exams are completely closed book. Although you are not permitted to take anything with you into the testing area, you are furnished with a blank sheet of paper and a pen (in some cases, an erasable plastic sheet and an erasable pen). Immediately before entering the testing center, try to memorize as much of the important material as you can, so you can write that information on the blank sheet as soon as you are seated in front of the computer. You can refer to this piece of paper during the test, but you'll have to surrender the sheet when you leave the room. Because your timer does not start until you begin the testing process, it is best to do this first while the information is still fresh in your mind.

You will have some time to compose yourself, write down information on the paper you're given, and take a sample orientation exam before you begin the real thing. I suggest you take the orientation test before taking your first exam (because the exams are generally identical in layout, behavior, and controls, you probably won't need to do this more than once).

Typically, the room has one to six computers, and each workstation is separated from the others by dividers. Most test rooms feature a wall with a large picture window. This permits the exam coordinator to monitor the room, prevent exam-takers from talking to one another, and observe anything out of the ordinary. The exam coordinator will have preloaded the appropriate Microsoft certification exam (for this book, Exam 70-216), and you'll be permitted to start as soon as you're seated in front of the computer.

All Microsoft certification exams allow a certain maximum amount of time in which to complete your work (this time is indicated on the exam by an on-screen counter/clock, so you can check the time remaining whenever you like). All Microsoft certification exams are computer-generated. In addition to multiple choice, you'll encounter select and place (drag and drop), create a tree (categorization and prioritization), drag and connect, and build list and reorder (list prioritization) on most exams. The questions are constructed to check your mastery of basic facts and figures about Microsoft Windows 2000 Network Administration and to require you to evaluate one or more sets of circumstances or requirements. Often, you'll be asked to give more than one answer to a question. You also might be asked to select the best or most effective solution to a problem from a range of choices, all of which are technically correct. Taking the exam is quite an adventure, and it involves real thinking. This book shows you what to expect and how to deal with the potential problems, puzzles, and predicaments.

In the next section, you learn more about the format of Microsoft test questions and how to answer them.

Exam Layout and Design: New Case Study Format

The format of Microsoft exams can vary. For example, many exams consist of a series of case studies, with six types of questions regarding each presented case. Other exams might have the same six types of questions but no complex multi-question case studies.

For the Design exams, each case study presents a detailed problem that you must read and analyze. Figure 1.1 shows an example of a case study. You must select the different tabs in the case study to view the entire case.

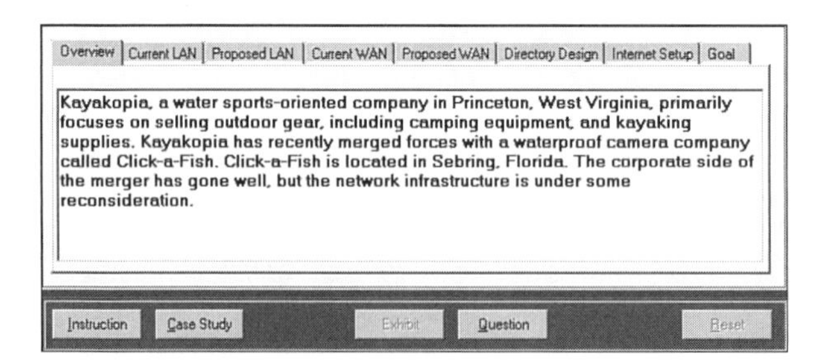

Figure 1.1 This is a typical case study.

Following each case study is a set of related questions. These questions can be one of six types (which are discussed next). Careful attention to details provided in the case study is the key to success. Be prepared to toggle frequently between the case study and the questions as you work. Some of the case studies also include diagrams (called *exhibits*) that you'll need to examine closely to understand how to answer the questions.

After you complete a case study, you can review all the questions and your answers. However, when you move on to the next case study, you cannot return to the previous case study and make any changes.

Following are the six types of question formats:

- Multiple choice, single answer
- Multiple choice, multiple answers
- Build list and reorder (list prioritization)
- Create a tree
- Drag and connect
- Select and place (drag and drop)

Exam formats can vary by test center location. You might want to call the test center to determine whether you can find out which type of test you'll encounter. Some exams will be offered in both forms on a random basis that cannot be predetermined.

Multiple-Choice Question Format

Some exam questions require you to select a single answer, whereas others ask you to select multiple correct answers. The following multiple-choice question requires you to select a single correct answer. Following the question is a brief summary of each potential answer and why it is either right or wrong.

Question 1

You have three domains connected to an empty root domain under one contiguous domain name: **tutu.com**. This organization is formed into a forest arrangement with a secondary domain called **frog.com**. How many Schema Masters exist for this arrangement?

❍ A. 1

❍ B. 2

❍ C. 3

❍ D. 4

The correct answer is A, because only one Schema Master is necessary for a forest arrangement. The other answers (B, C, and D) are misleading because you are led to believe that Schema Masters may be in each domain, or that you should have one for each contiguous domain namespace.

This sample question format corresponds closely to the Microsoft Certification Exam format (of course, questions are not followed by answer keys on the exam). To select an answer, you position the cursor over the radio button next to the answer and click the mouse button to select the answer.

Let's examine a question where one or more answers are possible. This type of question provides check boxes rather than radio buttons for marking all appropriate selections.

Question 2

How can you seize FSMO roles? [Check all correct answers.]

- ❑ A. The **ntdsutil.exe** utility
- ❑ B. The Replication Monitor
- ❑ C. The **secedit.exe** utility
- ❑ D. Active Directory Domains and FSMOs

Answers A and B are correct. You can seize FSMO roles from a server that is still running through the Replication Monitor, or in the case of a server failure, you can seize roles with the `ntdsutil.exe` utility. The `secedit.exe` utility is used to force group policies into play; therefore, answer C is incorrect. Active Directory Domains and FSMOs are a combination of truth and fiction; therefore, answer D is incorrect.

For this particular question, two answers are required. Microsoft sometimes gives partial credit for partially correct answers. For Question 2, you have to check the boxes next to answers A and B to obtain credit for a correct answer. Notice that picking the right answers also means knowing why the other answers are wrong.

Build-List-and-Reorder Question Format

Questions in the build-list-and-reorder format present two lists of items: one on the left and one on the right. To answer the question, you must move items from the list on the right to the list on the left. The final list must then be placed into a specific order.

These questions are usually in the form, "From the following list of choices, pick the choices that answer the question. Arrange the list in a certain order." To give you practice with this type of question, some questions of this type are included in this study guide. Here's an example of how they appear in this book; for a sample of how they appear on the test, see Figure 1.2.

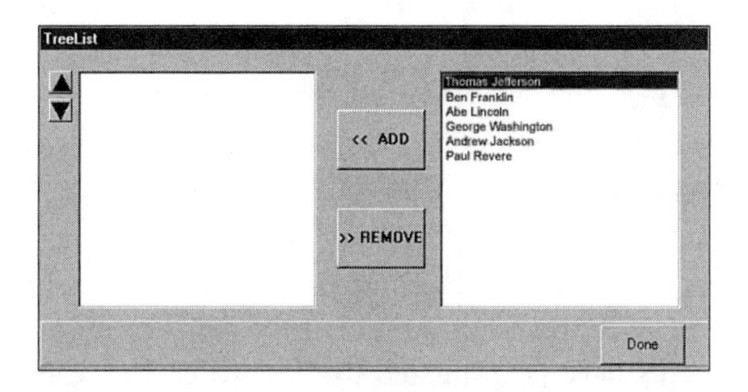

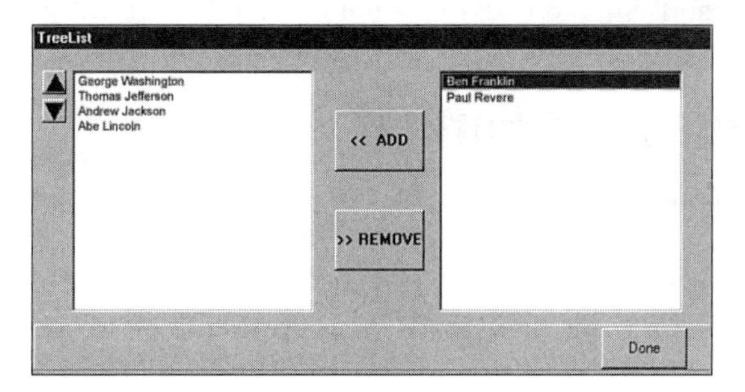

Figure 1.2 This is how build-list-and-reorder questions appear.

Question 3

From the following list of famous people, pick those that have been elected President of the United States. Arrange the list in the order in which they served.

Thomas Jefferson

Ben Franklin

Abe Lincoln

George Washington

Andrew Jackson

Paul Revere

The correct answer is:

George Washington

Thomas Jefferson

Andrew Jackson

Abe Lincoln

On an actual exam, the entire list of famous people would initially appear in the list on the right. You would move the four correct answers to the list on the left and then reorder the list on the left. Notice that the answer to the question did not include all items from the initial list. However, this might not always be the case.

To move an item from the right list to the left list, first select the item by clicking it, and then click the Add button (left arrow). After you move an item from one list to the other, you can move the item back by first selecting the item and then clicking the appropriate button (either the Add button or the Remove button). After items have been moved to the left list, you can reorder the list by selecting an item and clicking the up or down button.

Create-a-Tree Question Format

Questions in the create-a-tree format also present two lists: one on the left and one on the right. The list on the right consists of individual items, and the list on the left consists of nodes in a tree. To answer the question, you must move items from the list on the right to the appropriate node in the tree.

These questions are basically a matching exercise. Items from the list on the right are placed under the appropriate category in the list on the left. Here's an example of how they appear in this book; for a sample of how they appear on the test, see Figure 1.3.

Question 4

The calendar year is divided into four seasons:

Winter

Spring

Summer

Fall

Identify the season during which each of the following holidays occurs:

Christmas

Fourth of July

Labor Day

Flag Day

Memorial Day

Washington's Birthday

Thanksgiving

Easter

The correct answer is:

Winter

Christmas

Washington's Birthday

Spring

Flag Day

Memorial Day

Easter

Summer

Fourth of July

Labor Day

Fall

Thanksgiving

In this case, all the items in the list were used. However, this might not always be the case.

To move an item from the right list to its appropriate location in the tree, you must first select the appropriate tree node by clicking it. Then, you select the item to be moved and click the Add button. If one or more items have been added to a tree node, the node is displayed with a "+" icon to the left of the node name. You can click this icon to expand the node and view whatever was added. If any item has been added to the wrong tree node, you can remove it by selecting it and clicking the Remove button (see Figure 1.3).

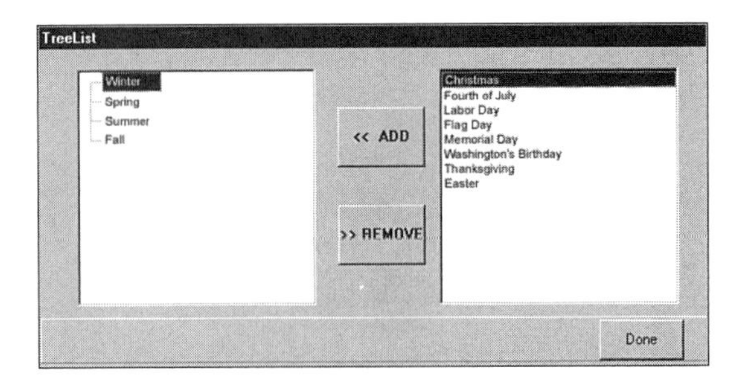

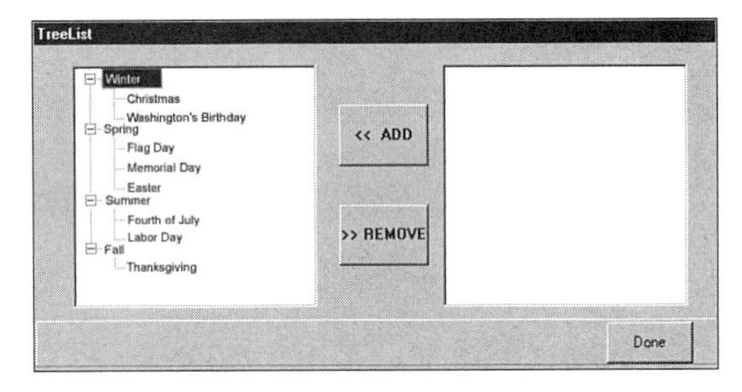

Figure 1.3 This is how create-a-tree questions appear.

Drag-and-Connect Question Format

Questions in the drag-and-connect format present a group of objects and a list of "connections." To answer the question, you must move the appropriate connections between the objects.

This type of question is best described using graphics. Here's an example.

Question 5

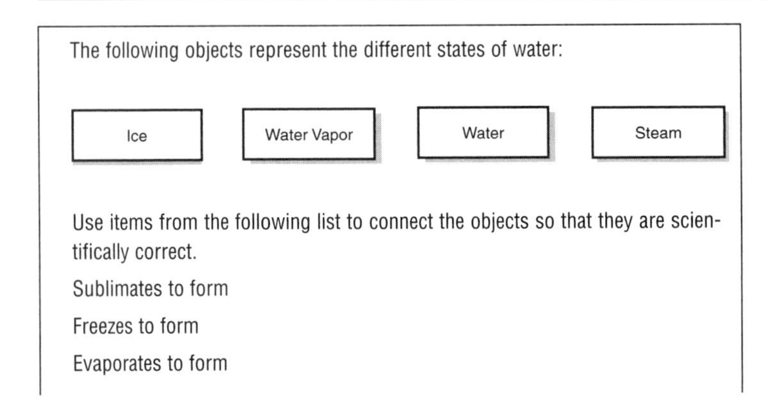

Boils to form
Condenses to form
Melts to form

The correct answer is:

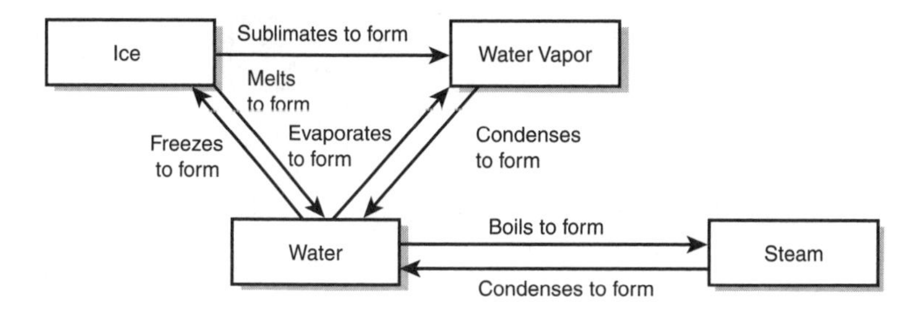

For this type of question, it's not necessary to use every object, but each connection can be used multiple times by dragging the answer to multiple locations. Dragging an answer away from its position removes it.

Select-and-Place Question Format

Questions in the select-and-place (drag-and-drop) format present a diagram with blank boxes and a list of labels that must be dragged to fill in the blank boxes. To answer the question, you must move the labels to their appropriate positions on the diagram.

This type of question is best described using graphics. Here's an example.

Question 6

Place the items in their proper order, by number, on the following flowchart. Some items may be used more than once, and some items may not be used at all.

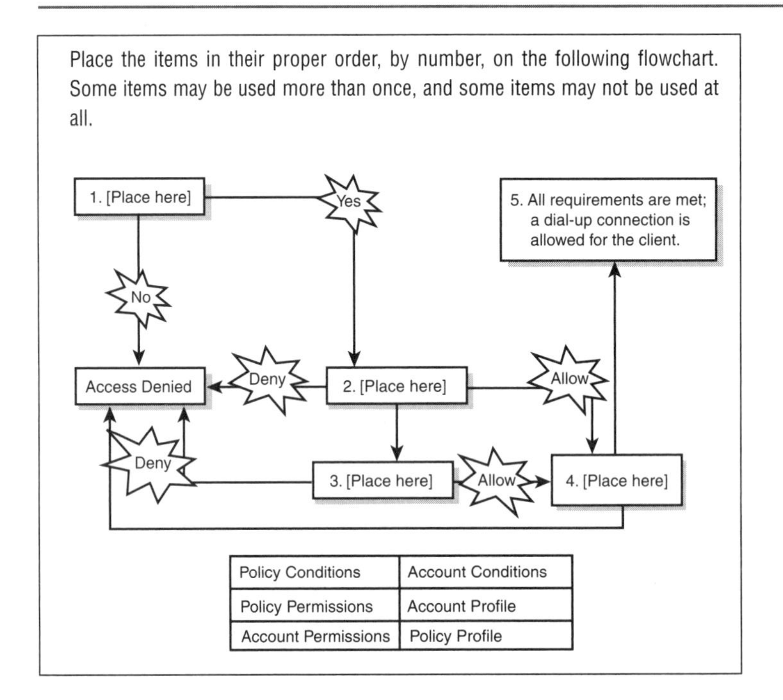

Policy Conditions	Account Conditions
Policy Permissions	Account Profile
Account Permissions	Policy Profile

The correct answer is:

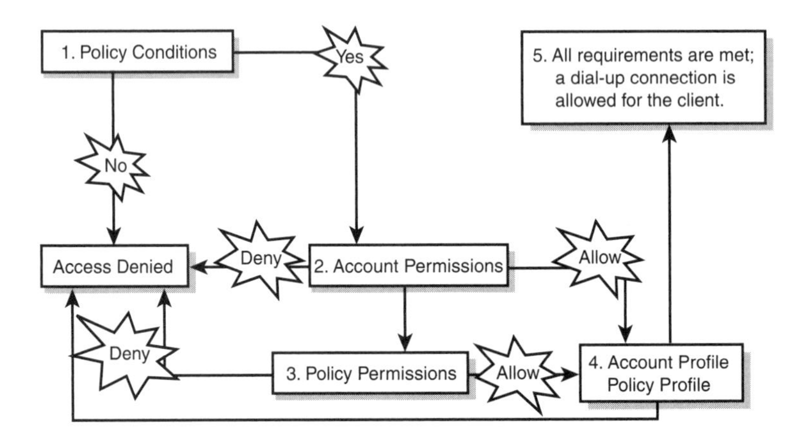

Microsoft's Testing Formats

Currently, Microsoft uses four testing formats:

- Case study
- Fixed length
- Adaptive
- Short form

As mentioned earlier, the case study approach is used with many of the newer Microsoft exams. These exams consist of a set of case studies that you must first analyze to answer questions related to the case studies. Such exams include one or more case studies (tabbed topic areas), each of which is followed by 4 to 10 questions. The question types for exams will be multiple choice, build-list-and-reorder, create a tree, drag and connect, and select and place. Depending on the test topic, some exams are totally case-based, whereas others are not at all.

Other Microsoft exams employ advanced testing capabilities that might not be immediately apparent. Although the questions that appear are primarily multiple-choice, the logic in *fixed-length tests*, which use a fixed sequence of questions, is more complex than that in older Microsoft tests. Some questions employ a sophisticated user interface (which Microsoft calls a *simulation*) to test your knowledge of particular software and systems in a simulated "live" environment that behaves just like the original. The Testing Innovations article at `www.microsoft.com/TRAINCERT/mcpexams/faq/innovations.asp` includes a downloadable series of demonstrations and samples.

For some exams, Microsoft has turned to a well-known technique, called *adaptive testing*, to establish a test-taker's level of knowledge and product competence. Adaptive exams look the same as fixed-length exams, but they determine the level of difficulty at which an individual test-taker can correctly answer questions. Test-takers with differing levels of knowledge or ability see different sets of questions; individuals with high levels of knowledge or ability are presented with a smaller set of more difficult questions, whereas individuals with lower levels of knowledge are presented with a larger set of easier questions. Two individuals may answer the same percentage of questions correctly, but the test-taker with a higher knowledge or ability level scores higher because his or her questions are weighted more heavily.

Also, lower-level test-takers may answer more questions than more knowledgeable colleagues. This explains why adaptive tests use ranges of values to define the number of questions and the amount of time needed to complete the tests.

Adaptive tests work by evaluating the test-taker's most recent answer. A correct answer leads to a more difficult question (also raising the test software's estimate of the test-taker's knowledge and ability level). An incorrect answer leads to a less difficult question (also lowering the test software's estimate of the test-taker's knowledge and ability level). This process continues until the test targets the test-taker's true ability level. The exam ends when the test-taker's level of accuracy meets a statistically acceptable value (in other words, when his or her performance demonstrates an acceptable level of knowledge and ability) or when the maximum number of items has been presented (in which case, the test-taker is almost certain to fail).

Microsoft also introduced a short-form test for its most popular tests. This test consists of 25 to 30 questions, with a time limit of exactly 60 minutes. This type of exam is similar to a fixed-length test because it allows readers to jump ahead or return to earlier questions and to cycle through the questions until the test is done. Microsoft does not use adaptive logic in this test; it claims that statistical analysis of the question pool is such that the 25 to 30 questions delivered during a short-form exam conclusively measure a test-taker's knowledge of the subject matter in much the same way as an adaptive test. The short-form test is like a "greatest hits exam" (that is, the most important questions are covered).

Some of the Microsoft exams may contain a combination of adaptive and fixed-length questions.

Because you won't know in which form the Microsoft exam might be, you should be prepared for an adaptive exam instead of a fixed-length or a short-form exam: The penalties for answering incorrectly are built into the test itself on an adaptive exam, whereas the layout remains the same for a fixed-length or short-form test, no matter how many questions you answer incorrectly.

The biggest difference between adaptive tests and fixed-length or short-form tests is that you can mark and revisit questions on fixed-length or short-form tests after you've read them. On an adaptive test, you must answer the question when it is presented and cannot go back to that question later.

Strategies for Different Testing Formats

Before you choose a test-taking strategy, you must determine which type of test it is: case studies, fixed length, short form, or adaptive.

- Case-study tests consist of a tabbed window that allows you to navigate easily through the sections of the case.
- Fixed-length tests consist of 50 to 70 questions with a check box. You can return to these questions if you want.
- Short-form tests have 25 to 30 questions with a check box. You can return to these questions if you want.
- Adaptive tests are identified in the introductory material of the test. They have no check box and can be visited (and answered) only once.

Some tests contain a variety of testing formats. For example, a test may start with a set of adaptive questions, followed by fixed-length questions.

You'll be able to tell for sure whether you are taking an adaptive, fixed-length, or short-form test by the first question. Fixed-length or short-form tests include a check box that allows you to mark the question for later review. Adaptive test questions include no such check box and can be visited (and answered) only once.

Case-Study Exam Strategy

Most test-takers find that the case-study type of exam is the most difficult to master. When it comes to studying for a case-study test, your best bet is to approach each case study as a standalone test. The biggest challenge you'll encounter is that you'll feel that you won't have enough time to get through all the cases that are presented.

Each case provides a lot of material that you'll need to read and study before you can effectively answer the questions that follow. The trick to taking a case study exam is to first scan the case study to get the highlights. Be sure you read the overview section of the case so that you understand the context of the problem at hand. Then, quickly move on and scan the questions.

As you are scanning the questions, make mental notes to yourself or notes on your paper so that you'll remember which sections of the case study you should focus on. Some case studies provide a fair amount of extra information that you don't really need to answer the questions. The goal with this scanning approach is to avoid having to study and analyze material that is not relevant.

When studying a case, read the tabbed information carefully. It is important to answer each question. You will be able to toggle back and forth from case to questions, and from question to question within a case testlet. However, after you leave the case and move on, you cannot return to it. I suggest that you take notes while reading useful information to help you when you tackle the test questions. It's hard to go wrong with this strategy when taking any kind of Microsoft certification test.

Fixed-Length and Short-Form Exam Strategy

A well-known principle when taking fixed-length or short-form exams is first to read through the entire exam from start to finish. Answer only those questions that you feel absolutely sure you know. On subsequent passes, you can dive into more complex questions more deeply, now knowing how many such questions you have left and the amount of time remaining.

There's at least one potential benefit to reading the exam completely before answering the trickier questions: Sometimes, information supplied in later questions sheds more light on earlier questions. At other times, information you read in later questions might jog your memory about facts, figures, or behavior that helps you answer earlier questions. Either way, you'll come out ahead if you answer only those questions on the first pass that you're absolutely confident about.

Fortunately, the Microsoft exam software for fixed-length and short-form tests makes the multiple-visit approach easy to implement. At the top-left corner of each question is a check box that permits you to mark that question for a later visit.

Marking questions makes later review easier, but you can return to any question by clicking the Forward or Back buttons repeatedly.

Here are some question-handling strategies that apply to fixed-length and short-form tests. Use them if you have the chance.

- When returning to a question after your initial read-through, read every word again; otherwise, your mind can miss important details. Sometimes, revisiting a question after turning your attention elsewhere lets you see something you missed, but the strong tendency is to see what you've seen before. Try to avoid that tendency at all costs.

- If you return to a question more than twice, try to articulate to yourself what you don't understand about the question, why answers don't appear to make sense, or what appears to be missing. If you chew on the subject a while, your subconscious might provide the missing details, or you might notice a "trick" that points to the right answer.

As you work your way through the exam, another counter that Microsoft provides comes in handy—the number of questions completed and questions outstanding. For fixed-length and short-form tests, it's wise to budget your time by making sure that you've completed roughly one-quarter of the questions one-quarter of the way through the exam period, and three-quarters of the questions three-quarters of the way through.

If you're not finished when only five minutes remain, use that time to guess your way through any remaining questions. Remember, guessing is potentially more valuable than not answering. Blank answers are always wrong, but a guess might turn out to be right. If you don't have a clue about any of the remaining questions, pick answers at random or choose all As, Bs, and so on. A guess is better than nothing at all.

At the very end of your exam period, you're better off guessing than leaving questions unanswered.

Adaptive Exam Strategy

If there's one principle that applies to taking an adaptive test, it's "get it right the first time." You cannot elect to skip a question and move on to the next one when taking an adaptive test, because the testing software uses your answer to the current question to select whatever question it plans to present next. You also cannot return to a question because the software gives you only one chance to answer it. You can, however, take notes as you work through the test. Sometimes, information supplied in earlier questions can help you answer later questions.

Also, when you answer a question correctly, you are presented with a more difficult question next, to help the software gauge your level of skill and ability. When you answer a question incorrectly, you are presented with a less difficult question, and the software lowers its current estimate of your skill and ability. This continues until the program settles into a reasonably accurate estimate of what you know and can do.

The good news is that if you know the material, you'll probably finish most adaptive tests in 30 minutes or so. The bad news is that you must really know the material well to do your best on an adaptive test. That's because some questions are so convoluted, complex, or hard to follow that you're bound to miss one or two, at a minimum. Therefore, the more you know, the better you'll do on an adaptive test, even accounting for the occasionally strange or unfathomable questions that appear on these exams.

Because you can't always tell in advance whether a test is fixed length, short form, adaptive, or a combination, you should prepare for the exam as if it were adaptive. That way, you will be prepared to pass, no matter what kind of test you take. If the test turns out to be fixed length or short form, remember the tips from the preceding section, which will help you improve on what you could do on an adaptive test.

If you encounter a question on an adaptive test that you can't answer, you must guess an answer quickly. (However, you might suffer for your guess on the next question if you guess correctly, because the software will give you a more difficult question!)

Question-Handling Strategies

For those questions that have only one right answer, usually two or three of the answers will be obviously incorrect, and two of the answers will be plausible. Unless the answer leaps out at you (if it does, reread the question to look for a trick; sometimes those are the ones you're most likely to get wrong), begin the process of answering by eliminating those answers that are most obviously wrong.

At least one answer out of the possible choices can usually be eliminated immediately because it matches one of these conditions:

- The answer does not apply to the situation.
- The answer describes a nonexistent issue, an invalid option, or an imaginary state.

After you eliminate all answers that are obviously wrong, you can apply your retained knowledge to eliminate further answers. Look for items that sound correct but refer to actions, commands, or features that are not present or not available in the situation that the question describes.

If you're still faced with a blind guess among two or more potentially correct answers, reread the question. Try to picture how each of the possible remaining answers would alter the situation. Be especially sensitive to terminology; sometimes the choice of words ("remove" instead of "disable") can make the difference between a right answer and a wrong one.

You should guess at an answer only after you've exhausted your ability to eliminate answers and are still unclear about which of the remaining possibilities is correct. An unanswered question offers you no points, but guessing gives you at least some chance of getting a question right; just don't be too hasty when making a blind guess.

If you're taking a fixed-length or a short-form test, you can wait until the last round of reviewing marked questions (just as you're about to run out of time or unanswered questions) before you start making guesses. You will usually have the same option within each case study testlet (but once you leave a testlet, you may not be allowed to return to it). If you're taking an adaptive test, you'll have to guess to move on to the next question if you can't figure out an answer some other way. Either way, guessing should be your technique of last resort!

Numerous questions assume that the default behavior of a particular utility is in effect. If you know the defaults and understand what they mean, this knowledge will help you cut through many Gordian knots. Simple "final" actions can be critical as well. If a utility must be restarted before proposed changes take effect, a correct answer might require this step as well.

Mastering the Inner Game

In the final analysis, knowledge gives confidence, and confidence breeds success. If you study the materials in this book carefully and review all the practice questions at the end of each chapter, you should become aware of those areas where additional learning and study are required.

After you've worked your way through the book, take the practice exam in the back of the book. Taking this test provides a reality check and helps you identify areas to study further. Be sure you follow up and review materials related to the questions you miss on the practice exam before scheduling a real exam. Don't schedule your exam appointment until after you've thoroughly studied the material and feel comfortable with the whole scope of the practice exam. You should score 80–85 percent or better on the practice exam before proceeding to the real thing (otherwise, obtain some additional practice tests so you can keep trying until you hit this magic number).

If you take a practice exam and don't get at least 80–85 percent of the questions correct, keep practicing. Microsoft provides links to practice exam providers and also self-assessment exams at **www.microsoft.com/traincert/mcpexams/prepare/**.

Armed with the information in this book and with the determination to augment your knowledge, you should be able to pass the certification exam. However, you need to work at it, or you'll spend the exam fee more than once before you finally pass. If you prepare seriously, you should do well.

The next section covers other sources you can use to prepare for the Microsoft Certification Exams.

Additional Resources

A good source of information about Microsoft Certification Exams comes from Microsoft itself. Because its products and technologies—and the exams that go with them—change frequently, the best place to go for exam-related information is online.

If you haven't already visited the Microsoft Certified Professional site, do so right now. The MCP home page resides at `www.microsoft.com/traincert/default.asp` (see Figure 1.4).

This page might be replaced by something new and different by the time you read this, because things change regularly on the Microsoft site. Should this happen, please read the sidebar titled "Coping with Change on the Web."

Coping with Change on the Web

Sooner or later, all the information I've shared with you about the Microsoft Certified Professional pages and the other Web-based resources mentioned throughout the rest of this book will become stale or be replaced by newer information. In some cases, the URLs you find here might lead you to their replacements; in other cases, the URLs will go nowhere, leaving you with the dreaded **"404 File not found"** error message. When that happens, don't give up.

There's always a way to find what you want on the Web if you're willing to invest some time and energy. Most large or complex Web sites (such as the Microsoft site) offer a search engine. On all of Microsoft's Web pages, a Search button appears along the top edge of the page. As long as you can get to the Microsoft site (it should stay at **www.microsoft.com** for a long time), use this tool to help you find what you need.

The more focused you can make a search request, the more likely the results will include information you can use. For example, you can search for the string

```
"training and certification"
```

to produce a lot of data about the subject in general, but if you're looking for the preparation guide for Exam 70-216, "Installing, Configuring, Managing, Monitoring, and Troubleshooting DNS in a Windows 2000 Network Infrastructure," you'll be more likely to get there quickly if you use a search string similar to the following:

```
"Exam 70-216" AND "preparation guide"
```

Likewise, if you want to find the Training and Certification downloads, try a search string such as this:

```
"training and certification" AND "download page"
```

Finally, feel free to use general search tools—such as **www.search.com**, **www.altavista.com**, and **www.excite.com**—to look for related information. Although Microsoft offers great information about its certification exams online, there are plenty of third-party sources of information and assistance that need not follow Microsoft's party line. Therefore, if you can't find something immediately, intensify your search.

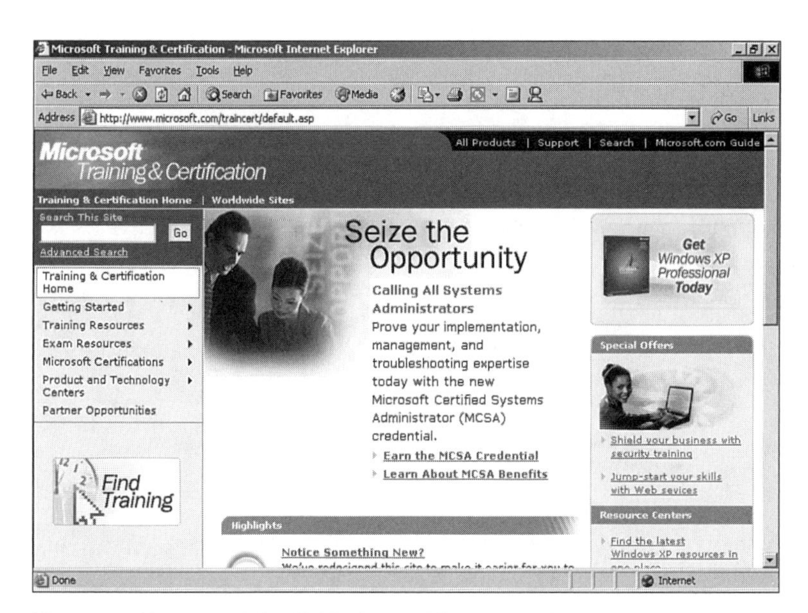

Figure 1.4 The Microsoft Certified Professional Training and Certification home page.

DNS

Terms you'll need to understand:

- ✓ DNS
- ✓ Zones
- ✓ Dynamic updates
- ✓ Delegation
- ✓ Caching-only server
- ✓ Root name server

Techniques you'll need to master:

- ✓ Understanding DNS
- ✓ Installing the DNS Server service
- ✓ Configuring a root name server
- ✓ Configuring zones
- ✓ Configuring a caching-only server
- ✓ Configuring a DNS client
- ✓ Understanding DNS zone types
- ✓ Configuring zones for dynamic update
- ✓ Testing the DNS Server service
- ✓ Implementing a delegated zone for DNS
- ✓ Manually creating DNS resource records

Introduction

Each machine on a computer network is assigned a unique network address. Computers communicate with each other across networks by connecting to these network addresses. These numbers are 12 digits long, however, and difficult for people to remember. To solve this dilemma, a system was developed to translate "friendly" names into the network addresses the computers use to locate each other and to communicate. These names are called *hostnames*, and each machine is assigned one. Groups of hosts form a domain. The software that translates these names to network addresses is called the Domain Name System (DNS).

Domain name servers have been in use on the Internet for many years. Prior to DNS, HOSTS files were used for name resolution, but as the Internet quickly grew in size and popularity, maintaining HOSTS files became impossible. When the Internet community realized there was a need for a more manageable, scalable, and efficient name resolution system, DNS was created.

Prior to Windows 2000, Network Basic Input/Output System (NetBIOS) names were used to identify computers, services, and other resources on Windows-based machines. In the early days of Windows networks, LMHOSTS files were used for NetBIOS name resolution. Later, these names were often resolved to Internet Protocol (IP) addresses using a NetBIOS Name Server (NBNS). Microsoft's version of the NBNS was called a Windows Internet Naming Service (WINS) server. With Windows 2000 and the introduction of Active Directory, hostnames are now used instead of NetBIOS names. In a Windows 2000 domain, DNS is required to resolve hostnames and locate resources, such as network services.

This chapter introduces the Windows 2000 implementation of DNS. You'll learn how to install and configure a DNS server, as well as how to maintain and monitor it. Having a thorough understanding of the topics presented here is important to both exam and on-the-job success.

Installing the DNS Server Service

At one time or another, most of us have typed a universal resource locator (URL) to get to one of our favorite Web sites. But, before you can view the Web site stored on a Web server, the name you typed must be resolved to an IP address, and this is where DNS servers come into play.

You have more than likely at some point heard the term *Fully Qualified Domain Name (FQDN)*. An FQDN consists of a hostname and a domain name. It uniquely identifies a host within a DNS hierarchy. For example, `www.bayside.net` is an FQDN. Every FQDN is broken down into different levels. In the preceding example, `.net` is the top-level domain and `bayside` is the second-level domain. The top-level domain normally identifies the type of organization, such as a government organization (gov) or an educational organization (edu). The second-level domain indicates a specific domain, and the third level can indicate a specific host within that domain. In any case, DNS servers are used to resolve FQDNs to IP addresses.

There are two processes that DNS can use to resolve queries: *recursive* and *iterative*. With a recursive query, the DNS client requires the DNS server to respond with the IP address of the request or an error message that the requested name does not exist. The DNS server cannot refer the client to another DNS server if it is unable to map the request to an IP address. When a DNS server receives a recursive request, it queries other DNS servers until it finds the information or until the query fails.

With an iterative query, the DNS server uses zone information and its cache to return the best possible answer to the client. If the DNS server does not have the requested information, it can refer the client to another DNS server.

For example, when a DNS client enters `www.bayside.net` into a browser, the following process occurs:

1. A DNS request is sent to the local DNS server. This might be a DNS server on the client's local network or a DNS server at the client's Internet service provider (ISP).

2. Before forwarding the request to a root server, the DNS server checks its local cache to determine whether the name has recently been resolved. If there is an entry in the local cache, the IP address is returned to the client.

3. If no entry exists in the cache for the hostname, the request is sent to a root name server.

4. The root name server refers the request to a name server responsible for the first-level domain within the hostname. For example, the root name server would refer the request to the `bayside.net` DNS server.

5. The request is referred to second-level DNS servers, and then third-level DNS servers, until one of them can resolve the request to an IP address and return the results to the client.

Now that you have a general idea of what happens when a DNS client attempts to connect to another computer using a hostname, you can take a look at how the DNS service is installed.

Installing DNS

DNS can be installed in several ways. It can be added during the installation of Windows 2000, after installation using the Configure Your Server option located on the Start menu, or through the Control Panel. The only real requirement for installing DNS is Windows 2000 Server, although, if you are using Dynamic Host Configuration Protocol (DHCP) on the network, it's generally a good idea to configure the DNS server with a static IP address instead of a DHCP client.

To install the DNS Server service using the Control Panel, perform the following steps:

1. Click Start, point to Settings, and click Control Panel.
2. Double-click the Add/Remove Programs applet. Click Add/Remove Windows Components.
3. Select Networking Services and click the Details button.
4. From the list of components, select Domain Name System. Click OK. Click Next.
5. After the necessary files are copied, click OK.

Windows 2000 DNS Server Roles

After you've installed the DNS service, you can configure the server in one of three main roles. The role the server plays depends on the configuration of zone files and how they are maintained. (Zone files are discussed later in the chapter.) The three main DNS server configuration roles are as follows:

- Caching-only server
- Primary server
- Secondary server

Keep in mind when you are planning server roles that a single DNS server can perform multiple roles. For example, a DNS server can be the primary server for one zone and at the same time be a secondary server to another DNS server.

Caching-Only Server

All DNS servers maintain a `cache.dns` file that contains a list of all Internet root servers. Any time a DNS server resolves a hostname to an IP address, the information is added to the cache file. The next time a DNS client needs to resolve the hostname, the information can be retrieved from the cache as opposed to the Internet.

Caching-only servers do not contain any zone information, which is the main difference between primary and secondary DNS servers. The main purpose of a caching-only server (other than providing name resolution) is to build the cache file as names are resolved. They resolve hostnames, cache the information, and return the results to the client. Because these servers hold no zone information, hostnames are either resolved from the cache or another DNS server is required to resolve them.

Caching-only servers are useful when you need to reduce network traffic. Again, because there is no zone information, there is no zone transfer traffic generated. Hostname traffic is also reduced as the cache file is built up.

It's important to understand when caching-only servers should be implemented. Caching-only servers are useful when there are remote locations that have slow WAN links. Configuring a caching-only server in these locations can reduce network traffic that would normally be generated between primary and secondary DNS servers, and speed up hostname resolution once the cache file is established.

Primary Server

A primary DNS server hosts the working copy of a zone file. If you need to make changes to the zone file, it must be done from the server that is designated as the primary server for that zone. For those of you who are familiar with Windows NT 4.0, this is similar to how the Primary Domain Controller (PDC) maintains the working copy of the directory database. Once a server is configured as a primary DNS server for a zone, it is said to be *authoritative* for that domain. Also, a single DNS server can be the primary DNS server for multiple zones.

A *zone file* contains the resource records for a portion of the DNS namespace. Resource records map hostnames to IP addresses. Both of these topics are covered later in the chapter.

Secondary Server

A secondary server gets all its zone information from a master DNS server. The secondary DNS server hosts a read-only copy of the zone file, which it gets from the primary server or another secondary DNS server. Through a process known as a *zone transfer*, the master DNS server sends a copy of the zone file to the secondary server.

Previous implementations of DNS supported only full transfers, in which an update to the zone file resulted in the entire zone database being transferred to the secondary servers. Windows 2000 supports incremental zone transfers, so the secondary servers can synchronize their zone files by pulling only the changes. This results in less network traffic.

For example, if Server2 is configured as a secondary server for `bayside.net`, Server2 would get all its zone information from Server1, the primary DNS server for the zone. Any changes that need to be made to the zone file would have to be performed on Server1. The updated zone file would then be copied to Server2. As already mentioned, a DNS server can be both a primary and a secondary server at the same time. Using this example, Server2 could also be configured as the primary server for `riverside.net`, and to provide fault tolerance for the zone file, Server1 could be configured as a secondary server for this zone.

Secondary DNS servers provide the following benefits:

- *Fault Tolerance*—Because the secondary server has a copy of the zone file, name resolution can continue if the primary DNS server is unavailable.
- *Reduction in Name Resolution Traffic*—Secondary servers can be placed in remote locations with a large number of users. Clients can then resolve hostnames locally instead of having to contact a primary DNS server using a WAN link.
- *Load Balancing*—Name resolution services for a zone can be provided by the secondary server as well, thereby reducing the load placed on the primary DNS server.

Windows 2000 DNS Interoperability with Non-Microsoft DNS Servers

It is worth discussing briefly how Windows 2000 interoperates with non-Microsoft DNS servers for both exam and on-the-job success. In a perfect world, every network would run one platform throughout the network. However, most networks run a mixture of platforms from Microsoft to Unix to Linux to take advantage of different features provided by each platform. This means there's a good chance that your Windows 2000 DNS servers might need to interoperate with other types of DNS servers.

To interoperate with a Windows 2000 DNS server, the non-Microsoft DNS server must support *SRV records* (which are used to locate servers running the Netlogon service). Windows 2000 DNS servers, Windows NT 4.0 DNS servers (with Service Pack 4 or later), and BIND 4.9.6 (or later) DNS servers all support the SRV records.

Although support for dynamic updates is not required to interoperate with a Windows 2000 DNS server, it does eliminate the need of having to manually enter SRV records. Windows 2000 DNS and BIND 8.1.3 both support dynamic updates.

There might be cases in which you need to integrate Windows 2000 DNS into an existing DNS infrastructure. Once DNS is installed on a Windows 2000 Server, a subdomain from the existing DNS server can be delegated to the new Windows 2000 DNS server (delegation is covered later in the chapter and entails making another DNS server authoritative for a portion of the DNS namespace). For example, for an existing domain called `bayside.net`, a subdomain called `Win2k.bayside.net` can be configured and delegated to the Windows 2000 DNS server. This means the Windows 2000 DNS server will be authoritative over the subdomain and will be responsible for resolving queries within the local domain.

To ensure name resolution outside the local domain, the Windows 2000 DNS server can be configured to use one of the existing DNS servers from the parent domain as a forwarder. This way, any queries outside the scope of the local domain are sent to one of the main DNS servers.

You can enable forwarders and configure the IP address of the DNS server to which non-local queries should be sent through the Properties window for the DNS server.

Configuring Zones

After you have installed the DNS Server service, your next step is to create and configure zones (unless you are implementing a caching-only server).

A *zone* is basically an administrative entity, which is a portion of the DNS database that is administered as a single unit. A zone can span a single domain or multiple domains. The DNS server that is authoritative for a zone is responsible for resolving any requests for that particular zone. The zone file maintains all the configuration information for the zone and contains the resource records for the domains in the zone.

Each new zone consists of a *forward lookup zone* and an optional *reverse lookup zone*. A forward lookup zone maps hostnames to IP addresses. When a client needs the IP address for a hostname, the information is retrieved from the forward lookup zone. A reverse lookup zone does the opposite and allows for reverse queries, or mapping an IP address to a hostname. Reverse queries are often used when troubleshooting with the `NSLookup` command.

Zone Types

Three types of zones can be configured: standard primary, standard secondary, and Active Directory–integrated. Each zone type is discussed further in the following list:

- *Standard primary zones*—This type of zone maintains the master writable copy of the zone in a text file. An update to the zone must be performed from the primary zone.
- *Standard secondary zones*—This zone type stores a copy of an existing zone in a read-only text file. To create a secondary zone, the primary zone must already exist, and you must specify a master name server. This is the server from which the zone information is copied.
- *Active Directory–integrated zones*—This zone type stores zone information within Active Directory. This allows you to take advantage of additional features, such as secure dynamic updates and replication. Active Directory–integrated zones can be configured on Windows 2000 domain controllers running DNS. Each domain controller maintains a writable copy of the zone information, which is stored in the Active Directory database.

When you install Active Directory on the first domain controller, a DNS server is required. If you choose to install DNS when Active Directory is installed, the zone is automatically configured as an Active Directory–integrated zone.

Creating Zones

The main tool used to configure and administer a DNS server is the *DNS manager*. From this management console, you can configure a DNS server by creating zones. To create a new zone, follow these steps:

1. Click Start, point to Programs, Administrative Tools, and click DNS. This opens the DNS management console.
2. Right-click the DNS server and click New Zone. The New Zone Wizard opens. Click Next.
3. Select the type of zone you want to create: *Active Directory–integrated*, *Standard primary*, or *Standard secondary* (see Figure 2.1). Click Next. Keep in mind that the option to create an Active Directory–integrated zone is only available if Active Directory is installed on the local machine.

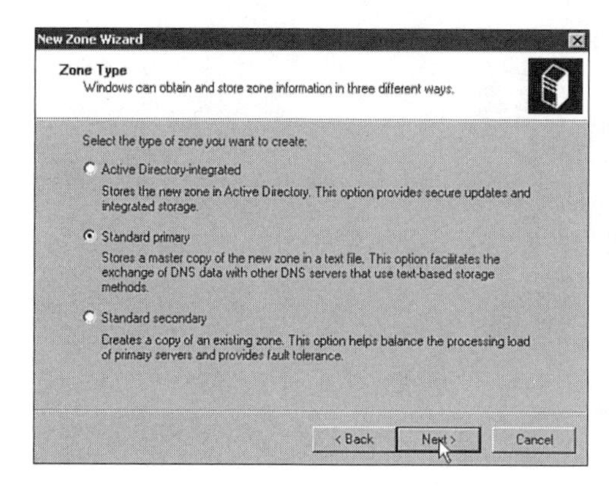

Figure 2.1 Configuring the zone type.

4. Select the type of zone you want to create: a forward lookup zone or a reverse lookup zone. Click Next.
5. If you select forward lookup zone, the Zone Name page appears. Type the name for the zone, such as `bayside.net`. Click Next.
6. If you selected to create a reverse lookup zone, type the network ID (see Figure 2.2). This is used to create the `in-addra.arpa` domain with subdomains named using the network ID of the IP address. DNS uses the reverse lookup zone for performing address to name translations. For example, a network ID of `192.168.1` would be translated into `1.168.192.in-addra.arpa`. Click Next.

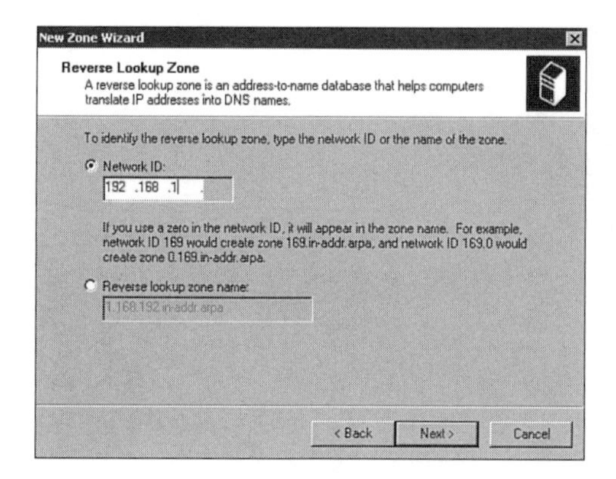

Figure 2.2 Creating a reverse lookup zone.

7. In the Zone File screen, select whether to create a new zone file or to use an existing one (see Figure 2.3). This option appears when creating a forward or reverse lookup zone. Click Next.

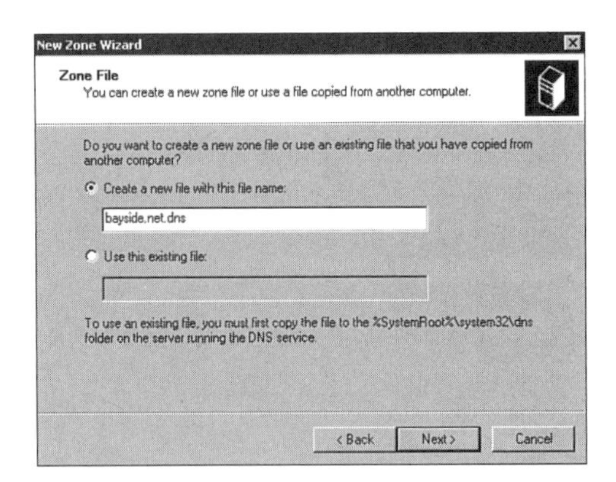

Figure 2.3 Configuring the zone filename.

8. Click Finish.

Configuring Zone Properties

After a zone has been successfully added to your DNS server, you can configure it via the zone's Properties dialog box. To do so, right-click the zone from within the DNS management console and click Properties. The Properties dialog box for the zone displays five tabs, as shown in Figure 2.4. (If the zone is Active Directory integrated, six tabs will be available.) Table 2.1 summarizes each of the tabs.

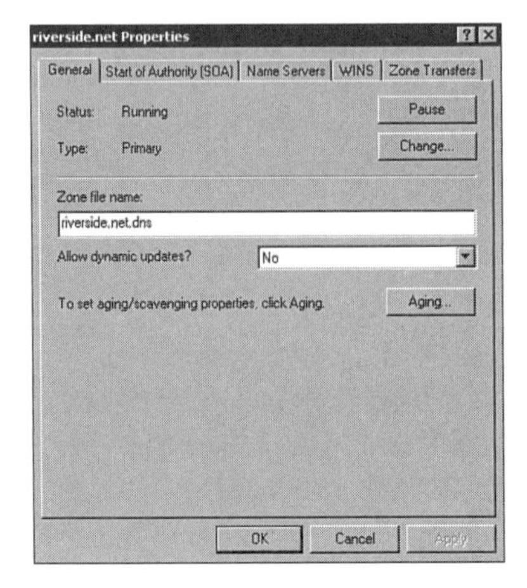

Figure 2.4 Configuring zone properties.

Table 2.1 Zone Property Tabs

Property Tab	Description
General	View the status of the zone, change the type of zone, change the zone filename, and configure dynamic updates.
Start of Authority (SOA)	Configure the zone transfer information and the email address of the zone administrator.
Name Servers	Specify the list of secondary servers that should be notified when changes to the zone file occur.
WINS	Enable the DNS server to query the list of WINS servers for name resolution.
Zone Transfers	Configure which secondary servers can receive zone transfers. You can specify any server, only those listed on the Name Servers tab, or the ones configured from this property sheet. Clicking the Notify button allows you to configure which secondary servers will be notified of changes.
Security	If the zone is Active Directory–integrated, the Security tab is available and can be used to configure permissions to the zone file.

Security has become a major topic both for exams and on-the-job realities. Be prepared to encounter at least one question on securing zone transfers between DNS servers. Using the Name Servers tab and the Zone Transfers tab, you can configure additional security by limiting which secondary servers can receive zone transfers and be notified of updates to the zone file.

Zone Transfers

Secondary servers get their zone information from a master name server. The master name server is the source of the zone file; it can be a primary server or another secondary server. If the master name server is a secondary server, it must first get the updated zone file from the primary server. The process of replicating a zone file to a secondary server is referred to as a *zone transfer*. Zone transfers occur between a secondary server and a master name server in two situations:

- When the master name server notifies the secondary server that a change has been made to the zone file. When the secondary server receives notification, it requests a zone transfer. If multiple secondary servers exist, they are notified at random so the master name server is not overburdened with zone transfer requests.
- When the refresh interval expires and the secondary server contacts the primary name server to check for changes to the zone file.

There are two types of zone transfers. The first is a *Full Zone Transfer (AXFR)*, in which the entire zone file is replicated to the secondary server. This type of zone transfer is supported by most implementations of DNS. If the secondary server's zone file is not current, which means changes were made, the entire zone file is replicated.

The second type of zone transfer is known as an *Incremental Zone Transfer (IXFR)*, in which only the changes made to a zone file are replicated to the secondary server, thereby reducing the amount of network traffic. You can control how often zone transfers occur from the Start of Authority (SOA) tab within the zone's Properties dialog box (see Figure 2.5). Table 2.2 summarizes the configurable options.

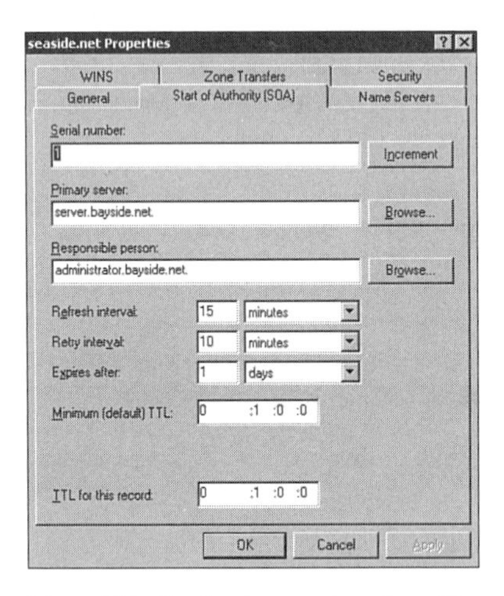

Figure 2.5 Configuring zone transfer settings.

Table 2.2 Zone Transfer Settings

Option	Description
Serial number	Lists the number used to determine whether the zone file has changed. Each time a change is made, this number is incremented by 1. You can force a zone transfer by manually increasing this number.
Primary server	Lists the hostname of the primary DNS server for the zone.
Responsible person	Lists the email address of the person responsible for administering the zone.
Refresh interval	Determines how often the secondary server will poll the primary server for updates. Consider increasing this value for slow network connections.

(continued)

Table 2.2 Zone Transfer Settings *(continued)*

Option	Description
Retry interval	Specifies how often the secondary server will attempt to contact the primary server if the server does not respond.
Expires after	Specifies when zone file information should expire if the secondary server fails to refresh the information. If a zone expires, zone data is considered to be potentially out of date and is discarded. Secondary master servers will not use zone data from an expired zone.
Minimum (default) TTL	Specifies how long records from the zone should be cached on other servers.
TTL for this record	Specifies how long DNS servers are allowed to store a record from the zone in their cache before it expires.

Active Directory–integrated zones replicate information differently than primary and secondary zones, because the zone information is stored in Active Directory. Zone transfers are not used to update the zone information. Instead, the DNS servers with Active Directory–integrated zones poll Active Directory at 15-minute intervals to check for updates.

Converting Zones

Using the General tab from the Zone Properties dialog box, you can change the current zone type (see Figure 2.6). You have the option of changing a primary or secondary zone to an Active Directory–integrated zone or an Active Directory–integrated zone to a primary zone or secondary zone. Before you attempt to change the zone type, be aware of the following points:

- To convert a zone to an Active Directory–integrated zone, the DNS Server service must be installed on a Windows 2000 domain controller.

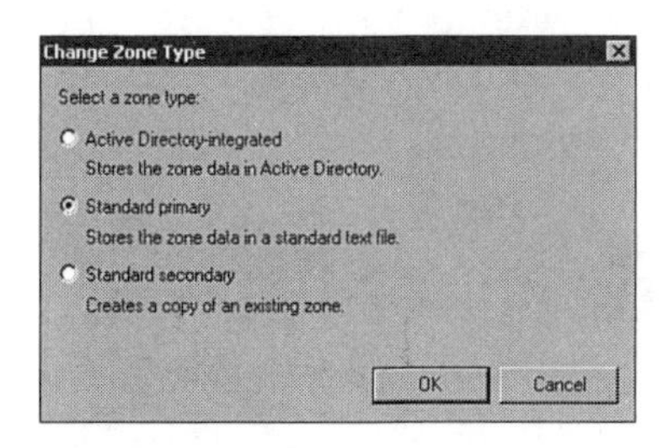

Figure 2.6 Changing the zone type.

- If you convert to a secondary zone, you must specify the IP address of the server from which the zone information will be retrieved.

- Changing a secondary zone to a primary zone will affect such things as dynamic updates, the use of the DNS Notify option, and zone transfers.
- When an Active Directory–integrated zone is converted to a primary zone, zone information is deleted from Active Directory and copied into a text file on the local DNS server.

Configuring a Caching-Only Server

As mentioned earlier in the chapter, one of the roles a DNS server can play is that of a *caching-only server*. Caching-only servers are used to resolve recursive queries, cache the results, and return the results to the requesting client. The server is not authoritative for any zone and resolves requests from its cache or another DNS server. As a DNS server retrieves the results for name resolution requests, it caches the results in the `cache.dns` file.

If DNS servers did not cache results, users would see an increase in response time, as well as more network traffic. If a DNS server received a request to resolve `www.bayside.net` and two minutes later another client made the same request, it would have to go through the referral process twice to resolve the same name. Because DNS is used on the Internet and by Windows 2000, this name resolution scenario would be very inefficient. Instead, by caching the results the DNS server can use the resource records within the cache to respond to subsequent name resolution requests made after the initial name request.

The main advantage to implementing a caching-only server is that no traffic is generated from zone transfers. Because the server is not authoritative for a zone, nor does it maintain a copy of an existing zone, no traffic is generated. This is useful for remote office locations that are connected with slow WAN links that cannot support traffic generated by zone transfers. The main disadvantage is, when the server is first configured, the `cache.dns` file only contains entries for the root name servers so it will take some time to build up the cache file as requests are resolved.

Time to Live Property in Resource Caching

One important aspect of caching resource records is the *Time To Live (TTL)* property. Each resource record stored in the cache is assigned a TTL. This is a numeric value that determines how long the resource record can remain in the cache without requiring a refresh from the primary server. When the TTL for an object in the cache expires, the DNS server can no longer respond to queries for that hostname using the cached record. This ensures that information in the cache is fairly up to date. The default TTL for a zone is set to 3600 seconds, or 1 hour.

Installing a Caching-Only Server

When it comes to installing a caching-only server, you don't need to perform much configuration. After the DNS server service is installed using the steps outlined earlier in the chapter, verify that the root hints are configured correctly. Remember, because the server isn't authoritative for any zones, no zone information needs to be configured. You can verify the configuration of the root hints by right-clicking the DNS server within the DNS management console, clicking Properties, and selecting the Root Hints tab.

Root hints are used by DNS servers to discover other DNS servers authoritative for a domain. For example, for a DNS server to resolve a query for **computer1.bayside.net**, it must be able to locate the root DNS servers for the namespace. The DNS servers for the **net** domain can provide referrals to the DNS server authoritative for the **bayside.net domain**.

Configuring a DNS Client

Successfully implementing DNS not only means installing and configuring a DNS server, but it also requires you to configure the DNS clients. Although this is not nearly as complex as configuring the DNS server, it's still important to understand for both exam and on-the-job success.

First, be sure the TCP/IP protocol is installed on the client machine. Depending on the platform of your clients, there will be some variance in how you install the protocol. If the client happens to be running Windows 2000, TCP/IP can be installed through the Properties screen for the local area connection.

DNS clients must be configured with the IP address of the preferred DNS server (and an alternative DNS server if one is available). You can do this manually through the Properties dialog box for the TCP/IP protocol (see Figure 2.7) or automatically using a DHCP server.

Clicking the Advanced button, shown in Figure 2.7, and selecting the DNS tab allows you to configure the advanced DNS settings (see Figure 2.8). If multiple DNS servers are available, you can specify the order in which DNS servers are contacted when clients need to resolve host names. The name server at the top of the list will be queried first. If the client receives no response, a query will be sent to the next DNS server in the list. The *DNS server addresses, in order of use* list box is useful for load balancing between DNS servers. For example, some DNS clients can be configured to contact the secondary DNS server first instead of the primary when resolving queries. For DHCP clients, the DNS servers and the order of use can be configured using the DNS Server service option 6.

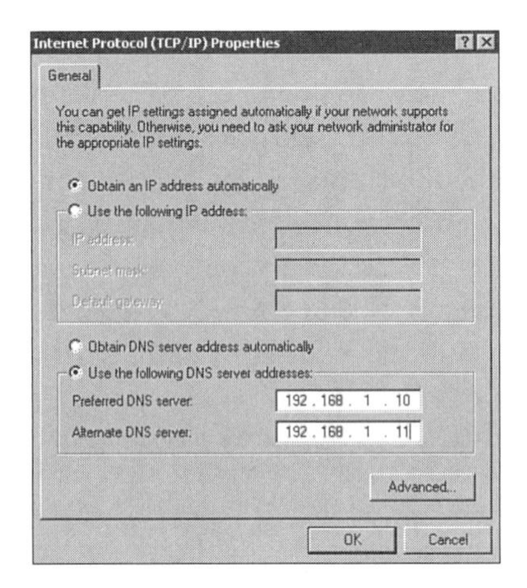

Figure 2.7 Manually configuring the IP address of the DNS server.

As you will see in Chapter 3, "DHCP," DHCP servers can assign clients IP addresses and subnet masks. Along with this, they can also assign optional parameters referred to as *scope options*. The DNS Server service option 6 is used to assign DHCP clients with the IP address of the DNS server. This eliminates the need of having to statically configure each workstation with the DNS server's IP address. This parameter can be configured by selecting the Scope Options container within the DHCP management console.

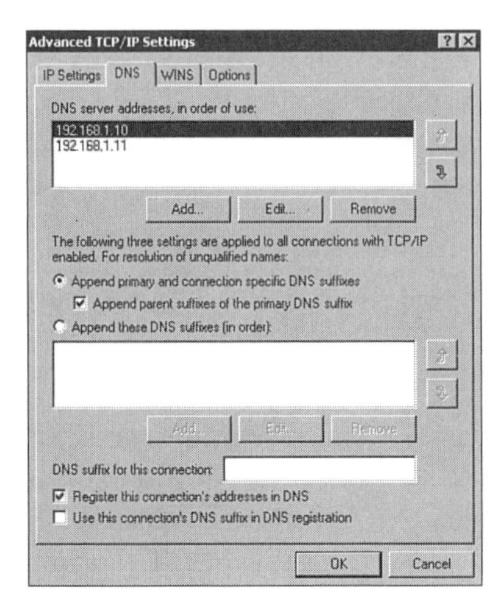

Figure 2.8 Configuring advanced DNS parameters.

You must also configure the list of DNS suffixes to append to unqualified DNS hostnames. These suffixes will be appended to the unqualified hostname when clients submit DNS queries for resolution. If suffixes are not appended to unqualified names, resolution will fail. You can have the primary and parent suffixes appended to the unqualified names. For example, if the primary DNS suffix is CHI.BAYSIDE.NET, when resolving the hostname of COMPUTER1, the query would be for COMPUTER1.CHI.BAYSIDE.NET and COMPUTER1.BAYSIDE.NET. In this case, the names are removed from left to right to resolve the name. You can also configure a list of suffixes to be appended by selecting the option to Append these DNS suffixes. By doing so, resolution for unqualified names is limited to those DNS suffixes listed.

With DHCP, you can use the DNS domain name option 15 to configure the DNS suffix for a workstation.

Notice the *Use this connection's DNS suffix in DNS registration* option at the bottom of the DNS property sheet. This option is available for Windows 2000 clients only and is selected by default. It enables the client for dynamic updates.

Many of you have probably heard of and used the **ipconfig** command to view your IP parameters. The command can also be used to remove entries from the client's DNS cache using the **/flushdns** parameter. This is useful when clients are unable to resolve hostnames after changes have been made to the DNS database. For example, if WRKST1 receives a new IP address from a DHCP server, this may result in a negative cache entry on WRKST2, causing WRKST1 to be resolved to the incorrect IP address. Flushing the DNS cache on WRKST2 would solve the problem because WRKST2 would then have to contact the DNS server to resolve the hostname.

Windows 2000 Dynamic Update

Windows 2000 clients can interact directly with a DNS server. With dynamic updates, clients can automatically register their own resource records with a DNS server and update them as changes occur. *Resources records* are the entries within the DNS server database files. Each resource record contains information about a specific machine such as the IP address or specific services running. The type of information within a resource record depends on the type of record created. For example, an A (address) record contains the IP address associated with a specific computer.

Dynamic update greatly reduces the administration associated with maintaining resource records. Dynamic updates eliminate the need for administrators to manually update these records. In terms of DHCP, with a short lease duration configured, the IP address assigned to DNS clients can change frequently.

Dynamic updates basically provide the following advantages:

- DHCP servers can dynamically register records for clients. This is particularly important because DHCP servers can perform updates on behalf of clients that do not support dynamic updates, such as Windows 95, 98, or NT4 clients.
- Reduces the administrative overhead because A records and PTR records can be dynamically updated by Windows 2000 clients. An A (address) record lists the IP address associated with a specific machine, whereas a PTR (pointer) record lists the specific machine associated with an IP address.
- Allows domain controllers to be dynamically registered through SRV records.

To support dynamic updates, a Windows 2000 DHCP server and a Windows 2000 DNS server must be on the network. Windows NT 4.0 DNS servers do not support dynamic updates. Windows 2000 DHCP servers are required to perform dynamic updates on behalf of those clients that do not support this feature.

How Dynamic Update Works

By default, any Windows 2000 client can update its own records with the DNS server. The DHCP client service attempts to update records with the DNS server when any of the following events occur:

- The workstation is rebooted.
- The client records are manually refreshed using the `ipconfig/registerDNS` command.
- A statically configured IP address is modified.
- The IP address leased from a DHCP server changes or is renewed.

Let's take a look at an example of what happens when a client performs a dynamic update. Assume that you change a `bayside.net` workstation's computer name from computer1 to computer2. Upon changing the computer name, you are then required to restart before the changes take effect. Once the workstation is rebooted, the following process occurs:

1. The DHCP client service sends the domain's authoritative DNS server a query using the new DNS domain name of the workstation.
2. The DNS server that is authoritative for the workstation's domain responds to the request.
3. The client uses the response information to determine the primary DNS server for the domain and sends a dynamic update request to the primary DNS server.
4. The update request is processed. The old host and pointer records are removed and replaced with the updated ones.

Configuring a Zone for Dynamic Update

Dynamic updates are configured on a per-zone basis. The zone must be either a primary or Active Directory–integrated zone.

To configure a zone for dynamic update, right-click the zone within the DNS management console and click Properties. In the Properties dialog box, select the General tab as shown in Figure 2.9. To enable dynamic updates, select one of the following options:

- *No*—Select this option to disable dynamic updates for the zone.
- *Yes*—Select this option to enable dynamic updates for the zone.
- *Only secure updates*—Select this option to enable dynamic updates for those users and groups authorized to do so. This option is only available for Active Directory–integrated zones.

For Windows 2000, the use of secure dynamic updates can be compromised by running a DHCP server on a domain controller when Windows 2000 DHCP server is configured to perform registration of DNS records on behalf of its clients. To avoid this issue, deploy DHCP servers and domain controllers on separate computers. If you are not concerned about security of reverse lookup (PTR) records, this precaution is advisable only if the DHCP server is configured to perform registration of host (A) records on behalf of its clients (which is not a default behavior).

When configuring dynamic updates, remember that the zone must be primary or Active Directory–integrated. Also, to use secure updates, the zone must be Active Directory–integrated. This feature is not supported by primary zones.

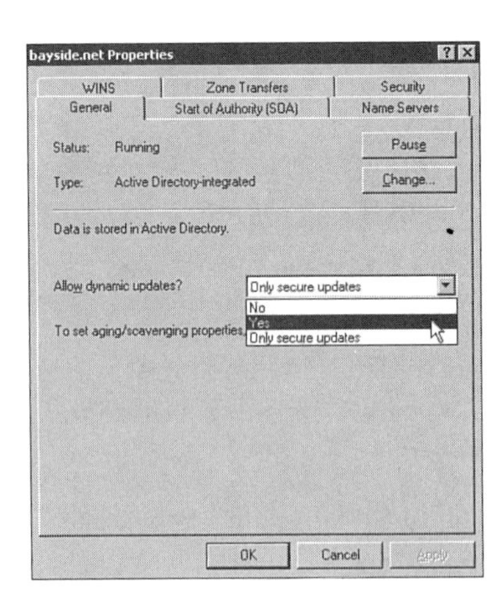

Figure 2.9 Configuring dynamic updates for a zone.

Using Secure Dynamic Updates

Windows 2000 supports secure dynamic updates for those zones that are Active Directory–integrated. Secure dynamic updates occur the same way as dynamic updates, except secure updates are accepted only from clients who are authorized to update the zone file. This means that the DNS server accepts updates only from clients that have accounts within Active Directory. Any computers that do not have accounts are not permitted to register any records, thereby eliminating the chance of unknown computers registering with the DNS server.

The benefit of this is obviously an increase in security. The resource records and zone files can be modified only by users who have been authorized to do so. It also provides administrators with a finer granularity of control, as they can edit the access control list (ACL) for the zone and specify which specific users and groups can perform dynamic updates. You edit the ACL for a zone by right-clicking the zone, selecting Properties, and choosing the Security tab.

One issue you need to be aware of is the situation in which you have enabled secure updates and also configured the DHCP server to perform updates on behalf of clients that do not support dynamic updates. If a DHCP server performs a secure update on behalf of the client, that DHCP server becomes the owner of the record. If another DHCP server on the network attempts to update the record, it cannot do so because it does not own the record. To get around this issue, you need to place the DHCP servers configured to perform dynamic updates into the DNSUpdateProxy group (as long as the DHCP server is not a domain controller), because members of this group bypass DNS security.

Testing the DNS Service

After your DNS server is installed and configured, you'll probably want to perform a few simple tests to verify that the name resolutions are functioning as they should.

One of the tools you can use to test your DNS server (as well as troubleshoot problems as they arise) is the `NSLookup` command. Using this command, you can send forward and reverse queries to your DNS server.

For a complete list of available options, type **nslookup /?** at the command prompt.

If you perform a forward query against the DNS server, the results should return the IP address associated with the hostname you specified (for example, `nslookup server1.bayside.net`). When performing a reverse query, the DNS server is queried to determine the hostname associated with a particular IP address (for example, `nslookup 192.168.1.15`).

You can also perform simple queries against your DNS server through the DNS management console. Through the console, you can perform a simple iterative query or a recursive query. To query the DNS server, follow these steps:

1. Within the DNS management console, right-click the DNS server and click Properties.
2. In the Properties dialog box, select the Monitoring tab (see Figure 2.10).

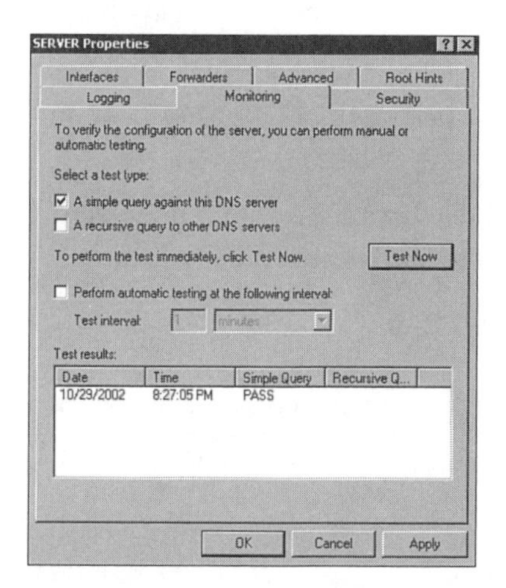

Figure 2.10 Testing the DNS server.

3. Select the type of test you want to perform: an *iterative* or *recursive* query.
4. Specify whether to perform automatic testing and at what interval.
5. After you make your selections, click the Test Now button. The results are displayed in the Test Results window. Click OK.

With an iterative query, the DNS server either resolves the hostname from the local cache or returns to the client a list DNS servers that might be able to resolve the hostname for the client. With a recursive query, the DNS server itself uses other DNS servers to resolve the hostname on behalf of the client.

Implementing a Delegated Zone for DNS

We've already covered creating and configuring zones; now we will take a brief look at delegating a zone. *Delegation* is the process of designating a portion of the DNS namespace to another zone. It gives administrators a way of dividing a namespace among multiple zones. For example, an administrator may place the `bayside.net` domain in one zone and place the `sales.bayside.net` subdomain in another delegated zone. The `bayside.net` zone would contain all the records for the sales subdomain if it is not delegated. By delegating, the `bayside.net` zone only contains information for `bayside.net`, as well as records to the name servers authoritative for the `sales.bayside.net` subdomain, but the host entries for any machines in `sales.bayside.net` are contained only on the delegated server.

In any case, when deciding whether to delegate, keep the following points in mind:

- It allows you to delegate management of part of the DNS namespace to other departments or locations.
- It allows you to distribute a large DNS database across multiple servers for load balancing, faster name resolution, and increased performance.
- It allows you to extend the namespace for business expansion.

To facilitate the delegation of zones, you need the appropriate delegation records that point to the name servers that are authoritative for the new zones.

Delegating a Zone

Before you delegate a zone, all the subdomains must first be listed in the current zone. After they've been added, you can use the following procedure to create a zone delegation:

1. From within the DNS management console, right-click the subdomain you want to delegate and select New Delegation. The New Delegation Wizard opens. Click Next.

2. Type a name for the delegated domain in the Delegated domain text box (see Figure 2.11). Click Next.

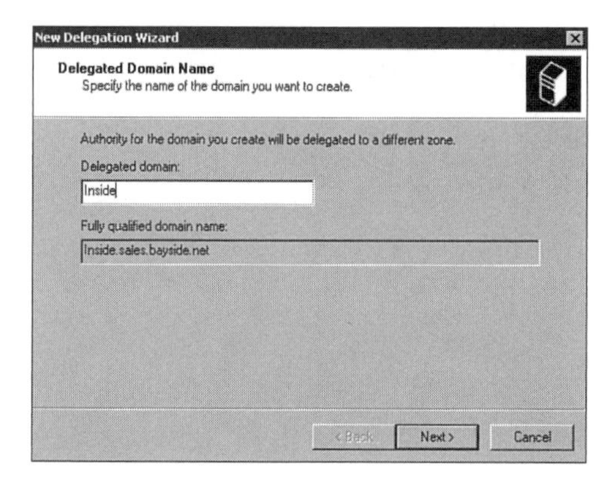

Figure 2.11 Configuring the name of a delegated domain.

3. Specify the name servers that will host the delegated domain by clicking the Add button (see Figure 2.12). The New Resource Record screen appears, allowing you to specify the name and IP address of the name servers. Click OK. Click Next.

4. Click Finish.

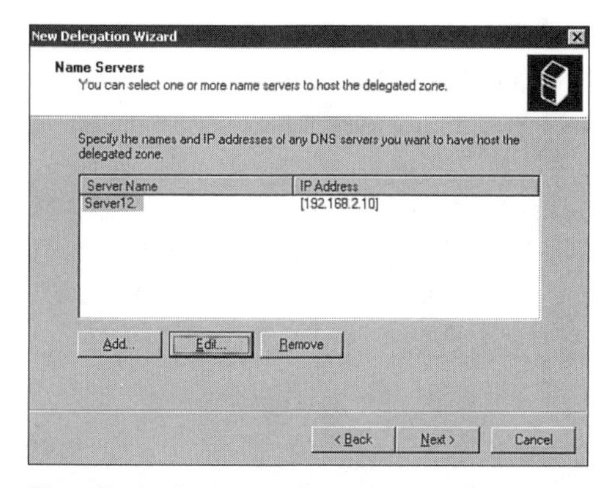

Figure 2.12 Configuring the name servers to host a delegated domain.

Manually Creating DNS Records

The final step in implementing DNS is to populate the zone files with resource records. Remember, if your clients are all running Windows 2000 and the zone is configured for dynamic updates, the clients can add and update their own resource records. You can also manually add resource records to a zone file through the DNS console.

Types of Resource Records

Several resource records can be created. Table 2.3 summarizes some of the more common resource records you might come across. To view all the resource records supported by Windows 2000 DNS, right-click a zone and select Other New Records (see Figure 2.13).

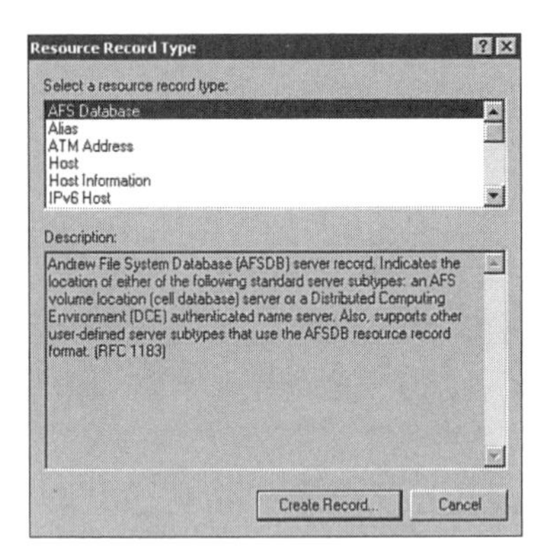

Figure 2.13 DNS resource records.

Table 2.3 Common DNS Resource Records

Resource Record	Description
Host Address (A) Record	Maps a DNS name to an IP address.
Mail Exchanger (MX) Record	Routes messages to a specified mail exchanger for a specified DNS domain name.
Pointer (PTR) Records	Points to a location in the DNS namespace. PTR records are normally used for reverse lookups.
Alias (CNAME) Record	Specifies another DNS domain name for a name that is already referenced in another resource record.

Creating a Resource Record

Now that you're familiar with some of the common resource record types, let's look at how to manually add a resource record to a zone file (it sounds much more complicated than it actually is).

To create a new host record, simply right-click the zone in which you want to create the record and select the New Host option. In the New Host dialog box, type the name and IP address for the host. To automatically create a pointer record, select the Create associated pointer (PTR) record check box (see Figure 2.14). After you've filled in the information, click the Add Host button. The record appears under the zone within the DNS management console, as shown in Figure 2.15.

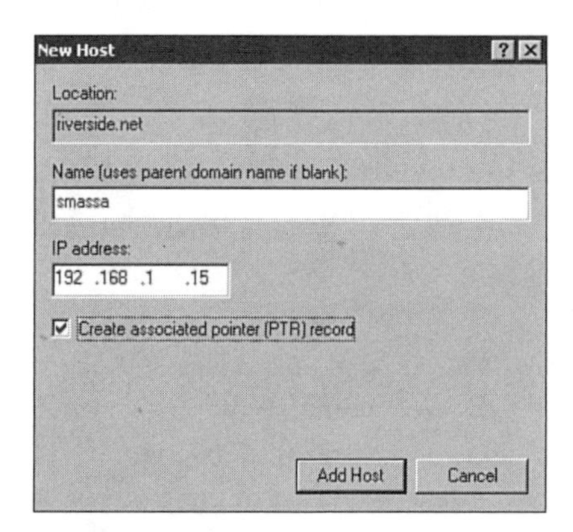

Figure 2.14 Adding a new host record.

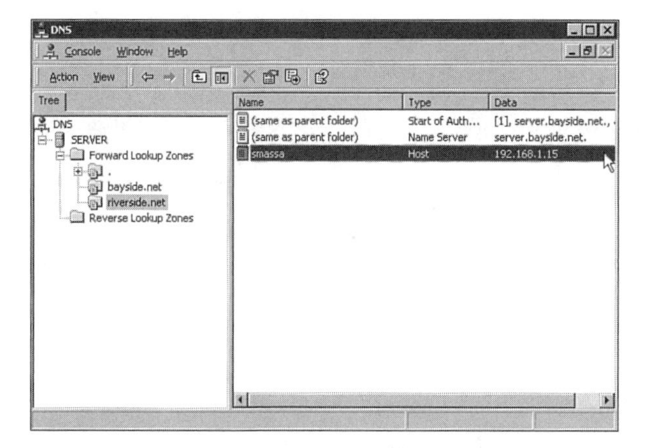

Figure 2.15 A new host record within a zone.

To create additional resource records, simply select the type of record you want to create and fill in the required information.

Managing and Monitoring DNS

Because of the important role DNS servers play in a Windows 2000 environment, it's important to properly manage and monitor them on a regular basis to ensure adequate performance. The following section introduces you to some of the management tasks you might have to perform on a DNS server and how to monitor your DNS server using Performance's System Monitor.

Managing DNS

Most management tasks performed on a DNS server are done through the DNS management console. When you highlight your DNS server within the DNS manager and click the Action menu, you see several options that can be used to manage different aspects of DNS. Some of the available options are summarized as follows:

- *Set Aging/Scavenging for all zones*—Use this option to configure refresh intervals for resource records. This allows you to refresh resource records on a set schedule, and it keeps bad records, such as invalid URLs, out of the database.
- *Scavenge Stale Resource Records*—Use this option to manually scavenge stale resource records. *Stale resource records* can accumulate within a zone over a period of time. For example, if a computer registers its own resource record and is shut down improperly, the record might not be removed from the zone file. Scavenging stale resource records can eliminate any problems such as outdated information.
- *Update Server Data Files*—Use this option to write all changes to the zone file stored within Active Directory to disk.
- *Clear Cache*—Use this option to clear the contents of the name server's cache.

From the All Tasks option listed on the Action menu, you can also perform tasks such as starting, stopping, and pausing the DNS Server service.

Monitoring DNS

Finally, you should monitor your DNS servers on a regular basis. Obviously, in large enterprise environments, you should monitor DNS servers more frequently. In any case, because DNS servers play such an important role within a Windows 2000 domain, it's important that solid performance is maintained.

The tool most often used to monitor how services are performing is the System Monitor tool located within the Performance console. When you install DNS, several counters are added specifically for monitoring this service (see Figure 2.16). Table 2.4 outlines some of the common DNS performance counters.

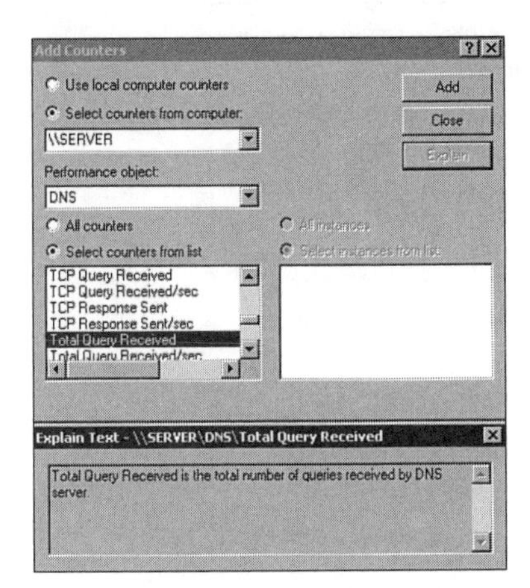

Figure 2.16 DNS performance counters in the Add Counters dialog box.

Table 2.4 Common DNS Performance Counters

Counter	Description
Caching Memory	Monitors the total caching memory used by the DNS server.
Dynamic Update Received/sec	Determines the number of dynamic update requests received by the server per second.
Dynamic Update Requests	Counts the total number of dynamic updates received by the server.
Recursive Queries	Monitors the total number of recursive queries received by the server.
Total Queries Received	Calculates the total number of queries received by the server.

Practice Questions

Question 1

Riverside consists of a number of different client platforms including Windows 2000, Windows NT 4.0, and Windows 95. You want to reduce the need to manually update resource records. All zones on the DNS servers are configured as primary and secondary zones. How can you configure dynamic updates so that all records are updated regardless of the platform a client is running? [Choose all that apply.]

- ❑ A. Convert all zones to Active Directory–integrated zones.
- ❑ B. Configure the zones to accept dynamic updates.
- ❑ C. Configure the DHCP servers to perform updates for clients that do not support dynamic updates.
- ❑ D. Install the Active Directory client on all pre-Windows 2000 workstations.
- ❑ E. Configure the properties of TCP/IP on all workstations so hostnames are automatically registered.

Answers B and C are correct. To support dynamic updates in this example, the primary zones must be configured to accept dynamic updates and the DHCP servers must be configured to update records for clients that cannot perform the updates themselves. Answer A is incorrect. The only reason why you would need to change the zone to an Active Directory–integrated zone is to support secure updates. Answer D is incorrect because the Active Directory client does not provide the functionality of performing dynamic updates. Answer E is incorrect because this option is available only on Windows 2000 platforms.

Question 2

What is the purpose of a reverse lookup zone?

- ❍ A. It maps hostnames to IP addresses.
- ❍ B. It maps MAC addresses to IP addresses.
- ❍ C. It maps IP addresses to MAC addresses.
- ❍ D. It maps IP addresses to hostnames.

Answer D is correct. Reverse lookup zones are used to map IP addresses to their associated hostnames. Answer A is incorrect because this is the purpose of a forward lookup zone. Answers B and C are incorrect. ARP is responsible for mapping IP addresses to MAC addresses via a broadcast.

Question 3

Sean is configuring the first domain controller in a Windows 2000 domain. During the installation of Active Directory, he chooses to have DNS installed and configured automatically. What type of zone is configured during the installation?

- ❍ A. Caching-only zone
- ❍ B. Active Directory–integrated zone
- ❍ C. Standard primary zone
- ❍ D. Standard secondary zone

Answer B is correct. When DNS is installed and configured during the installation of Active Directory, the zone is automatically configured as an Active Directory–integrated zone. Therefore, answers A, C, and D are incorrect.

Question 4

Two DNS servers are currently configured on the Windows 2000 network and are connected by high-speed links. Both servers are configured with identical hardware. Currently, one server is configured as a primary server and the other as a secondary. Both DNS servers are also Windows 2000 domain controllers. You want to convert the zone to Active Directory–integrated so updates can take place on either server. How should you proceed?

- ❍ A. In the Properties dialog box for the DNS server, select the General tab and click the Change button.
- ❍ B. In the Properties dialog box for the zone, select the Zone Type tab and click the Change button.
- ❍ C. In the Properties dialog box for the zone, select the General tab and click the Change button.
- ❍ D. In the Properties dialog box for the DNS server, select the Zone Type tab and click the Change button.

Answer C is correct. To change the zone type, right-click the zone within the DNS management console and click Properties. In the Properties dialog box, be sure the General tab is selected and click the Change button. Answer A is incorrect because the zone type is configured at the zone level. Answers B and D are incorrect because there is no Zone Type tab available in either the server's Properties dialog box or the zone's Properties dialog box.

Question 5

Due to internal reorganization within your network, you had to make recent changes to the host records within DNS. Some of the clients on the network now report that they are unable to connect to some hosts. Which of the following commands can you use to solve the problem?

❍ A. **ipconfig /deletedns**

❍ B. **ipconfig /registerdns**

❍ C. **ipconfig /flushdns**

❍ D. **ipconfig /displaydns**

Answer C is correct. Using the `ipconfig /flushdns` command allows you to flush and reset the contents of the client resolver cache. This is useful if changes have been made to DNS making the cached entries now invalid. Answer A is incorrect as there is no such parameter. Answer B is incorrect because this parameter is used to renew a client's registration with DNS. Answer D is incorrect because this parameter simply displays the contents of the cache.

Question 6

Sean has just finished installing a DNS server on a Windows 2000 member server in the **bayside.net** domain. He needs to add a record into the zone file for the mail server on the domain. Which type of resource record should be created?

❍ A. PTR

❍ B. A

❍ C. CNAME

❍ D. MX

Answer D is correct. Mail servers are identified within a zone file using Mail Exchanger (MX) records. Answer A is incorrect because PTR records are used to associate an IP address with its hostname. Answer B is incorrect because A records are used to map hostnames to IP addresses. Answer C is incorrect because CNAME records are used to assign alias names to those names that are already referenced in another record.

Question 7

A DNS server has been installed on a member server within a Windows 2000 domain. You want to provide fault tolerance for your zone so that name resolution can still continue in the event the DNS server goes offline. You plan to add another DNS server to the domain. In what type of role should the new DNS server be configured?

❍ A. Secondary server

❍ B. Master Name server

❍ C. Caching-only server

❍ D. Backup Name server

Answer A is correct. The new server should be configured as a secondary server. It will then maintain a copy of the DNS zone file. If the original DNS server goes offline, name resolution can still occur. Answer B is incorrect because Master Name servers are the source of the zone file for secondary servers. Answer C is incorrect because caching-only servers do not hold any zone information. Answer D is incorrect because there is no such DNS server role called a Backup Name Server.

Question 8

Your corporate office contains the primary DNS server. One of the branch locations has a large number of users, so you install a secondary server to decrease name resolution response time. Because the link between the remote office and the corporate office is slow, you want to increase the interval at which the secondary server will poll the primary server for updates. How can you do this?

❍ A. In the Properties dialog box for the DNS server, select the Zone transfers tab and increase the refresh interval.

❍ B. In the Properties dialog box for the zone, select the Start of Authority (SOA) tab and increase the refresh interval.

❍ C. In the Properties dialog box for the zone, select the Start of Authority (SOA) tab and increase the retry interval.

❍ D. In the Properties dialog box for the zone, select the General tab and increase the retry interval.

Answer B is correct. To increase the rate at which the secondary server polls for updates, select the Start of Authority (SOA) tab from the zone's Properties dialog box and increase the refresh interval. Answer A in incorrect because the interval at which a secondary server polls for updates is configured at the zone level. Answer C is incorrect because the retry interval defines how often the secondary server continues to poll if the server does not respond. Answer D is incorrect because you must configure the refresh interval and it must be done from the Start of Authority (SOA) tab.

Question 9

You have received so many complaints lately from users in different branch offices that it is taking a long time for Internet names to be resolved. All the calls seem to be coming from locations with slow connections to the main office. What should you do?

- ❍ A. Upgrade the connections to high-speed links.
- ❍ B. Upgrade all client workstations to Windows 2000 to take advantage of dynamic updates.
- ❍ C. Install secondary servers at each of the different locations.
- ❍ D. Increase the refresh interval on the DNS server at the main office location.

Answer C is correct. Placing secondary servers at each of the locations allows each site to take advantage of caching and local name resolution. Answer A is incorrect because it would be more efficient to configure a secondary server than to upgrade the connections. Answer B is incorrect because dynamic updates have no impact on name resolution response time. Answer D is incorrect because configuring the refresh interval will have no impact if there are no secondary servers configured.

Question 10

You recently upgraded all the client workstations on the network to Windows 2000 Professional. Two DNS servers on the network run Windows NT 4.0—one is a primary server and the other is a secondary. There is also a Windows 2000 DHCP server. You notice that the DNS zone file is not being dynamically updated by the Windows 2000 clients. What must you do?

- ❍ A. Configure the DHCP server to perform the updates.
- ❍ B. Install Service Pack 6 on the DNS servers.
- ❍ C. Configure the clients to perform dynamic updates through the properties of TCP/IP.
- ❍ D. Upgrade the DNS servers to Windows 2000.

Answer D is correct. Windows NT 4.0 DNS servers do not support dynamic DNS; therefore, the servers need to be upgraded to Windows 2000. Thus, answers A, B, and C are incorrect.

Need to Know More?

Search the online version of TechNet and the Windows 2000 Server Resource Kit using keywords such as `DNS`, `Zones`, and `Dynamic Updates`.

Ruth, Andy, *Concise Guide to Windows 2000 DNS*, Que Publishing, 2000. ISBN: 0-7897-2335-2. This book provides concise, in-depth information on installing and configuring DNS.

Larson, Matt, and Cricket Liu, *DNS on Windows 2000*, O'Reilly and Associates, 2001. ISBN: 0596002300. The topics in this book cover all aspects of Windows 2000 DNS, from conceptual information to installing the DNS Server service.

DHCP

Terms you'll need to understand:

- ✓ DHCP
- ✓ Lease duration
- ✓ Scopes
- ✓ Superscopes
- ✓ Multicast scopes
- ✓ Scope options

Techniques you'll need to master:

- ✓ Installing DHCP
- ✓ Understanding the DHCP lease process
- ✓ Creating scopes, superscopes, and multicast scopes
- ✓ Configuring the lease duration
- ✓ Configuring optional IP parameters that can be assigned to DHCP clients
- ✓ Understanding how DHCP interacts with DNS
- ✓ Configuring DHCP for DNS integration
- ✓ Authorizing a DHCP server in Active Directory
- ✓ Managing a DHCP server
- ✓ Monitoring a DHCP server

Introduction

The TCP/IP protocol is an Active Directory operational requirement. This means that all computers on a Windows 2000 network require a unique IP address to communicate with the Active Directory. Static IP addresses can add a lot of administrative overhead. Not only can management of static IP addresses become time consuming, but such management also increases the chances of misconfigured parameters. Imagine having to manually type 10,000 IP addresses and not make a single error. The *Dynamic Host Configuration Protocol (DHCP)* can be implemented to centralize the administration of IP addresses. Through DHCP, many of the tasks associated with IP addressing can be automated. However, implementing DHCP also introduces some security issues because anyone with physical access to the network can plug in a laptop and obtain IP information about the internal network.

In this chapter, you'll learn how to implement a DHCP server, including the installation process, authorization of the server, and the configuration of DHCP scopes. The chapter ends by looking at how to manage a DHCP server and monitor its performance.

Implementing the DHCP Server Service

Every workstation (actually every device with a network interface card) on an IP network requires a unique IP address and a corresponding subnet mask. You have two options for configuring IP addresses. The first is to visit each workstation and configure each one with a static IP address, as well as any other required parameters, such as a default gateway and subnet mask.

To illustrate how difficult it could be, imagine a large network with 5,000+ users. It is possible to visit each workstation and manually configure IP addresses initially, but the work doesn't stop there. What if later you need to make a change to one of the parameters, such as the IP address of the DNS server? Once again, you'd have to visit each workstation. The more efficient way to do this is to implement a DHCP server to centralize administration and automate IP address assignment.

To automate the allocation of IP addresses and other parameters, at least one computer must have the DHCP Server service installed and configured. The service can be installed on a Windows 2000 domain controller, Windows 2000 member server, or a standalone server that is a member of a workgroup.

Although it is preferred to use Windows 2000 DHCP, you can also implement Windows NT 4.0 DHCP.

Requirements for a DHCP Implementation

To successfully implement the DHCP Server service on a Windows 2000 network, the following requirements must be met:

- The server that will run DHCP should not be configured as a DHCP client. Instead, configure the server with static IP parameters before installing DHCP.
- The DHCP Server service must be installed.
- The DHCP server must be configured with a range of IP addresses (also known as a *scope*) to be leased to DHCP clients. Each DHCP server requires at least one scope.
- The DHCP server must be authorized within Active Directory.

To be a DHCP client, workstations must be running one of the following operating systems, all of which are supported by Windows 2000 DHCP:

- Windows 95 or later
- Windows NT 3.51 or later
- Windows 2000 or later
- LAN Manager 2.2c for MS-DOS
- Windows for Workgroups 3.11 running TCP/IP32
- MS-DOS with the Microsoft Network Client 3.0 with real mode TCP/IP drivers

Installing DHCP

There are a number of ways that the DHCP Server service can be installed. It can be added as an optional service during the installation of Windows 2000, it can be installed after installation via the Control Panel, or it can be installed by choosing the Configure Your Server option from the Start menu.

To install the DHCP Server service via the Control Panel, follow these steps:

1. Click Start, point to Settings, and click Control Panel.
2. Select the Add/Remove Programs applet. Click Add/Remove Windows Components.

3. From the list of components, highlight Networking Services and click the Details button.

4. In the Networking Services dialog box, select the Dynamic Host Configuration Protocol (DHCP) check box and click OK (see Figure 3.1). Click Next.

5. Click Finish.

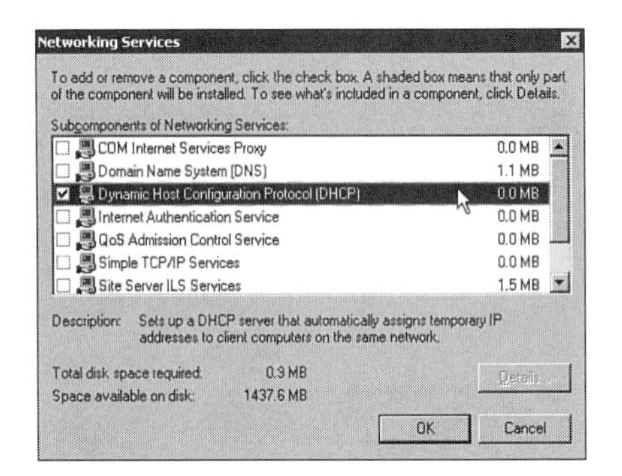

Figure 3.1 Installing DHCP using the Add/Remove Programs applet.

If your server is configured as a DHCP client, you will be prompted during the service to configure a static IP address. If you opt to leave the server as a DHCP client, a message will appear warning you that the configuration is not recommended.

The IP Address Lease Process

When a DHCP server is available on the network (that is, it has an active scope and has been authorized in Active Directory), it can assign IP addresses and other optional parameters to DHCP-enabled clients. The process of leasing an IP address occurs in four phases:

As you will see later in the chapter, a DHCP server must be authorized within Active Directory before it can function. This prevents any unauthorized DHCP server from being started on the network. A DHCP server must also be configured with at least one scope. The *scope* is the range of IP addresses that can be leased to DHCP clients.

1. The DHCP client broadcasts a `DHCPDISCOVER` message on the network containing its MAC address and NetBIOS name. If no DHCP servers respond to the request, the client will continue to broadcast up to four times at 2, 4, 8, and 16 seconds. If during this time a response is not received, the client will continue to broadcast every five minutes.

2. Each DHCP server on the network that receives the request will respond with a DHCP offer message. Included in the message is an offered IP address.
3. If multiple DHCP servers respond, the client selects the first offer it receives and broadcasts a DHCPREQUEST for the IP address. The message is broadcast on the network because the client has not yet been assigned an IP address, only offered one.
4. The DHCP server responds with a DCHPACK granting the client's request to use the IP address. The DHCPACK also contains information about any DHCP options that have been configured on the server (such as the IP address of the DNS server).

Remember, if a DHCP server is unavailable, the DHCP client will continue to broadcast the DHCP discover message until a DHCP server responds. However, during this time, the client will assign itself an IP address in the range of 169.254.0.0–169.254.255.255. This is known as *automatic IP addressing*. The client can communicate on the network but only with other clients on the same subnet also using an IP in this range. If clients are running Windows XP, you can configure the IP address they use when a DHCP server is unavailable.

Creating and Managing Scopes, Superscopes, and Multicast Scopes

Now that you're familiar with how to install the DHCP Server service, let's take a look at how to configure it. The first step in configuring your DHCP server is to create a scope.

Creating a Scope

Before a DHCP server can provide clients with IP addresses, the server must be configured with a scope. A *scope* is a range of IP addresses that can be leased to DHCP clients on a given subnet. For example, if you have multiple subnets, each with DHCP clients, you have to create multiple scopes.

In addition to IP addresses, a scope can also assign optional parameters to DHCP clients, including the IP address of DNS servers, WINS servers, and routers, and so on.

Before creating scopes, consider the following guidelines:

- If there are multiple DHCP servers on the network, each server requires at least one scope.

- If a workstation on the network requires a static IP address, it must be excluded from the scope. This eliminates the chance of duplicate IP addresses.
- A DHCP server can be configured with multiple scopes.
- Scope information is not shared between DHCP servers. With this in mind, make sure the IP addresses in each scope do not overlap, again to eliminate the possibility of duplicate IP addresses.
- If a client reservation is configured on one DHCP server, it must be configured on all DHCP servers from which the client can lease an IP address.

Chances are you will run into scenarios that include multiple DHCP servers. You can provide redundancy on the network for DHCP servers without the possibility of duplicate IP addresses. To accomplish this, use the *80/20 rule*, in which 80 percent of the IP addresses for one subnet are added to a scope on one DHCP server and the remaining 20 percent are added to a scope on another DHCP server. Because both servers have IP addresses available for the subnet, clients (or some of them) can still obtain an IP address should one of the servers become unavailable.

Creating a scope is a relatively simple process that can be accomplished through the DHCP management console. Once you select the New Scope option, a wizard prompts you for the required parameters. To create a new scope, perform the following steps:

1. From within the DHCP management console, right-click the DHCP server and select New Scope. The New Scope Wizard opens. Click Next.
2. Type a name and description for the new scope that will help you to easily identify it within the console. Click Next.
3. Type the range of IP addresses that will be available to clients on a particular subnet, as shown in Figure 3.2. The subnet mask is automatically defined but can be changed if your network is subnetted. Click Next.
4. Type a range or single IP address that you want excluded (see Figure 3.3). IP addresses that are excluded will not be leased to DHCP clients. Click Next.
5. Specify the lease duration (the length of time a DHCP client can use an IP address before it must be renewed). The default is eight days, as shown in Figure 3.4.

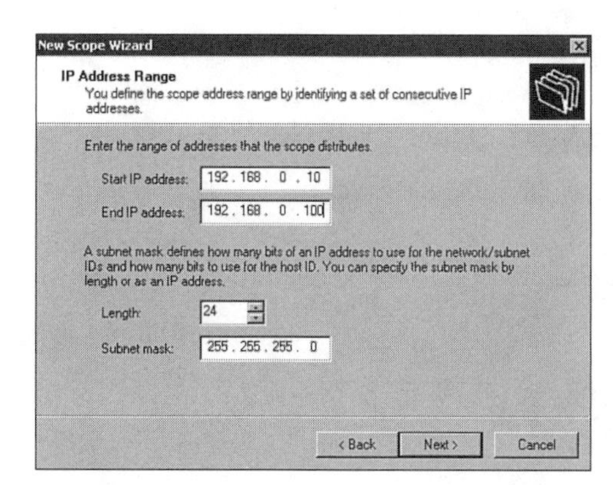

Figure 3.2 Defining the range of IP addresses within a scope.

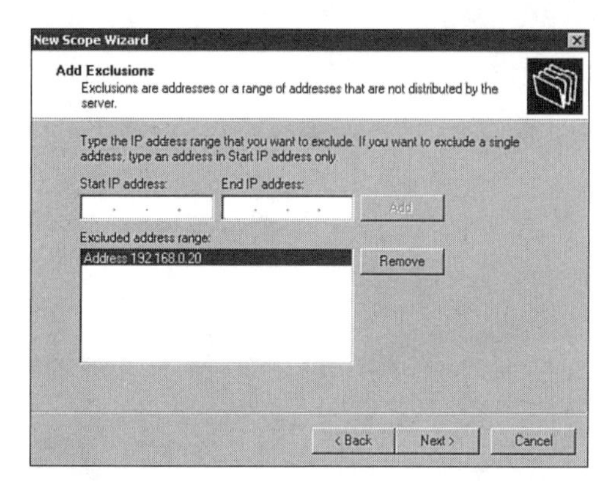

Figure 3.3 Excluding IP addresses from a scope.

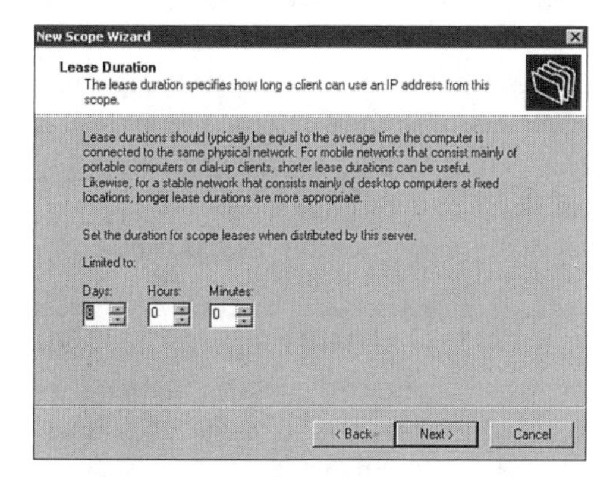

Figure 3.4 IP address lease duration.

6. The Configure DHCP Options screen allows you to select whether to configure additional DHCP options at this time (see Figure 3.5). If you do not, the options can be configured at another time as you will

see later in the chapter. The default option is Yes, I Want to Configure These Options Now. To configure the options at a later time, select No, I Will Configure These Options Later. Click Next.

7. Click Finish.

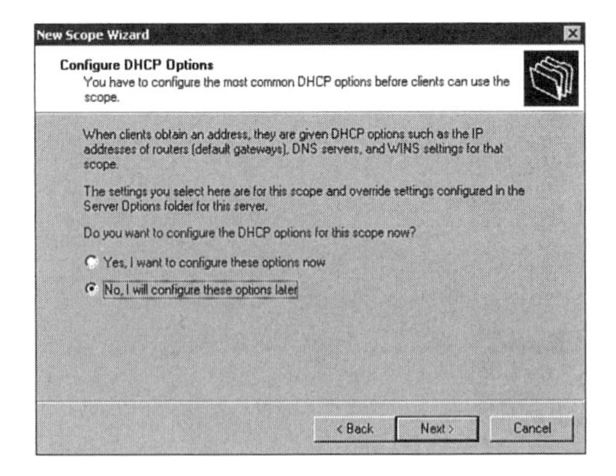

Figure 3.5 DHCP scope options.

Lease Duration

The *lease duration* determines how long the client can continue to use the leased IP address before it must be renewed. The default lease duration is set to eight days, as you saw when you installed the DHCP Server service.

The lease duration can be customized to meet the requirements of your network. For example, if the number of IP addresses exceeds the number of DHCP clients on the network, you can configure a longer lease duration. However, if the number of IP addresses available in the scope is comparable to the number of DCHP-enabled clients, you should configure a shorter lease duration to ensure an address will always be available for new and renewing clients. Also, if your network consists of a number of mobile users who move between subnets, consider configuring a shorter lease time.

When a client receives an IP address from a DHCP server, a renewal process occurs as the lease approaches expiration. After 50% of the configured lease duration has elapsed, the client attempts to contact the DHCP server. The client that's requesting to renew its IP address broadcasts a DHCPREQUEST message. The DHCP server, if available, responds with a DHCPACK, granting the client's request to renew the IP address. Also, information about other DHCP options is included in this reply. If any information has changed since the client first obtained its lease, the client updates its configuration accordingly.

If the server from which the client originally leased the IP address does not respond, the client again attempts to renew the IP address when 87.5% of the lease duration has elapsed. At this point, the client attempts to renew its current lease with any available DHCP server. If a server responds with a DHCP offer message (DHCPOFFER) to update the current client lease, the client can renew its lease based on the offering and continue operation.

If the lease expires and no server has been contacted, the client must immediately discontinue using its leased IP address. The client then follows the same process used during its initial start up operation to obtain an IP address.

The lease duration can be configured when you create a new scope. If you need to change it afterward, you can do so by right-clicking the scope within the DHCP console and choosing the Properties option. From the General tab, you can change the lease duration as shown in Figure 3.6.

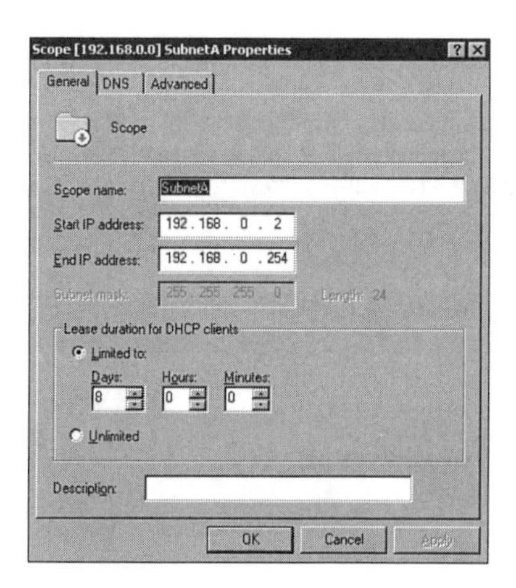

Figure 3.6 Reconfiguring the lease duration.

Activating a Scope

After a scope has been created, it appears within the DHCP management console with a red arrow beside it. Before any addresses from the scope can be leased to clients, the scope itself must be activated. This is a simple process that you can perform from within the console. To do so, right-click the scope and select the Activate option. The red arrow disappears, indicating that clients can now receive IP addresses from the scope.

Each DHCP server requires at least one active scope to function on a network. However, before a DHCP server can lease IP addresses to clients, the server must be authorized to do so in Active Directory. Authorization of a DHCP server is a new feature in Windows 2000. It eliminates the possibility of a DHCP server being brought online mistakenly or maliciously and assigning incorrect IP address information to clients. Keep in mind as well that any Windows NT DHCP servers that are upgraded to Windows 2000 must also be authorized before they can lease IP addresses to clients.

Client Reservation

There might be instances when a workstation on the network requires the same IP address every time. For example, if you have only a few IP addresses, you might need to reserve one for high-priority users. With a client reservation, the workstation can still be DHCP enabled, but the DHCP server will always assign the client the same IP address. In terms of administration, IP addressing remains centralized and the clients are assigned optional parameters through the DHCP server.

If multiple DHCP servers are configured with a range of IP addresses that cover the range of the reserved address, the client reservation must be duplicated on all DHCP servers. If not, the client might receive an incorrect IP address (one other than the address that has been reserved for the client).

Configuring Scopes

After a scope has been created, you can configure several DHCP options. The options can be configured at one of four levels:

- Server
- Scope
- Class
- Client

Server Level Scope Configuration

Options configured at the server level are applied to all DHCP clients regardless of the subnet they are on. Any options that should be applied to all DHCP clients should be configured at this level. For example, to configure all clients on the network to use the same DNS server, the option can be configured at the server level. When you are configuring scope options, any options configured at the scope or client level will override those configured at the server level. To configure server-level options, right-click the Server Options container listed under the DHCP server and select Configure options.

Scope Level Scope Configuration

If you want to configure DHCP options so they apply only to DHCP clients on a specific subnet, the options should be configured at the scope level. For example, the IP address of the default gateway for a subnet should be applied at the scope level. Configuring scope-level options can be done by right-clicking the Scope Options container and selecting Configure options.

Class Level Scope Configuration

Windows 2000 now includes a fourth method for applying DHCP options. With User and Vendor Class Options, DHCP options can be applied to a group of clients with similar needs (such as a group of mobile users or a group of clients sharing the same vendor). User class options can be used to assign options to DHCP clients that have common needs for similar DHCP options configurations. For example, a user class may be used to configure options for mobile users. Vendor class options can be used to assign DHCP options on the basis of vendor information. For example, specific options can be assigned to clients running a specific version of Windows.

Client Level Scope Configuration

Finally, if you want to apply DHCP options only to a specific DHCP client, you can configure the options at the client level. You can configure options at this level only for clients that have a client reservation, which means they are DHCP clients but always lease the same IP address. Any option you configure at this level will override any option configured at the server and scope levels. To configure a client option, right-click the client reservation and select Configure options.

Be sure you are familiar with the order in which scope options are applied. The order is server, scope, class, and then client.

Now that you're familiar with how DHCP options can be applied, let's take a look at the different DHCP options that can be assigned to clients.

DHCP Options

As already mentioned, a DHCP server can assign parameters other than just an IP address and subnet mask to a DHCP client. You can see all the available DHCP options through the Properties dialog box for the server, scope, class, or client reservation (see Figure 3.7) Table 3.1 provides a description of the commonly used DHCP options.

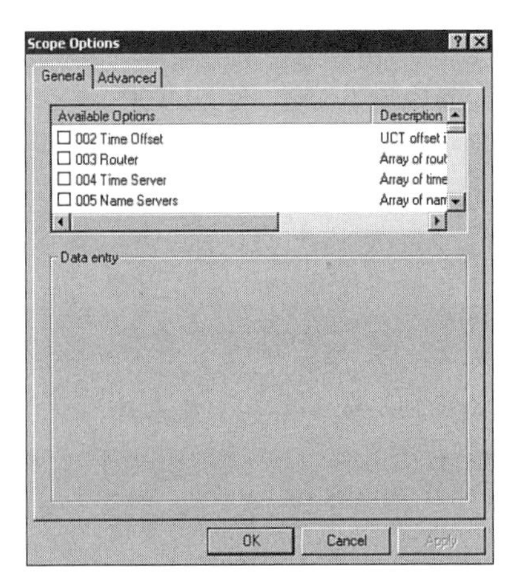

Figure 3.7 DHCP options.

Table 3.1 Common DHCP Options

Option	Description
006 DNS Servers	Specifies the IP address of the DNS servers available to clients on the network.
015 DNS Domain Name	Specifies the DNS domain name used for client resolutions.
003 Router	Specifies the IP address of the router or default gateway.
044 WINS/NBNS Servers	Specifies the IP address of the WINS servers on the network available to clients.
046 WINS/NBT Node Type	Specifies the name resolution type. The available options include 1 = B-node (broadcast), 2 = P-node (peer), 4 = M-node (mixed), and 8 = H-node (hybrid).

Most of the options outlined in Table 3.1 can be configured locally on the client. By doing so, any options configured on the DHCP server are overwritten by those configured locally.

Superscopes

Aside from a regular scope, you can also create a second type of scope known as a *superscope*. In a multinetted environment (one that has multiple logical IP subnets defined on a single physical network), superscopes allow a DHCP server to assign leases to clients on multiple subnets.

For example, a physical network is divided into two subnets, Subnet A and Subnet B, connected by a router. Subnet B contains two multinets. A single DHCP server is located on Subnet A. The DHCP server contains a single scope with a range of IP addresses to lease to clients on Subnet A. To have the DHCP server assign IP addresses to clients on Subnet B, you can create a superscope and add to it the IP address ranges for the multinets on Subnet B. The scope configuration on the DHCP server could be similar to the following:

```
Subnet A
   Scope 1: 192.168.1.2-192.168.1.254
Subnet B
   Superscope for Subnet B
      Scope 2: 192.168.2.2-192.168.2.254
      Scope 3: 192.168.3.2-192.168.3.254
```

One of the biggest advantages of creating superscopes is to ease administration of a multinetted environment. Identifying which scopes go with which networks can be a difficult administration task. Creating superscopes and grouping scopes in some logical manner can make them easier to administer; for example, grouping all the scopes from a single floor in a large office building into a superscope eases the administration process.

Superscopes are also used to support DHCP clients on a single physical network segment (such as a single Ethernet LAN segment) on which multiple logical IP networks are used. When more than one logical IP network is used on each physical subnet or network, such configurations are called *multinets*.

Creating a Superscope

To create a new superscope within the DHCP management console, follow these steps:

1. Right-click the DHCP server and select the New Superscope option. The New Superscope Wizard opens. Keep in mind that the superscope option is available only if a regular scope already exists. Click Next.

2. Type a descriptive name for the superscope (something that makes it easy to identify). Click Next.

3. From the list of available scopes, select those to include in the superscope. You can only add active scopes. Click Next.

4. Click Finish.

After the superscope has been created, it must be activated by right-clicking the scope and selecting the Activate option.

Multicast Scopes

Multicasting is the process of sending a message to a group of recipients as opposed to *unicasting*, in which a message is sent to a specific recipient.

Normally, DHCP is used to assign each DHCP client a single unique IP address from a range of IP addresses configured in a scope. Windows 2000 extends the functionality to allow you to create multicast scopes so that messages destined to a multicast IP address can be sent to all clients in a multicast group.

Multicast scopes are supported through a protocol known as the *Multicast Address Dynamic Client Allocation Protocol (MADCAP)*. MADCAP controls how the DHCP servers dynamically assign IP addresses on a TCP/IP network.

The multicast server (in this case, the DHCP server) is configured with a group of Class D IP addresses (in the range of 224.0.0.0–239.255.255.255) that can be assigned to multicast clients. The server is also responsible for maintaining the group membership list and updating the list as members join and leave a group.

Creating Multicast Scopes

To create a multicast scope, follow these steps:

1. Within the DHCP management console, right-click the DHCP server and choose the New Multicast Scope option. The New Multicast Scope Wizard opens. Click Next.
2. Type a name and description for the scope. Click Next.
3. Specify a range of IP addresses and a TTL (see Figure 3.8). Click Next.

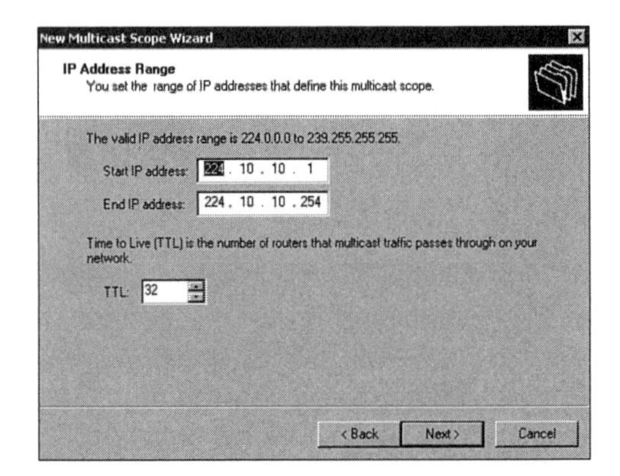

Figure 3.8 Configuring a range of multicast addresses.

4. Type any IP addresses you want to exclude from the range. Click Next.
5. Specify a lease duration, which defines how long a client can lease a multicast address from the scope. Click Next.
6. Click Yes to activate the scope. Click Next.
7. Click Finish.

Configuring DHCP for DNS Integration

The Windows NT 4.0 environment uses NetBIOS names to identify clients and servers on a network. These names can be resolved to IP addresses using `LMHOSTS` files or a WINS server. Because the WINS database is dynamic, integrating DHCP and WINS on a network is simple. In addition, because the DNS database is static, implementing DHCP and DNS on a Windows NT network requires a WINS server.

The Windows 2000 environment requires DNS, which is used to locate clients, servers, and services on the network. Traditionally, administrators had to manually enter the host records. To overcome this and allow DHCP and DNS to be integrated on a network without the use of a WINS server, Windows 2000 workstations configured as DHCP clients can be automatically registered in the DNS database.

Updating Client DNS Information with DHCP Servers

The workstation platform determines how the client interacts with the DHCP and DNS servers. Recall from earlier in the book that Windows 2000 clients can send update requests directly to a DNS server to update its own pointer and address records, known as a *dynamic update*. Alternatively, the client can request that the DHCP server make the update on its behalf.

Using an additional DHCP option included in the `DHCPRequest` message, the Client FQDN option (option 81), and the client's fully qualified domain name (FQDN), a Windows 2000 DHCP client can pass its FQDN to the DHCP server and inform the server how to perform the update. The client can either perform the update or inform the DHCP server (using option 81 included with the DHCPRequest message) that it should perform the update on its behalf.

Clients running platforms earlier than Windows 2000 do not support dynamic updates and are unable to interact directly with a DNS server like a Windows 2000 client can. When a pre-Windows 2000 client (or a non-Microsoft client) receives an IP address from a DHCP server, the DHCP server can be configured to perform the updates on behalf of these clients. As you just saw, Windows 2000 clients can have this functionality configured as well, but the difference here lies in the fact that non-Windows 2000 clients cannot update their records with the DNS server themselves, as do Windows 2000 clients.

Be sure you know which clients support dynamic DNS and understand how to configure DHCP for those clients that cannot update their own records.

Configuring DHCP/DNS Integration

To configure DHCP for DNS integration, right-click the DHCP server within the management console and choose Properties. If you select the DNS tab, you'll see a dialog box similar to the one shown in Figure 3.9. Three settings can be configured for DNS integration, which are described as follows:

- *Automatically update DHCP client information in DNS*—This option is selected by default. The DHCP server will register host records and pointer records when requested to do so by the client. In an environment that runs only Windows 2000, the default setting is sufficient because Windows 2000 clients are capable of updating their own records directly with the DNS server. Two suboptions are listed. The Update DNS only if DHCP client requests option is selected by default. If you have pre-Windows 2000 DHCP clients on the network, select the option to always update DNS.
- *Discard forward (name-to-address) lookups when lease expires*—This option is enabled by default as well. Once the IP address lease expires (the client is no longer using it), the DHCP server sends a request to the DNS server that the DNS record for the client should be discarded.
- *Enable updates for DNS clients that do not support dynamic updates*—If you have pre-Windows 2000 or non-Microsoft clients on the network, select this option to have the DHCP server perform DNS updates on behalf of the clients.

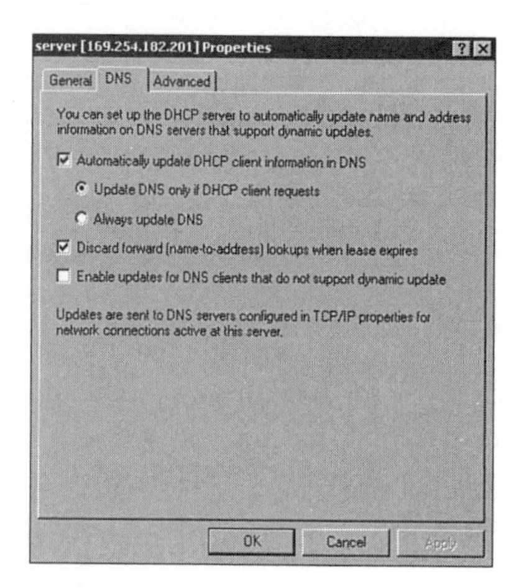

Figure 3.9 Configuring DHCP integration with DNS.

Authorizing a DHCP Server in Active Directory

Windows 2000 introduces many new features designed to increase network security. One of these new features is the detection of rogue DHCP servers on the network. Before a DHCP server can begin leasing IP addresses to DHCP clients, it must first be authorized to do so within Active Directory. This eliminates the possibility of someone adding a Windows 2000 DHCP server to the network that hasn't been approved by the appropriate authority. Any DHCP server that hasn't been authorized is detected and the DHCP service will fail to start.

Detection of rogue servers eliminates the possibility of a Windows 2000 DHCP server with inaccurate IP addressing information being introduced onto a network. However, this feature applies only to Windows 2000 DHCP servers. A Windows NT 4.0 rogue server would not be detected.

Authorizing the DHCP Server

A DHCP server can be authorized through the DHCP management console by an member of the Enterprise Admins group. To authorize a DHCP server, perform the following steps:

1. Click Start, point to Programs, Administrative Tools, and click DHCP.
2. Within the DHCP management console, right-click the DHCP server and click Authorize.
3. Once authorized, the DHCP server can respond to client requests for IP address parameters.

If a DHCP needs to be removed from the network, you should unauthorize the server so it no longer has the capability to lease IP addresses to clients. To do so, right-click the DHCP server within the DHCP console and select the Unauthorize option. Click Yes to confirm your actions. The DHCP server will then be removed from Active Directory.

Because the detection of rogue servers is new in Windows 2000, be prepared to answer at least one question pertaining to the authorization of DHCP servers. Note that only enterprise admins can authorize a DHCP server.

Managing and Monitoring DHCP

After a DHCP server has been installed, it most certainly must be maintained. This entails performing management tasks and monitoring the server on a regular basis to ensure adequate performance over time. A number of tools are available that you can use to perform these tasks, including:

- DHCP Manager for managing the DHCP service
- System Monitor for monitoring real-time performance of a DHCP server
- Event Viewer for viewing any messages generated by the DHCP service
- Network Monitor for monitoring DHCP-related network traffic

Using the DHCP Manager

As you've seen throughout this chapter, the DHCP Manager is where most DHCP server-management tasks are performed.

The Action menu within the management console has a number of options. Some of the options are outlined in the next section beginning with "Displaying Statistics."

Displaying Statistics

When you highlight the DHCP server and choose Display Statistics from the Action menu, the Server Statistics dialog box opens (see Figure 3.10), providing you with a summary of what is happening on the server.

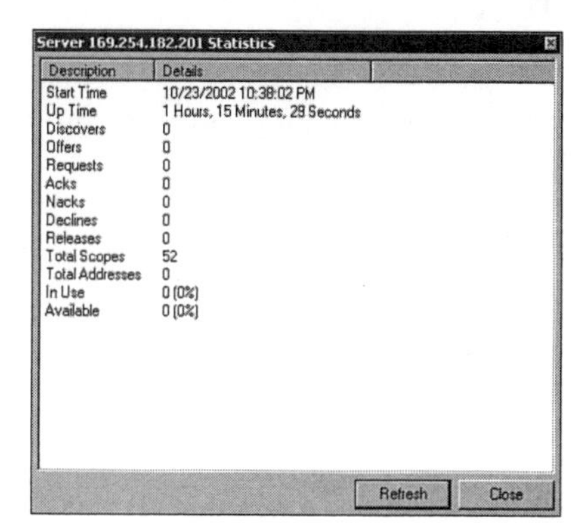

Figure 3.10 Viewing DHCP server statistics.

The statistics window displays the following items:

- *Start Time*—The time when the service was last started
- *Up Time*—Length of time since the service was last restarted
- *Discovers*—The number of `DHCPDISCOVER` messages received by the server
- *Offers*—The number of offers the DHCP server has sent out
- *Requests*—The number of `DHCPREQUEST` messages received by the server
- *Acks*—The number of acknowledgements the server has sent out
- *Nacks*—The number of negative acknowledgements the server has sent out
- *Declines*—The number of decline messages the server has sent out
- *Releases*—The number of release messages the server has received
- *Total Scopes*—The number of scopes that are currently active on the server
- *Total Addresses*—The number of IP addresses the server has available for lease to DHCP clients
- *In Use*—The number of IP addresses currently leased to clients
- *Available*—The number of IP addresses left in the pool

Reconciling Scopes

The Reconcile All Scopes option is useful when you need to fix any inconsistencies in the DHCP database, such as when not all IP address leases are being reflected in the DHCP database. Information in the database is compared with information stored in the Registry.

Selecting the Reconcile All Scopes option opens the Reconcile All Scopes dialog box. Click the Verify button to check the database for inconsistencies. Any errors are displayed (see Figure 3.11).

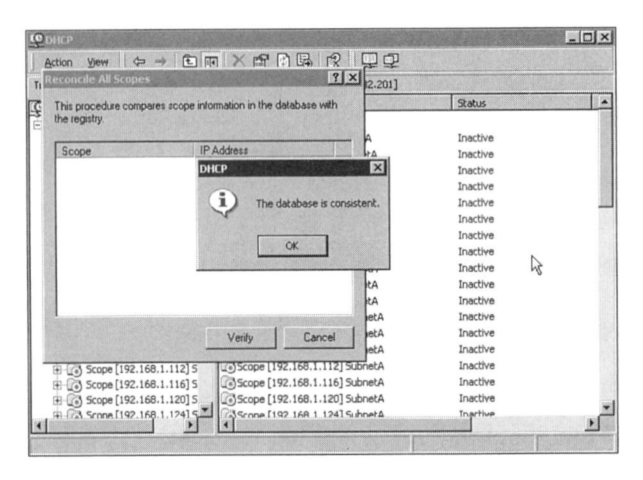

Figure 3.11 Checking the DHCP database for inconsistencies.

Other Management Tasks in the DHCP Manager Action Menu

You can also perform a number of other tasks from the Action menu, including

- *Unauthorize*—Use this option to unauthorize a DHCP server. The server will no longer appear in the list of authorized servers within Active Directory.
- *Start/Stop*—Use these options to stop and start the DHCP Server service.
- *Pause/Resume*—Use these options to pause and resume the DHCP server.
- *Restart*—Use this option to restart the DHCP Server service. Doing so resets all the server statistics discussed earlier.

The last three options described in the preceding list can be found under the All Tasks menu option.

Finally, selecting the Properties option from the Action menu opens the Properties dialog box for the DHCP server. The Properties dialog box contains three tabs:

- General
- DNS
- Advanced

You have already seen the DNS tab earlier in the chapter; the next two sections cover the other two tabs in further depth.

The General Tab

On the General tab, you can configure how often the statistics gathered for the server are refreshed (see Figure 3.12), whether to write DHCP information to the System log within Event Viewer, and whether to display the BOOTP configuration information in the DHCP management console.

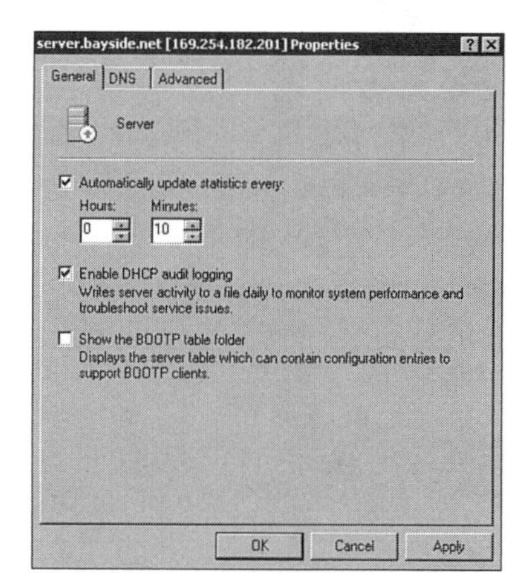

Figure 3.12 Configure DCHP server properties.

The Advanced Tab

On the Advanced tab (see Figure 3.13), you can configure conflict detection, which specifies the number of times the DHCP server should attempt to determine whether an IP address is already in use before assigning it to a DHCP client. You can also change the location of the DHCP database and audit log, as well as check the connections used to service DHCP clients.

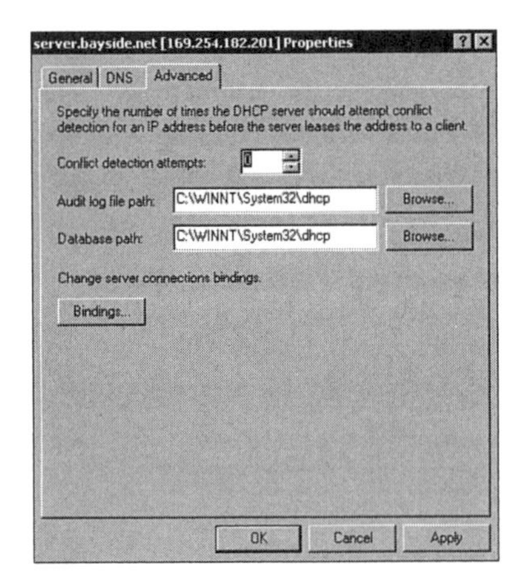

Figure 3.13 Configuring the Advanced properties of a DHCP server.

Tools for Monitoring

It's always good practice to monitor server performance, whether it's a DHCP server, a domain controller, or a DNS server. Windows 2000 comes with a number of tools that can be used to monitor different aspects of a DHCP server. The following section looks at monitoring real-time performance of a DHCP server, logging DHCP related events, and monitoring DHCP related traffic.

System Monitor

The tool most commonly used for monitoring is the System Monitor found in the Performance MMC within the Administrative Tools menu. Once the DHCP Server service is installed, a number of counters are added that allow you to monitor specific aspects of DHCP (see Figure 3.14). Some of the more commonly used counters include:

- *Packets Received/Sec*—Monitors the rate at which packets are received by the DHCP server. This counter monitors all request types received by the server.
- *Requests/Sec*—Monitors the rate at which DHCP requests are received by the DHCP server. If this value is high, consider increasing the lease duration.

- *Offers/Sec*—Monitors the rate at which offers are sent by the DHCP server.
- *Releases/Sec*—Monitors the rate at which releases are received by the DHCP server.
- *Active Queue Length*—Monitors the number of packets in the processing queue of the DHCP server.
- *Conflict Check Queue Length*—Monitors the number of packets in the DHCP server queue waiting on conflict detection.

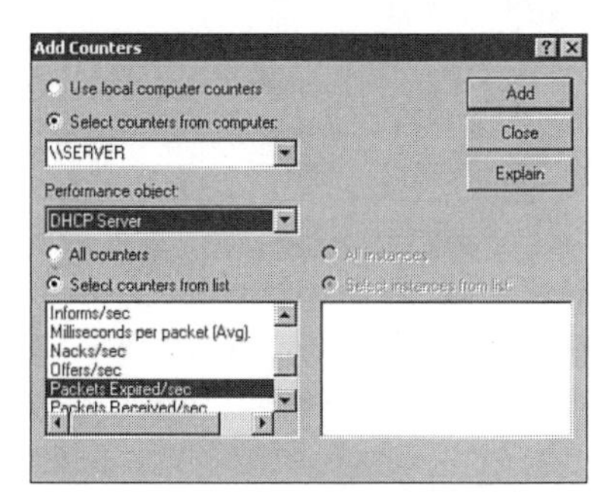

Figure 3.14 DHCP performance counters.

Event Viewer

If the DHCP server is configured to log activity, you can use the System Log within the Event Viewer to monitor and troubleshoot events. When an event does occur, such as the DHCP Server service being restarted, it is written to the log file and provides useful information, including a description of the event and when it occurred.

Network Monitor

Network Monitor is a "sniffer" that can be used to capture network traffic coming to and from a computer. In terms of DHCP, you can use it to view and analyze traffic between a DHCP server and DHCP clients, such as the IP address lease process.

Practice Questions

Question 1

You recently installed the DHCP Server service on one of your Windows 2000 member servers in the domain. You notice that the DHCP service is constantly being shut down. What is causing the problem to occur?

- ❍ A. The DHCP server has not been configured with a scope.
- ❍ B. The scope on the DHCP server has not been activated.
- ❍ C. The DHCP server has not been authorized within Active Directory.
- ❍ D. There is a DHCP server on the network with a duplicate scope.

Answer C is correct. If a DHCP server has not been authorized within Active Directory, it is considered to be a rogue server and the service will continue to shut down until it is authorized. Answers A, B, and D are incorrect because none of these problems would cause the DHCP service to shut down.

Question 2

You recently upgraded all workstations from Windows 98 to Windows 2000 Professional. Your network has a DNS server, a WINS server, and a Windows NT 4.0 DHCP server. The reason for upgrading the clients to Windows 2000 Professional is to take advantage of dynamic updates. After you upgrade the clients to Windows 2000, you notice the DNS records are not being updated. What must you do to take advantage of dynamic updates?

- ❍ A. Within the DHCP Manager, configure the DHCP server to upgrade the records for clients.
- ❍ B. The DNS server must be configured to accept updates from the Windows 2000 Professional clients.
- ❍ C. The WINS server must be removed from the network.
- ❍ D. The DHCP server must be upgraded to Windows 2000 Server.

Answer D is correct. Windows NT 4.0 DHCP does not support dynamic DNS. The existing DHCP server must be upgraded to Windows 2000 Server. Therefore, answers A and B are incorrect. Answer C is incorrect because removing the WINS server will not have any impact on whether dynamic updates can occur.

Question 3

You are having problems with your DHCP server—it does not seem to be functioning correctly. You'd like to begin troubleshooting this by logging all DHCP activity to the System log. How can you enable this logging option?

- ❍ A. Open the Properties dialog box for the DHCP server and select the Enable Audit Logging check box on the Advanced tab.
- ❍ B. Open the Properties dialog box for the DHCP server and select the Automatically Update Statistics check box on the Advanced tab.
- ❍ C. Open the Properties dialog box for the DHCP server and select the Enable Audit Logging check box on the General tab.
- ❍ D. Nothing needs to be done. The DHCP server logs all activity to the System log by default.

Answer C is correct. To have DHCP activity logged to the System log, open the Properties dialog box for the DHCP server and make sure the General tab is active. Select the Enable DHCP Logging check box. Answer A is incorrect because logging is configured on the General tab. Answer B is incorrect because selecting the option to Automatically Update Statistics does not enable logging. Answer D is incorrect because logging is not enabled by default.

Question 4

Your network consists of multiple subnets connected by routers. You have finished installing a Windows 2000 DHCP server. You create the necessary scopes and configure the **003** router option to assign all clients the IP address of their local router. All clients successfully lease an IP address. However, you soon discover that users on Subnet A are the only ones capable of communicating outside their local subnet. What could be causing the problem?

- ❍ A. All the scopes have not yet been activated.
- ❍ B. The DHCP option is configured at the server level.
- ❍ C. The DHCP server has not yet been authorized.
- ❍ D. The **003** router option must first be activated.

Answer B is correct. Each subnet will have its own gateway so the `003` router option should be configured at the scope level instead of the server level. Answers A and C are incorrect because all clients are successfully leasing IP addresses. Answer D is incorrect because DHCP options do not have to be activated.

Question 5

Your company placed you in charge of configuring a Windows 2000 DHCP server. The network was recently upgraded to Windows 2000 and Active Directory. The network consists of three domains. You are a member of the Administrator group in each of the domains. You install the DHCP server and create the necessary scopes. When you attempt to authorize the DHCP server, you receive an "**access denied**" message. What is causing the problem to occur?

- ❍ A. You are not a member of the Administrators group in the forest root domain.
- ❍ B. Active Directory is unavailable.
- ❍ C. You are not logged on as the local Administrator on the DHCP server.
- ❍ D. You are not a member of the Enterprise Admins group.

Answer D is correct. To authorize a DHCP server, the user account you are logged on with must be a member of the Enterprise Admins group. Therefore, answers A and C are incorrect. Answer B is incorrect because if Active Directory was unavailable, you would receive a different error message altogether.

Question 6

You are a junior network administrator. One of your tasks is to maintain a newly installed DHCP server. The scopes have not yet been created. The senior administrator documents all the required scopes and asks you to create them on the server. You notice several DHCP options are to be configured, but it is not specified what type of scope options to configure. You are trying to recall how scope options are applied. Which of the following correctly lists the order in which they are applied to clients?

- ❍ A. Server, Scope, Class, Client
- ❍ B. Server, Class, Scope, Client
- ❍ C. Server, Scope, Client, Class
- ❍ D. Scope, Server, Client, Class

Answer A is correct. The correct order in which DHCP options are applied is server, scope, class, and then client. Therefore, answers B, C, and D are incorrect.

Question 7

Bayside Consulting firm currently consists of 400 workstations. One hundred clients are running Windows 95 and the remaining clients are running Windows 2000 Professional. You use a Windows 2000 DHCP server to automate the task of assigning IP addresses. All clients on the network are successfully receiving IP addresses from the server. When you check the DNS zone file, you notice that only the Windows 2000 Professional clients have records. How can you most easily resolve the problem?

❍ A. Upgrade the Windows 95 clients to Windows 2000 Professional.

❍ B. Configure the properties of the DHCP server to always update DNS.

❍ C. Configure the properties of the DHCP server to enable updates for DNS clients that do not support dynamic updates.

❍ D. Configure the Windows 95 workstations to update their own records.

Answer C is correct. By selecting the option to enable updates for DNS clients that do not support dynamic updates, the DHCP server can update the address and pointer records on behalf of the Windows 95 clients. Therefore, answer B is incorrect. Answer A is incorrect because it would not provide the easiest solution. Answer D is incorrect because Windows 95 clients cannot interact directly with a DNS server regardless of their configuration.

Question 8

Your organization recently increased the number of workstations on the network. To simplify the process of assigning IP addresses, you are implementing DHCP. The budget allows for the purchase of two new servers that will both run DHCP. Two subnets exist, and a DHCP server will be placed in each one. How can you ensure that clients can still lease IP addresses in the event that one of the DHCP servers is unavailable?

❍ A. Configure replication to occur between the two DHCP servers.

❍ B. Nothing needs to be configured, because DHCP servers on the same network share scope information.

❍ C. Configure each server with a range of IP addresses for both subnets.

❍ D. Configure all clients with the IP address of both DHCP servers.

Answer C is correct. To provide fault tolerance, each DHCP server should be configured with a range of IP addresses for both subnets. Each DHCP server should have a scope with 80% of the IP addresses for its local subnet and a scope with 20% of the IP addresses in the remote subnet. This provides fault tolerance without the chance of duplicate IP addresses. Answers A and B are incorrect because DHCP servers do not share scope information. Answer D is incorrect because clients are not configured with the IP addresses of a DHCP server. A DHCP server is located using a broadcast.

Question 9

You install the DHCP Server service on a Windows 2000 member server. The DHCP server is authorized in Active Directory and all the required scopes are created. Clients on the network cannot lease IP addresses from the server. What is causing the problem to occur?

❍ A. The scope has not been authorized.

❍ B. The DHCP server has not been activated.

❍ C. The DHCP server does not need to be authorized because it's running on a member server.

❍ D. The scope has not been activated.

Answer D is correct. Before clients can lease an IP address, the scope must be activated. Answer A is incorrect because scopes are not authorized. Answer B is incorrect because servers are authorized, not activated. Answer C is incorrect because DHCP servers must still be authorized when the service is installed on a member server.

Question 10

Your network consists of 100 Windows 2000 computers, 25 Windows 95 computers, and 3 Windows 2000 servers. DHCP is used on the network to automate TCP/IP configurations on all client computers. You want to meet the following requirements:

- All client computers will be accessible by the FQDN.
- Host and PTR records should be automatically updated in DNS by Windows 2000 clients.
- Records should be automatically removed from DNS when IP address leases expire.
- The DHCP server will update DNS for those clients that do not support dynamic updates.

You perform the following tasks:

- Configure the DHCP server to discard forward lookups when leases expire.
- Configure the DHCP server to update DNS only if the DHCP client requests it.
- Configure the 015 DNS Domain Name option.

Which of the requirements are met? [Choose all that apply.]

- ❑ A. All client computers are accessible by their FQDNs.
- ❑ B. Host and pointer records are automatically updated in DNS by Windows 2000 clients.
- ❑ C. Records are automatically removed from DNS when leases expire.
- ❑ D. The DHCP server will update DNS for those clients that do not support dynamic updates.

Answers B and C are correct. By selecting the option to discard forward lookups when leases expire, records in the DNS zone file will be automatically removed when the lease duration expires. Windows 2000 clients by default will update their own records in the DNS database. Answers A and D are incorrect because Windows 95 clients cannot update their own records, and the DHCP server isn't configured to do so on their behalf. As a result, not all clients will be accessible by their FQDN.

Need to Know More?

Search the online version of TechNet and the Windows 2000 Server Resource Kit using keywords such as `DHCP`, `IP Addresses`, and `Dynamic Updates`.

Alcott, Neall, *DHCP for Windows 2000*, O'Reilly & Associates, Inc., Sebastopol, CA, 2001. ISBN: 1565928385. This book provides comprehensive, in-depth information about how DHCP works and provides good examples on its implementation.

Lemon, Ted, and Ralph E. Droms, *The DHCP Handbook: Understanding, Deploying, and Managing Automated Configuration Services*, Indianapolis, IN, Macmillan Technical Publishing, 1999. ISBN: 1578701376. This book covers many aspects of DHCP from conceptual information to its installation and configuration.

Remote Access

Terms you'll need to understand:

- ✓ Virtual private network
- ✓ Authentication
- ✓ Encryption
- ✓ Remote Access Service (RAS)
- ✓ Multilink
- ✓ RADIUS
- ✓ Internet Authentication Server

Techniques you'll need to master:

- ✓ Configuring inbound connections
- ✓ Understanding the components of a remote access policy
- ✓ Understanding how remote access policies are evaluated
- ✓ Creating a remote access policy
- ✓ Configuring a remote access profile
- ✓ Configuring a virtual private network
- ✓ Understanding and configuring Multilink connections
- ✓ Configuring routing and remote access for DHCP integration
- ✓ Understanding and configuring the different authentication and encryption protocols
- ✓ Managing and monitoring remote access

Introduction

As technology advances and allows users to be more mobile, the need for remote access is quickly increasing. It is almost a necessity to provide users with access to network resources from remote locations, such as home offices and client and business sites. Organizations need the flexibility of providing mobile users access to network resources without a compromise in security or a drastic increase in administrative overhead.

This chapter covers important topics relating to Windows 2000 remote access. You learn how to configure a remote access server and provide access to the network without compromising security. You also learn about some of the management and monitoring tasks that go along with remote access.

It's crucial that you have a thorough understanding of all the topics presented in the chapter, because remote access is one of the most popular exam areas and you'll likely run into several remote access questions.

Configuring and Troubleshooting Remote Access

Windows 2000 includes a *remote access service*, allowing remote clients to connect to a remote access server and use resources as though they were directly attached to the network. RAS can also be used to configure virtual private networks (VPNs), thus expanding your LAN over the Internet.

Windows 2000 remote access provides two connectivity methods:

- *Dial-up*—Using dial-up remote access such as an ISDN or phone line, clients can connect to a remote access server.
- *VPN (virtual private network)*—Clients connect to a remote access server configured as a VPN server using an IP-based internetwork (most often the public Internet).

Enabling Routing and Remote Access

Routing and Remote Access Service (RRAS) is installed by default with Windows 2000. However, before you can begin using RRAS, it must first be enabled. To enable RRAS, follow these steps:

1. Click Start, point to Programs, Administrative Tools, and click Routing and Remote Access.
2. Right-click the server and select Configure and Enable Routing and Remote Access. Click Next.
3. The Routing and Remote Access Server Setup Wizard opens. From the list of common configurations, select one of the available options (see Figure 4.1). To configure a virtual private network, select the Virtual private network (VPN) server option. The remaining options are outlined in Table 4.1. Click Next.

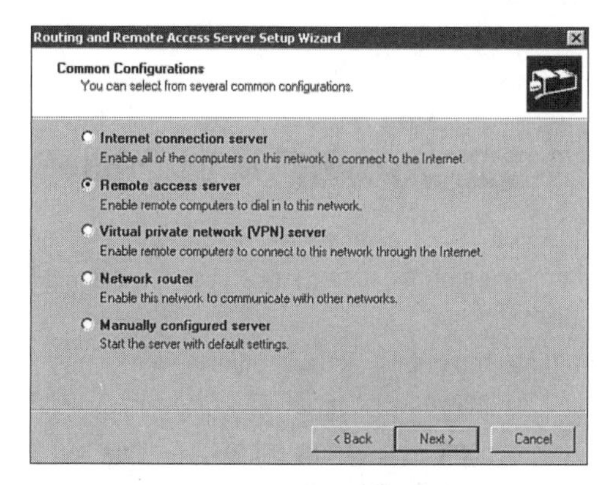

Figure 4.1 Enabling a remote access server.

4. Verify that the protocols required by remote clients are installed on the server. If necessary, you can add additional protocols. Click Next.
5. On the IP Address Assignment screen, select how remote access clients will receive an IP address (see Figure 4.2). IP addresses can be assigned automatically using a DHCP server on the internal network or you can configure a range of IP addresses on the remote access server to assign to remote access clients. If you choose the second option, the resulting wizard screen allows you to configure the range of IP addresses available to remote clients. Click Next.
6. Specify whether to use a RADIUS server. If you choose to use a RADIUS server, the resulting wizard screen allows you to specify the name of the primary and alternative RADIUS servers and the shared secret. Click Next.
7. Click Finish.

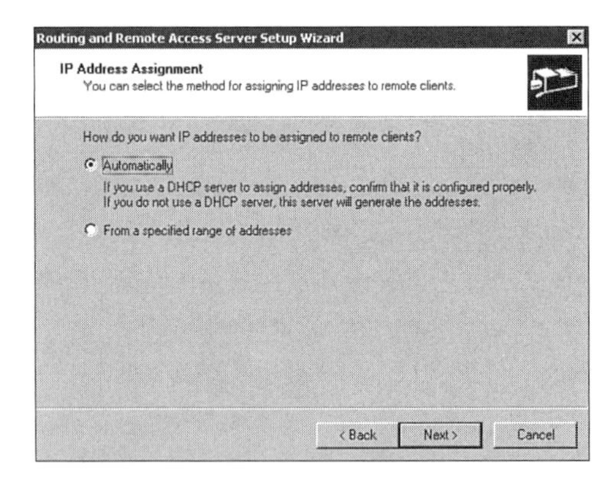

Figure 4.2 Configuring IP address assignments for remote clients.

Table 4.1 Common Remote Access Configurations

Configuration	Description
Internet connection server	Enables computers on the network to access the Internet through this server.
Remote access server	Enables remote computers to dial into the server and access the local network.
Virtual private network (VPN) server	Enables remote computers to connect to this server and access the local network using the Internet.
Network router	Enables communication between the local network and remote networks.
Manually configure server	Starts the server with the default settings.

After you click Finish to exit the wizard, a warning message appears if you chose to use a DHCP server to assign IP addresses to remote clients (see Figure 4.3). The message warns you that to have DHCP messages relayed from remote clients to a DHCP server on the internal network, the remote access server must be configured as a DHCP Relay Agent. (This issue is covered in more detail in the section "Configuring Remote Access for DHCP," later in this chapter.)

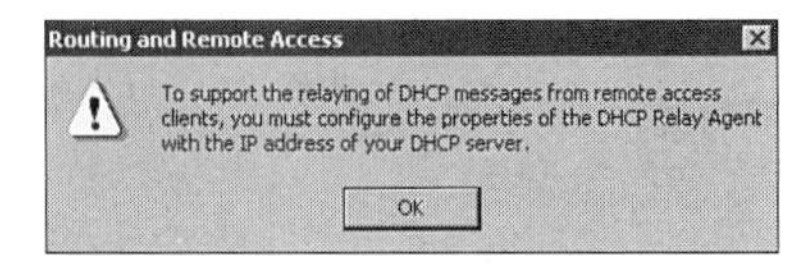

Figure 4.3 Routing and Remote Access warning message.

NT 4 RAS in a Windows 2000 Environment

Before configuring RAS, it is worth mentioning a few points in regard to the co-existence of a Windows NT 4.0 RAS server on a Windows 2000 network. The problem that occurs is that Windows NT RAS servers attempt to retrieve user account information from Active Directory using null credentials, which Active Directory does not allow. To maintain the NT RAS servers in an Active Directory environment, one of the following requirements must be met:

- Permission within Active Directory must be relaxed to allow the Everyone group Read access to Active Directory objects. This can be done by adding the Everyone group to the Pre-Windows 2000 Compatible Access group.
- The RAS service is running on a backup domain controller (BDC) in a mixed-mode Windows 2000 domain.
- The NT RAS server is configured to retrieve dial-in account property information from a BDC (again, the domain must be running in mixed mode).

Configuring Inbound Connections

The two main communication protocols used by dial-up remote access clients are PPP and SLIP. The *point-to-point protocol (PPP)* has become an industry standard communication protocol because of its popularity. PPP provides support for multiple network protocols, including TCP/IP, IPX/SPX, and NetBEUI. PPP supports a number of authentication protocols, discussed later in this chapter in the section entitled "Configuring a Virtual Private Network (VPN)."

Serial Line Internet Protocol (SLIP) is a legacy communication protocol used primarily to connect to UNIX systems. One of the major disadvantages of SLIP is the lack of security (for example, sending passwords in clear text). Windows 2000 remote access supports the use of SLIP for outbound connections only. SLIP also does not support the DHCP functionality on a RAS server to assign dial in clients an IP address.

The two protocols used for accessing a VPN server are Point-to-Point Tunneling Protocol (PPTP) and Layer 2 Tunneling Protocol (L2TP), which are discussed later in this chapter. PPTP is used over a PPP connection to create a secure tunnel.

You can configure PPP using the PPP tab in the Properties window of the remote access server (see Figure 4.4). You can enable the Multilink connections option to allow remote access clients to aggregate multiple phone lines into a single logical connection, which increases bandwidth. For example, combining two B channels from an ISDN BRI connection. Although Multilink enables multiple connections to act as a single logical connection, it does not provide a way of dynamically adding and dropping links based on bandwidth requirements.

This feature is provided by the Bandwidth Allocation Protocol (BAP). BAP enables multilink connections to be added and dropped as bandwidth requirements change. For example, if the bandwidth utilization for a link goes beyond a configured level, a BAP request message can be sent by the client requesting an additional link. The Bandwidth Allocation Control Protocol (BACP) works in conjunction with the Link Control Protocol (LCP) to elect a favored "peer" so if multiple BAP requests are received simultaneously, a favored peer can be identified. From the properties window shown in Figure 4.4, you can also enable or disable BAP, BACP, LCP, and software compression for PPP connections.

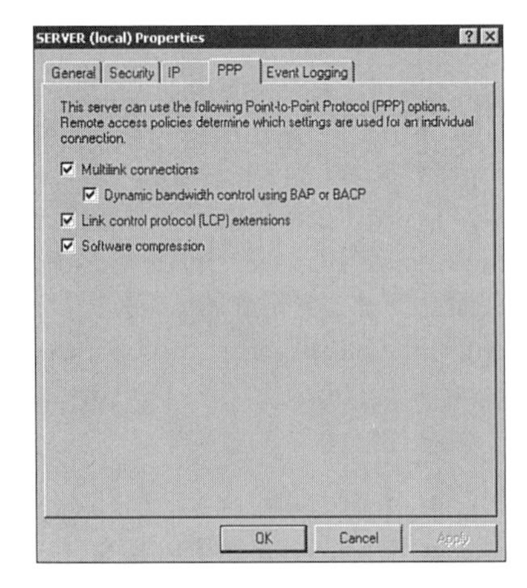

Figure 4.4 Configuring PPP.

To apply Multilink at the remote access policy level, you must first enable it at the server level. This means if Multilink is not enabled through the Properties window for the remote access server, you cannot apply Multilink in a remote access policy.

Configuring Ports

Configuring inbound connections allows a remote access server to accept incoming connections from remote access clients. Once RRAS has been enabled (see the steps discussed in the "Installing Routing and Remote Access" section near the start of the chapter to refresh your memory on how to enable the server), five PPTP and five L2TP ports are automatically created. Additional ports can be created if necessary. You can configure the ports by right-clicking the Ports icon under the RAS server and selecting Properties. Select the ports you want to configure and click the Configure button. Keep in mind that the configuration changes made apply to all five ports. The configurable options are the same for PPTP and L2TP ports (see Figure 4.5). From this properties window, you can also increase the number of ports by changing the Maximum ports setting.

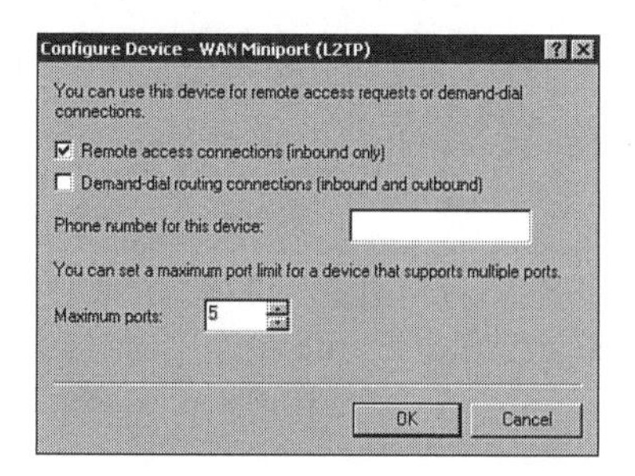

Figure 4.5 Configuring ports.

In the Configure Device dialog box shown in Figure 4.5, you can configure the ports for inbound use only, or inbound and outbound use if the server is used for demand-dial routing. This is also where you can configure additional ports by setting the maximum ports value.

Demand-dial routing enables on-demand connections using physical or virtual links. The benefit of a demand-dial connection as opposed to a dedicated link is reduced cost and increased security. For example, you can use demand-dial routing to allow two offices in different geographical locations to communicate without incurring the cost of a dedicated link. This way the connection is only established when necessary.

Modem and serial ports are also created for any modems installed on the server and any serial or parallel connections. These ports can also be configured in the Ports Properties dialog box.

Configuring a Remote Access Policy

A *remote access policy* allows you to control which users are permitted remote access to the network and the characteristics of the connection. Windows 2000 introduces some major changes from Windows NT 4.0 in terms of remote access, one of which is the use of remote access policies. Prior to Windows 2000, remote access was controlled through the Properties dialog box of a user account. Windows 2000 uses user account properties *and* remote access policies to control remote access.

With remote access policies, administrators can permit or deny connection attempts based on a number of criteria (such as the time of day or group membership), giving administrators much more flexibility and granular control. Once a connection has been granted, administrators can further control the session by defining the maximum session time and encryption settings.

A remote access policy consists of the following elements that work together to provide secure access to remote access servers:

- Conditions
- Permissions
- Profile

After remote access is enabled, a default remote access policy is automatically created. The default policy allows remote access any time on any day of the week, denies remote access permission to all users, and has no remote access profile settings configured.

You can create additional policies by right-clicking the Remote Access Policies icon within the Routing and Remote Access management console and selecting the New Remote Access Policy option. The wizard walks you through policy configuration elements, all of which are discussed in the next section.

Remote Access Conditions

Conditions define the parameters that must match those configured on the remote access client before remote access will be granted. These can include parameters such as the time of day and Windows group membership. Before the permissions of a remote access policy are evaluated, the connection attempt must match the condition within a remote access policy. If multiple policies are configured, the first policy that matches the conditions of the connection attempt is then further evaluated for permissions and profile settings. Table 4.2 summarizes some of the commonly used conditions that can be configured for a remote access policy.

Table 4.2 Conditions That Can Be Configured in a Remote Access Policy	
Condition	**Description**
Called Station ID	The number dialed by the remote access client
Calling Station ID	The number from which the remote access client called
Day and Time Restrictions	The days of the week and time of day users are allowed remote access
Windows Groups	The Windows groups the user must belong to

To configure the conditions of a remote access policy, follow these steps:

1. Open the Routing and Remote Access management console and click Remote Access Policies.
2. Right-click the remote access policy and click Properties.
3. From the Properties dialog box for the policy, click the Add button.
4. In the Select Attribute dialog box, select the attributes you want to configure and click Add (see Figure 4.6).

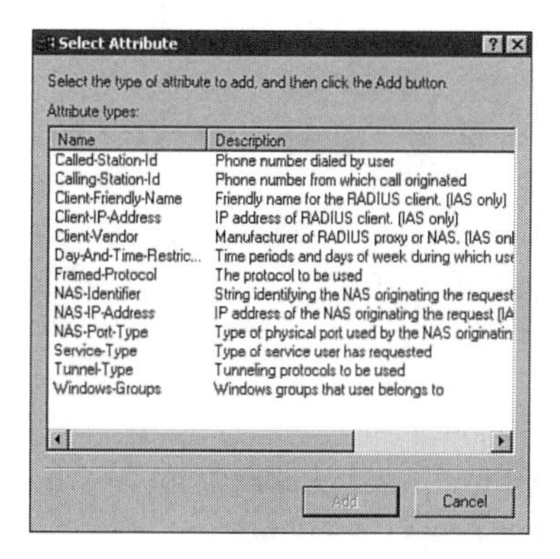

Figure 4.6 Configuring remote access conditions.

Remote Access Permissions

If the connection attempt matches the conditions of a remote access policy, the permissions of that policy are then evaluated. The remote access permissions determine whether a specific user is granted or denied remote access. Windows 2000 uses a combination of the dial-in properties of a user account and the permissions in the remote access policy to determine whether the connection attempt is allowed. Remote access permissions can be explicitly allowed or denied through user account properties. When configuring remote access permissions using the Dial-in tab in the

Properties dialog box for a user account, you have three options (see Figure 4.7):

➤ Allow access

➤ Deny access

➤ Control access through Remote Access Policy

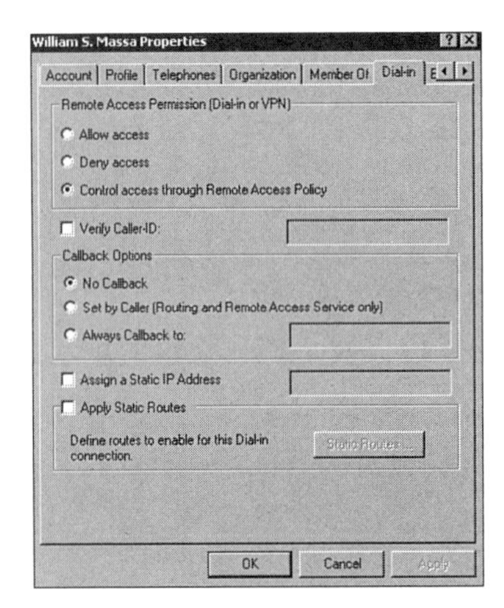

Figure 4.7 Configuring remote access permissions through the user account properties.

If the Control Access Through Remote Access Policy option is unavailable, switch the domain from mixed mode to native mode. When operating in mixed mode, this option is not available. Once the domain mode is changed, this is the default option.

If you explicitly allow remote access by selecting the Allow access option, the connection attempt can still be denied if the properties configured for the user account do not match the remote access policy or if the profile settings are not met.

If you choose to have remote access permissions controlled through the policy, permission can be granted or denied through the policy's Properties window (see Figure 4.8). If you are using the default policy, remote access permission is denied by default. You have to change this setting to allow access.

From the Dial-in tab, several other settings can be configured, including caller ID, callback options, and static IP routes. Again, if you configure the settings for the user account, they must match the settings configured on the client or the connection attempt will be denied.

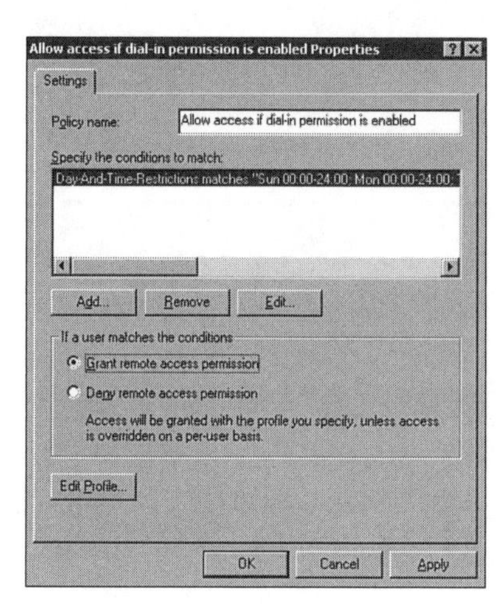

Figure 4.8 Controlling access through the remote access policy.

Using the callback feature, a RAS server can be configured to call a remote access client back at a preconfigured number or at a number set by the caller. This provides an added level of security because users are only allowed to dial into the remote access server from the number specified.

Configuring a Remote Access Profile

The final element of the remote access policy is the remote access profile. Once the remote access client has been granted permission, the profile determines the settings of the connection. Once again the settings in the profile must match those of the connection attempt, or it will be denied.

To configure the profile settings, click the Edit Profile button in the policy's Properties window. This opens the Edit Dial-in Profile dialog box, as shown in Figure 4.9. Several tabs are available, as summarized in Table 4.3.

Table 4.3 Remote Access Profile Settings

Property Tab	Description
Dial-in Constraints	Configure the disconnect if idle time, maximum session time, day and time restrictions, and media and number restrictions.
IP	Define how IP addresses are assigned to clients and configure packet filtering for inbound and outbound connections.
Multilink	Enable and configure Multilink and Bandwidth Allocation Protocol.
Authentication	Configure the authentication methods available for the connections in the remote access policy.
Encryption	Configure the different levels of encryption for the policy.
Advanced	Specify additional connection parameters.

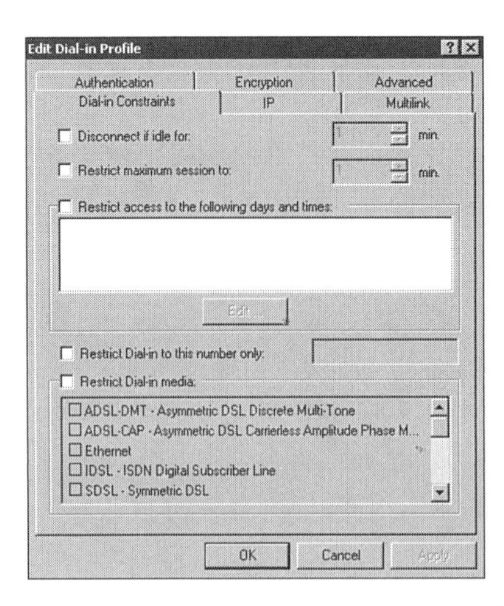

Figure 4.9 Configuring a remote access profile.

Remote Access Policy Evaluation

Given the many options and the complexity of remote access policy elements, it's important to have a good understanding of how policies are applied when a remote access client attempts a connection. Assuming you are running in native mode, the following points outline the connection process:

- When a user attempts to connect, the RAS server determines whether a policy exits. The first policy in the ordered list of remote access policies is checked. If there is no policy configured (and the default policy has been deleted), the connection attempt is rejected. If a policy does exist, the evaluation process continues.
- The conditions of the first policy in the list are evaluated. If the connection attempt matches all the conditions, the evaluation process continues. If all conditions do not match the connection attempt, the next policy in the list is evaluated. If no more policies exist, the connection attempt is rejected.
- If the connection attempt matches the conditions in one of the policies, the user's permissions are evaluated. If the user's account property is set to Deny Access or if the permission within the policy is set to Deny Access, the connection attempt is rejected. If the policy or the account property is set to Allow Access, the process continues.
- The settings of the remote access profile and the properties of the user account are evaluated against the connection attempt. If the connection attempt matches both the profile and account settings, the user is granted remote access. If not, the connection attempt is rejected.

Remote access policies are a popular topic on the exam. Be sure you are familiar with how remote access policies and the policy elements are evaluated. Also keep in mind that remote access policies are not stored within Active Directory but on each individual server.

When running in mixed mode, keep in mind that the permission settings configured using the Dial-in tab for a user account override those in the policy, unless set to Deny Access. For example, if the account property is set to Allow Access but the profile denies it, the user is granted access and the process of evaluation continues. On the other hand, if the account property is set to Deny Access and the profile permits access, the connection attempt is rejected. By default, the Administrator and Guest accounts on a standalone remote access server or in a Windows 2000 native-mode domain are set to control access through the Remote Access Policy. For a Windows 2000 mixed-mode domain, they are set to Deny access. Any new accounts created on a standalone remote access server or in a Windows 2000 native-mode domain are set to Deny Access.

Configuring a Virtual Private Network (VPN)

A *virtual private network (VPN)* enables you to connect to a remote server using an internetwork such as the Internet. Once a remote access client has established a connection to the Internet, a connection is created with the VPN server using a tunneling protocol (PPTP or L2TP). The tunnel provides secure communication between the user and the private network. One of the biggest advantages to implementing a VPN is a reduction in cost. Remote clients can dial in to a local ISP and then connect to the remote server instead of incurring possible long-distance charges.

There are two types of tunneling protocols that can be used to connect to a VPN server: the *Point-to-Point Tunneling Protocol (PPTP)* and the *Layer 2 Tunneling Protocol (L2TP)*. Both protocols are automatically installed by default. PPTP is used over PPP connections on an IP-based network and supports the encryption and encapsulation of IP, IPX, and NetBEUI packets. L2TP can encapsulate IP traffic over a variety of networks, including Frame Relay, ATM, and X.25.

Both PPTP and L2TP encrypt data being transferred. PPTP has built-in encryption technologies and uses MPPE 40-bit to 128-bit encryption. L2TP uses IPSec for data encryption. IPSec uses the Data Encryption Standard (DES) to encrypt data with supported key lengths between 56 bits (DES) and 168 bits (3Des).

In terms of authentication, a user attempting to establish a VPN connection can be authenticated using EAP, MS-CHAP, CHAP, SPAP, or PAP. If you are using L2TP over IPSec, computer- and user-level authentication is provided. The mutual authentication of computers occurs through the exchange of computer certificates, which means that certificates must be installed on both the VPN client and the VPN server. The user-level authentication can be performed by EAP, CHAP, MS-CHAP, SPAP, and PAP.

Table 4.4 summarizes the differences between the two tunneling protocols.

Table 4.4 Differences Between PPTP and L2TP

PPTP	L2TP
Used only for IP-based networks	Supports any point-to-point connection, including IP, ATM, and frame relay
Uses PPP encryption	Encryption is handled by IPSec
Allows IP, IPX, and NetBEUI traffic to be encrypted	Allows IP traffic to be encrypted
Tunnel Authentication	No tunnel authentication
Works through NAT	Does not support NAT

To enable a Windows 2000 server as a VPN server, use the same process outlined when enabling a remote access server, only select the option to configure a VPN server. Once a VPN server is enabled, five PPTP and five L2TP ports are automatically created. Additional ports can be created and configured using the process outlined in the section titled "Configuring Inbound Connections" earlier in this chapter.

Configuring Multilink Connections

Windows 2000 includes a feature known as *Multilink* that allows you to combine multiple phone lines connected to multiple modems into a single logical connection to increase bandwidth.

Multilink functionality is enhanced through the Bandwidth Allocation Protocol (BAP) and the Bandwidth Allocation Control Protocol (BACP), which basically work together to provide bandwidth on demand.

To enable Multilink for individual remote access policies, click the Edit Profile button in the Properties dialog box for the policy and select the Multilink tab (see Figure 4.10).

The following three options are available for configuring Multilink settings:

- *Default to Server Settings*—This setting establishes that the use of Multilink is determined by the settings configured at the remote access server level.

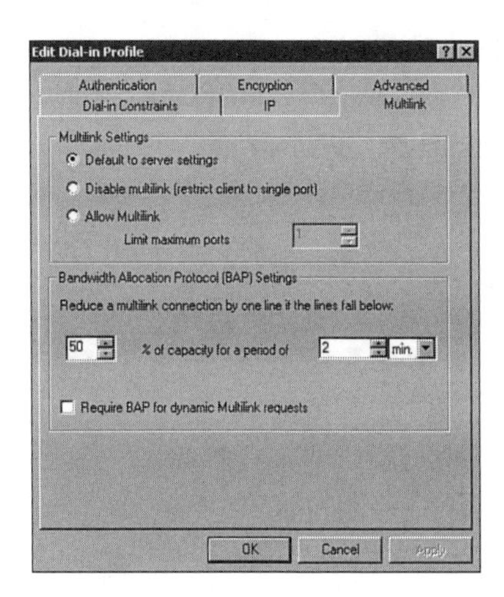

Figure 4.10 Configuring Multilink for a remote access policy.

- *Disable Multilink (restrict client to single port)*—This option restricts remote access clients to a single phone line.
- *Allow Multilink*—This option enables Multilink for the profile and configures the maximum number of ports that can be used by a dial-in client. You can also specify the criteria that must be met for a line to be dropped, as well as enable BAP for dynamic Multilink requests.

Configuring Multilink through a remote access profile applies those settings to that policy only. Before Multilink can be used, it must be enabled using the PPP tab within the Properties dialog box for the remote access server.

Configuring Routing and Remote Access for DHCP

As you saw when enabling RRAS, you can configure the remote access server with a range of IP addresses to assign to remote access clients. (If you do, make sure the range does not conflict with the range of IP addresses configured on the DHCP server to avoid duplicate addresses.) You can also configure the RAS server to obtain IP addresses from the DHCP server to lease to clients.

When you select to use a DHCP server, the remote access server obtains, by default, 10 IP addresses to lease to clients. If all 10 IP addresses are in use, the remote access server obtains 10 more from the DHCP server. (The default number is 10 but can be changed through the Registry.) The benefit of using DHCP with RAS is that IP address assignment remains centralized.

For DHCP to be used with RAS, the DHCP Relay Agent must be configured on the RAS server. When you configure the DHCP Relay Agent, clients still receive IP addresses from the RAS server but they can use `DHCPInform` messages to obtain optional parameters, such as the IP addresses of WINS and DNS servers, directly from the DHCP server. The relay agent component allows the RAS server to relay the `DHCPInform` messages between the remote access clients and the DHCP server.

To configure DHCP to work with remote access, follow these steps:

1. Within the Routing and Remote Access management console, right-click General under the IP Routing icon and select New Routing Protocol.
2. In the Select Routing Protocol window, select the DHCP Relay Agent and click OK.
3. Right-click the DHCP Relay Agent icon listed under IP routing and select New Interface. Select the network connection over which DHCP messages will be routed and click OK.
4. Right-click the DHCP Relay Agent and select Properties. Type the IP addresses of the DHCP server or servers to which the RAS server should forward the `DHCPInform` requests (see Figure 4.11).

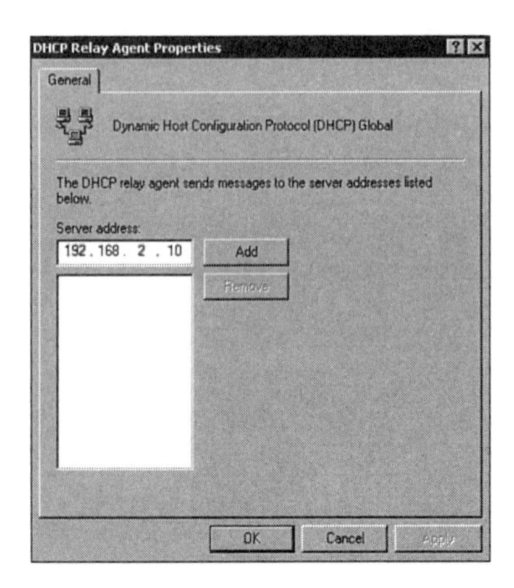

Figure 4.11 Configuring the RAS server with the IP address of the DHCP server.

5. Right-click the interface to bring up the property window (see Figure 4.12). From the property window, you can disable or enable the relaying of DHCP packets and configure the hop count and the boot threshold.

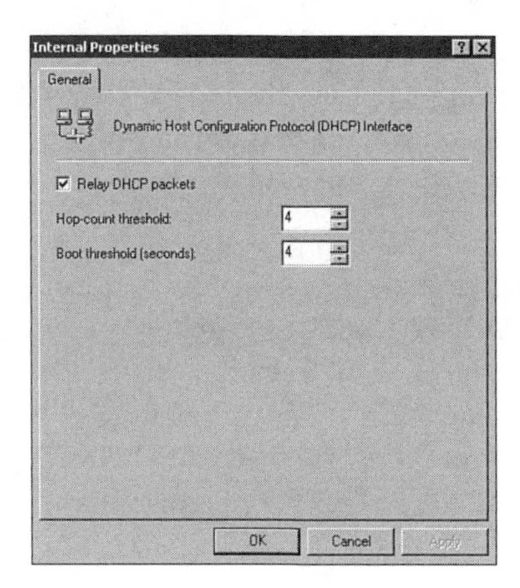

Figure 4.12 Configuring the DHCP Relay Agent.

Managing and Monitoring Remote Access

As with all servers performing a specific role on a network, you should perform management and monitoring tasks to ensure the server is functioning as it should. The following section covers the function of an *Internet Authentication Service (IAS)* server and how it can simplify the administration of multiple RAS servers, as well as how to monitor a RAS server for performance.

Managing Remote Access

Several management tasks have already been covered in this chapter, such as managing remote access through policies and managing IP address assignment using a DHCP server and the DHCP Relay Agent. However, one topic that has been mentioned but not discussed, which you may come across on the exam, is that of an *IAS RADIUS server*.

As your networks increase in size, you may need to implement multiple remote access servers. To ease the administrative overhead of managing multiple RAS servers, you can implement Remote Authentication Dial-in User Service (RADIUS) to centralize the authentication of remote access clients and the storage of accounting information.

Windows 2000 can be configured for RADIUS by installing the Internet Authentication Service (IAS) through the Add/Remove programs applet in the Control Panel. When configured for RADIUS, a remote access server will forward authentication requests from RAS clients to the IAS server. IAS provides the benefit of centralizing user authentication and centralizing the storage of auditing and accounting information collected from the RAS Servers.

When RADIUS is implemented, the remote access server is configured as a RADIUS client. You can configure a RADIUS client when enabling routing and remote access. Any authentication requests to the remote access server by dial-up users is sent to the server running IAS. The server running IAS will provide authentication, auditing, and accounting services for RADIUS clients.

Monitoring Performance

The performance of a remote access server can be monitored using System Monitor (found in the Performance console). Several counters are available for monitoring RAS (see Figure 4.13). Table 4.5 summarizes some of the available counters. Two performance objects are available for monitoring RAS: *RAS Total* and *RAS Ports*. Use RAS Total to monitor the RAS server and RAS Ports to monitor the status of individual ports.

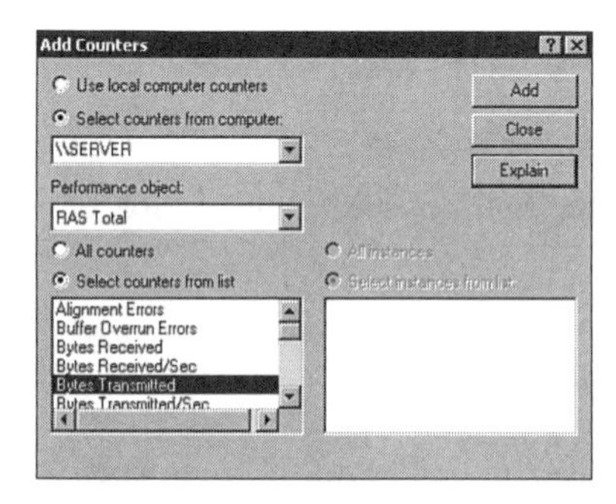

Figure 4.13 Remote access performance counters.

Table 4.5 Performance Counters for Monitoring Remote Access

Counter	Description
Bytes Received	The total number of bytes received.
Bytes Transmitted	The total number of bytes sent.
CRC Errors	The total number of frames with Cyclic Redundancy errors.
Frames Received	The total number of frames received.

(continued)

Table 4.5 Performance Counters for Monitoring Remote Access (*continued*)

Counter	Description
Frames Transmitted	The total number of frames transmitted.
Serial Overrun Errors	The total number of serial overrun errors. These errors occur when the hardware cannot handle the rate at which data is being received.
Timeout Errors	The total number of timeout errors.
Total Errors	The total number of errors, including timeout errors, serial overrun errors, and so on.

Another way in which you can monitor a RAS server is through logging. Using the Event Logging tab in the server's Properties dialog box, you can have information pertaining to Remote Access Service written to the System log. The logging of errors and warnings is enabled by default, as shown in Figure 4.14. From here you can disable logging, log errors only, or log detailed information. You can also enable PPP logging.

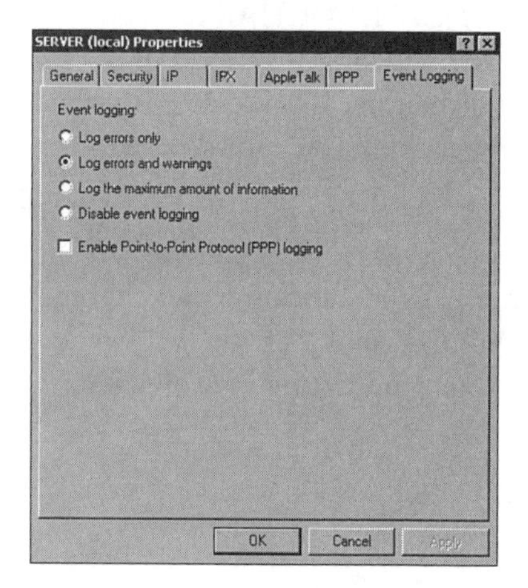

Figure 4.14 Enabling remote access logging.

Configuring Remote Access Security

With remote access, you are basically opening the door for remote access clients to access the internal network. With this arises the topic of security. You need to be able to allow certain clients remote access while keeping the door closed to everyone else. You also want to ensure that the data being sent between a remote access client and a remote access server is secure. To meet these requirements, Windows 2000 supports a number of authentication and encryption protocols.

Configuring Authentication Protocols

Windows 2000 supports a number of authentication protocols that can be used to authenticate dial-up clients. Knowing the features and differences between each is important to achieving success on the exam.

- *Password Authentication Protocol (PAP)*—PAP is the least secure of all the authentication protocols because it sends the username and password in clear text.
- *Shiva Password Authentication Protocol (SPAP)*—SPAP can be used to authenticate against Shiva remote access servers. It can also be used to authenticate against Windows 2000 Servers. This protocol is typically more secure than PAP but not as secure as CHAP or MS-CHAP.
- *Challenge Handshake Authentication Protocol (CHAP)*—CHAP does not send the username and password across the network. Instead, it uses a challenge response with a one-way hash algorithm. It is an industry standard protocol that can be used to authenticate non-Windows–based clients.
- *Microsoft Challenge Handshake Authentication Protocol (MS-CHAP)*—A Microsoft version of CHAP that uses mutual authentication and encryption for Windows-based clients. MS-CHAP version 2 provides stronger encryption and separate encryption keys for sending and receiving data.
- *Extensible Authentication Protocol (EAP)*—EAP is an extension of the PPP protocol that provides support for other authentication mechanisms, such as SmartCards.

Using the Properties dialog box for the remote access server, as shown in Figure 4.15, you can configure which authentication protocol the remote access server can use to authenticate remote clients. Clicking the Authentication Methods button opens the Authentication Methods dialog box, in which you can select the authentication protocols available on the server.

Once you've enabled the authentication protocols at the server level, you can specify which of the authentication protocols are available for each remote access policy using the Authentication tab in the policy's properties dialog box (see Figure 4.16).

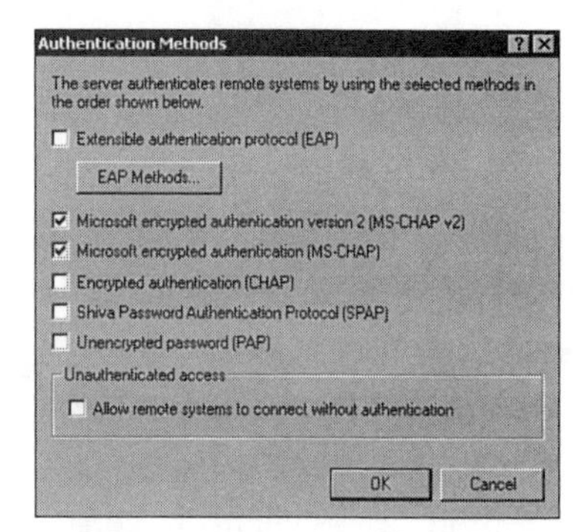

Figure 4.15 Configuring authentication methods.

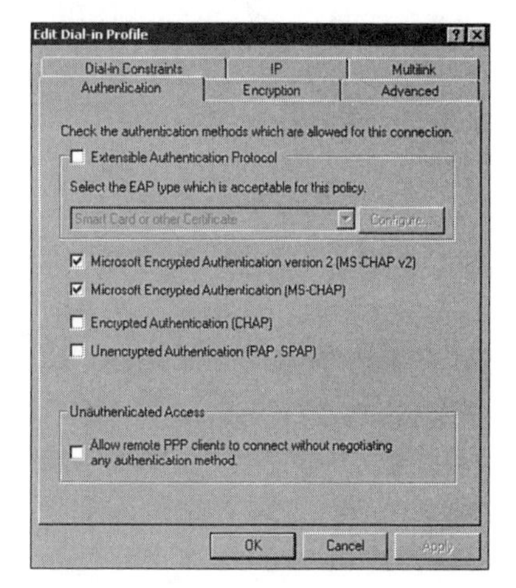

Figure 4.16 Configuring authentication methods in a remote access policy.

Configuring Encryption Protocols

If you're sending sensitive data across the network, you may want to add another level of security by implementing some form of data encryption. The two types of encryption available are as follows:

- *Microsoft Point-to-Point Encryption (MPPE)*—MPPE can use 40-bit, 56-bit, and 128-bit encryption keys. MPPE encryption can be used for PPP connections, including PPTP VPN connections. MPPE is used in conjunction with EAP-TLS and MS-CHAP authentication protocols.
- *IP Security (IPSec)*—IPSec is used with L2TP connections. It supports the Data Encryption Standard (DES) and triple DES (3DES).

Some older Microsoft operating systems do not support 56-bit encryption. To support these clients, you must use 40-bit encryption instead; otherwise, 56-bit encryption should be used. In addition, 128-bit encryption is only supported in North America.

You configure encryption for a dial-up connection at the policy level. To do so, open the Properties dialog box for the remote access policy and select the Encryption tab (see Figure 4.17). Select one or more of the following encryption levels:

- *No Encryption*—Select this option to allow remote access clients to connect without requiring a form of encryption.
- *Basic*—Specifies whether remote access clients can connect using MPPE 40-bit or IPSec 56-bit DES encryption.
- *Strong*—Specifies whether remote access clients can connect using MPPE 40-bit or IPSec 56-bit DES encryption.

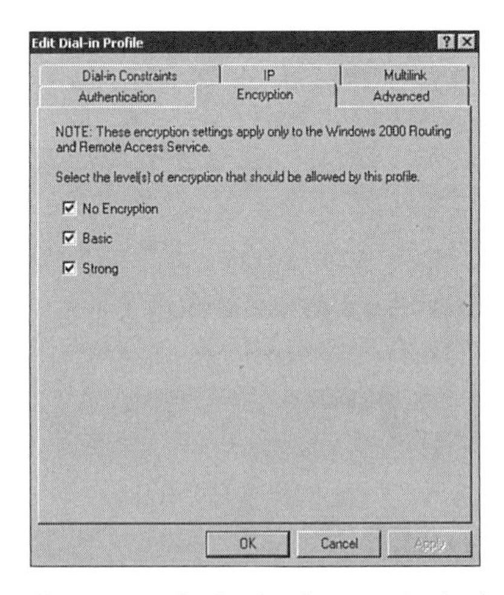

Figure 4.17 Configuring the encryption level.

Creating a Remote Access Policy

Earlier in the chapter, you looked at the elements of a remote access policy. Those were conditions, permissions, and profile settings. As already mentioned, once RRAS is enabled, a default policy is automatically created called Allow Access If Dial-in Permission Is Granted. However, there may be instances whereby you need to configure additional policies to meet security requirements and the needs of the remote access clients.

To create a new remote access policy, right-click the Remote Access Policies container within the Routing and Remote Access management console and click New Remote Access Policy. You are prompted to specify a name for the policy and configure the conditions, permissions, and profile settings. Once complete, the policy will be listed under the Remote Access Policies container. The policy settings can be changed at any time using the policy's Properties dialog box.

Policies are evaluated in the order in which they appear within the management console. The order can be changed by right-clicking a policy and choosing the Move Up or Move Down options.

Practice Questions

Question 1

Dayton Distributing plans to use Routing and Remote Access to give users the capability to access resources from other locations while still maintaining a high level of security. Specifically, the company president needs to be able to access resources from her home office and other locations. Network administrators also use remote access when they are working from home. A Windows 2000 server is added to the network and configured as a remote access server. When configuring the dial-in properties of user accounts, what options should be selected for callback?

- ❍ A. Choose No Callback for the president's account and Set by Caller for the network administrators' accounts.
- ❍ B. Choose Set by Caller for the president's account and No Callback for the network administrators' accounts.
- ❍ C. Choose Always Callback to for the president's account and Set by Caller for the network administrators' accounts.
- ❍ D. Choose Set by caller for the president's account and Always Callback to for the network administrator's accounts.

Answer D is correct. Because the president needs remote access from various locations, the Set by Caller option should be selected. To limit where network administrators can dial in from, select Always Callback to. In this way, the remote access server will always call them back at the configured phone number, ensuring that is where they are attempting remote access from. Selecting No Callback disables this feature. Therefore, answers A, B, and C are incorrect.

Question 2

Your junior network administrator installed and configured a remote access server. Certain users need to be able to dial directly into the server to access network resources. To test the configuration, you attempt to connect to the server but are unsuccessful. When you open the Routing and Remote Access snap-in, you notice the default remote access policy has been deleted. What should you do?

- ❍ A. Disable Routing and Remote Access and then enable the service.
- ❍ B. Create a remote access policy.
- ❍ C. Configure the dial-in properties of the user accounts.
- ❍ D. Configure the remote access profile settings.

Answer B is correct. If the default remote access policy is deleted and no other policy exists, users will not be permitted remote access. Therefore, a remote access policy must be created to solve the problem. Answer A is incorrect because disabling and then enabling Routing and Remote Access would re-create the default policy, but this is not the easiest solution. The remote access server would have to be reconfigured afterward. Answer C is incorrect because dial-in permission can be granted through the properties of a user account but a policy must still exist. Answer D is incorrect because profile settings cannot be configured until a policy is created.

Question 3

Some of the users within your organization have home offices, which they work from during the weekdays. They require access to network resources, and all users can dial directly into the remote access server. For security purposes, you want to limit the dial-in hours from 8 A.M. to 6 P.M. How should you proceed?

❍ A. Configure the properties of each user account.

❍ B. Configure the properties of the remote access server.

❍ C. Configure the conditions of the remote access policy.

❍ D. Configure the port properties.

Answer C is correct. You can set day and time restrictions for remote users by configuring the conditions of the remote access policy. Answer A is incorrect because day and time restrictions are no longer configured through the properties of a user account as they were in Windows NT 4.0. You cannot configure day and time restrictions by configuring the properties of the remote access server or the ports; therefore, answers B and D are incorrect.

Question 4

You are in the process of configuring profile settings for a remote access policy. You configure the settings as shown in the following figure. Which of the following statements are true? [Choose all that apply.]

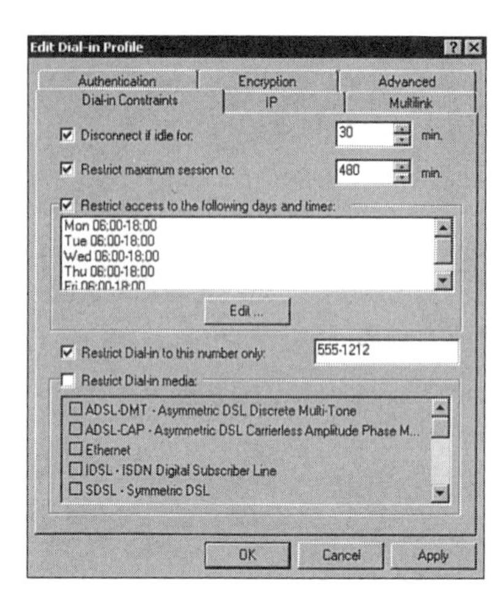

- ❑ A. Users will be disconnected after eight hours of inactivity.
- ❑ B. Users will be disconnected after 30 minutes of inactivity.
- ❑ C. Users can remain connected as long as necessary.
- ❑ D. Users can dial in only between 6 P.M. and 6 A.M.
- ❑ E. Users can dial in only between 6 A.M. and 6 P.M.
- ❑ F. Users can dial any number for remote access.

Answers B and E are correct. The profile settings configured will disconnect a session after 30 minutes of idle time, restrict the maximum session to 8 hours, allow users remote access during the hours of 6 A.M. and 6 P.M., and allow users to dial in to a specified number. Therefore, answers A, C, and D are incorrect.

Question 5

You configured a Windows 2000 server as a remote access server. While enabling the service, you chose to use DHCP for IP address assignment. WINS is still used on the internal network, because you are still in the process of upgrading to Windows 2000. Clients report that they can successfully connect but are unable to access network resources using a UNC path. What must be done to resolve the problem?

❍ A. You must configure a range of IP addresses on the RAS server, as well as assign any optional IP parameters to the clients.

❍ B. You must manually configure the IP settings on the remote access clients.

❍ C. You must install the DHCP Relay Agent on the DHCP server.

❍ D. You must install the DHCP Relay Agent on the RAS server.

Answer D is correct. The clients need to be configured with the IP address of the WINS server. To do this, the DHCP Relay Agent must be installed on the RAS server so it can forward `DHCPInform` messages between the clients and the DHCP server. Answer A is incorrect because optional parameters cannot be configured on the RAS server. Clients can be configured with the IP address of the WINS server; however, it's easier from a management perspective to centralize IP address assignment and use a relay agent instead. Therefore, answer B is incorrect. Answer C is incorrect because the DHCP Relay Agent isn't installed on a DHCP server.

Question 6

You are installing a RAS server on the network to provide business managers with remote access. The following requirements should be met:

- Only business managers should be permitted access.
- Users in this group should have access any time of the day except weekends.
- Remote clients should be automatically assigned an IP address.
- Remote clients should be assigned optional parameters needed to communicate on the internal network.

You perform the following tasks:

- Enable Routing and Remote Access.
- Configure the RAS server with a range of IP addresses.
- Configure the user account properties to control access through a remote access policy.

- Delete the default remote access policy and create a new one.
- Create a new group called **remoteusers** and add the business managers to it.
- Edit the conditions of the profile to only allow access to the **remoteusers** group and allow use from Monday through Friday with no restrictions on time.
- Set the permissions of the policy to allow access.

Which of the following requirements are met? [Choose all that apply.]

❑ A. Only business managers are permitted access.

❑ B. Users can dial in anytime between Monday and Friday.

❑ C. All remote users are assigned an IP address.

❑ D. All remote users are assigned any required optional parameters.

Answers A, B, and C are correct. By creating a new group for the business managers and configuring the conditions of the policy to allow access only to this group, the first requirement is met. Configuring the day and time restrictions gives users access anytime during the weekdays. Configuring a range of IP addresses on the RAS server ensures that remote access clients will receive an IP address. Answer D is incorrect because the RAS server needs to be configured to use DHCP and have the DHCP Relay Agent installed for clients to be dynamically assigned optional components.

Question 7

Some of your remote access users require more bandwidth than others. You have created a new remote access policy specifically for these clients. You want to allow the use of Multilink for these users. How should you proceed?

❍ A. In the Properties dialog box for the remote access server, select the Multilink tab.

❍ B. In the Properties dialog box for the user accounts, select the Dial-in tab and select the Allow Multilink option.

❍ C. Through the Properties window for the policy, use the Multilink tab from the Edit Dial-in Profile dialog box.

❍ D. From the Properties window for the policy, click the Add button to configure Multilink as a policy condition.

Answer C is correct. To enable Multilink in a remote access policy, you must use the Multilink tab found in the Edit Dial-in Profile dialog box within the properties of the remote access policy. Therefore, answers A, B, and D are incorrect.

Question 8

You have multiple RAS servers on your network. You want to centralize the authentication of remote access clients and accounting information. Which of the following services should you install?

❍ A. IAS

❍ B. IIS

❍ C. RADIUS

❍ D. RRAS

Answer A is correct. To centralize the authentication of remote access clients and accounting information, the Internet Authentication Service (IAS) should be installed. Answer B is incorrect because IIS is for Web hosting. Answer C is incorrect because RADIUS is the protocol used by IAS to provide authentication and accounting services. Answer D is incorrect because Routing and Remote Access Service is used to provide a variety of services, including remote access, VPN, and routing.

Question 9

What is the main purpose of IPSec?

❍ A. Ensure data integrity through encryption.

❍ B. Establish a VPN tunnel over a PPP connection.

❍ C. It's an authentication protocol.

❍ D. It's used by Multilink to dynamically add and drop lines.

Answer A is correct. IPSec is used in conjunction with L2TP to encrypt data. Answer B is incorrect because PPTP and L2TP are used to establish VPN tunnels. Answer C is incorrect because it is not a protocol used to authenticate users. Answer D is incorrect because BAP is the protocol used by Multilink.

Question 10

For security purposes, SmartCards are being implemented for all remote access users. Which of the following protocols is required to support SmartCard authentication?

❍ A. PAP

❍ B. EAP

❍ C. MS-CHAP

❍ D. SPAS

Answer B is correct. The Extensible Authentication Protocol is required to support SmartCard authentication. Answers A, C, and D are incorrect because they do not support SmartCard authentication.

Need to Know More?

Check out `http://www.microsoft.com/technet/` and `http://www.microsoft.com/technet/treeview/default.asp?url=/technet/prodtechnol/windows2000serv/reskit/deploy/sdgintro.asp`. Search the online version of TechNet and the Windows 2000 Server Resource Kit using keywords such as `Routing and Remote Access` and `VPN`.

Charles, Kackie, *Windows 2000 Routing and Remote Access Services*, New Riders Publishing, Indianapolis, IN, 2000. ISBN: 0735709513. Provides in-depth information on configuring Routing and Remote Access.

Shinder, Deborah Littlejohn, and Thomas W. Shinder, *Managing Windows 2000 Network Services*, Syngress Media, Inc., Rockland, MA, 2000. ISBN: 1928994067. Provides good information on network services, including Routing and Remote Access.

Network Protocols

Terms you'll need to understand:

✓ TCP/IP
✓ Subnet mask
✓ IPSec
✓ Packet filter
✓ NWLink
✓ Frame type
✓ Ipconfig
✓ Ping
✓ Network Monitor

Techniques you'll need to master:

✓ Understanding TCP/IP addressing
✓ Installing and configuring TCP/IP
✓ Testing TCP/IP using Ipconfig and Ping
✓ Understanding NWLink
✓ Installing and configuring NWLink
✓ Configuring network bindings
✓ Configuring IP packet filters
✓ Managing and monitoring network traffic
✓ Understanding and implementing IPSec

Introduction

Network protocols enable communication between computers on a network. The type of protocols you install largely depends on the type of servers on the network, as well as the services and applications you install. For example, a number of network services now require TCP/IP to be present before they can be installed. In any case, knowing how to install and configure network protocols is an important part of any network administrator's job, as well as important to achieving exam success.

This chapter looks at two main protocols: *TCP/IP* and *NWLink*. You learn how to install them and properly configure them. The chapter also examines managing and monitoring network traffic as well as implementing, configuring, and managing IPSec.

Installing, Configuring, and Troubleshooting Network Protocols

Windows 2000 supports a variety of network protocols, the most popular of which is the *Transmission Control Protocol/Internet Protocol (TCP/IP)*. The different protocols enable a Windows 2000 Server to interoperate in a number of network environments, and to support multiple client platforms, as well as different services and applications. Because network communication is dependent on network protocols, it's important to have the knowledge necessary to install, configure, and troubleshoot them. The following sections cover the fundamentals regarding the two main network protocols supported by Windows 2000: TCP/IP and NWLink.

Installing and Configuring TCP/IP

TCP/IP is an industry standard suite of protocols and utilities that enables communication between hosts on a network. Because of the increasing popularity of TCP/IP, it is quickly becoming the protocol of choice in many network environments. You will find that most operating systems today, including Windows 2000, provide support for TCP/IP.

How a suite of protocols performs is described through the Open Systems Interconnection (OSI) Model. The OSI Model consists of seven layers. The protocols within a protocol suite, such as TCP/IP, operate at different layers of the model, performing different functions to enable network communication. The seven layers of the OSI model are as follows:

- *Application*—This is the top layer of the model. It defines how network applications perform network-related functions.
- *Presentation*—Protocols operating at this layer are responsible for converting and encrypting data.
- *Session*—This layer is responsible for establishing, maintaining, and ending communication sessions.
- *Transport*—Protocols functioning at this layer provide flow control and error checking.
- *Network*—This layer is responsible for addressing and routing.
- *Data Link*—This layer controls the logical network topologies, physical protocol assigned to the data, as well as sequencing.
- *Physical*—This layer defines the physical characteristics of the network.

The suite of protocols that make up TCP/IP also map to a model referred to as the Department of Defense (DoD) model. This model defines communication in four layers. Each of the four layers maps to the different layers within the OSI model and each layer of the model also defines a specific role or function. The different protocols making up the suite each function at a specific layer and work together to provide network communication. The four layers of the DoD model include:

- *Application*—This is the top layer of the model where applications such as FTP, SMTP, and HTTP gain access to the network.
- *Transport*—Protocols operating at this layer are responsible for establishing sessions between two hosts. The two protocols that function at this level include the Transmission Control Protocol (TCP) and the User Datagram Protocol (UDP). The main difference between the two protocols is that TCP is connection-orientated, which means that it provides reliable delivery, whereas UDP is connectionless and does not.
- *Internet*—The main responsibilities of protocols operating at this layer are addressing and routing. The protocols working at this layer include the Internet Protocol (IP), which is responsible for addressing and routing, Address Resolution Protocol (ARP), which maps IP addresses to MAC addresses, Internet Control Message Protocol (IMCP), and Internet Group Management Protocol (IGMP).
- *Network*—This is the bottom layer of the model and is responsible for sending and receiving frames over the physical medium.

IP Addressing

For packets to be routed on an IP network, every host requires a unique IP address (hosts can include workstations, servers, routers, printers, or any other device with a network interface card). The IP address is a 32-bit number, represented in decimal format, that identifies each host.

An IP address consists of two parts: the *network ID* and the *host ID*. The network ID is used to identify a specific network or subnet, whereas the host ID identifies the hosts on a given network or subnet. For example, an IP address of `132.10.26.2` has a network ID of `132.10` and a host ID of `26.2`.

The network ID determines whether a destination host is on the local network. If the network ID of the destination host does not correspond to the network ID of the local host, the packet is forwarded to the default gateway. From there, the default gateway uses the information in its routing tables to determine to which network or subnet the packet should be forwarded. This is called an *adjacency test.*

IP addresses are organized into different address classes that define the number of bits out of the 32 that are used to identify the network. These classes also identify the number of bits used to identify the hosts on a network. By examining the address classes, you can also determine the number of networks and the number of hosts. Table 5.1 summarizes the different address classes.

Table 5.1 TCP/IP Address Classes

Address Class	Range	Number of Network IDs	Number of Host IDs
Class A	1–126	126	16,777,214
Class B	128–191	16,834	65,534
Class C	192–223	2,097,152	254

Table 5.1 summarizes three of the address classes. There are also Classes D and E. Class D is reserved for multicasting and Class E is reserved for testing purposes, but neither of these is relevant to Windows networking. You can determine the class of an IP address by mapping the first decimal value (the number before the first period) to one of the ranges outlined in Table 5.1. For example, `198.221.10.254` is a Class C address.

When assigning IP addresses, each host also requires a *subnet mask*, which determines which part of an IP address is used as the network ID and which is used to identify a host. For example, the default subnet mask for a Class C address is `255.255.255.0`, which means the first three decimal places (called octets) identify the network and the last octet identifies the host. The subnet mask is also used to determine whether the destination host is on the local or a remote subnet. The subnet mask of the local host is compared against the IP address of the destination host and, through a process known as "anding," it is determined whether the destination IP address is local or remote. (This is called an *adjacency test.*)

Installing TCP/IP

During the installation of Windows 2000, TCP/IP is automatically installed by default when a network adapter is detected, unless you override the default settings. If it wasn't installed during setup or if you need to add it again, you can do so through the Network and Dial-up Connections applet within the Control Panel. The following steps will help you install TCP/IP:

1. Right-click the Local Area Connection within the Network and Dial-up Connections applet and select Properties.
2. From the Properties window, click the Install button.
3. The Select Network Component Type window appears. Select Protocol from the list and click Add (see Figure 5.1).
4. From the Select Network Protocol window, select Internet Protocol (TCP/IP). Click OK.
5. Click Close.

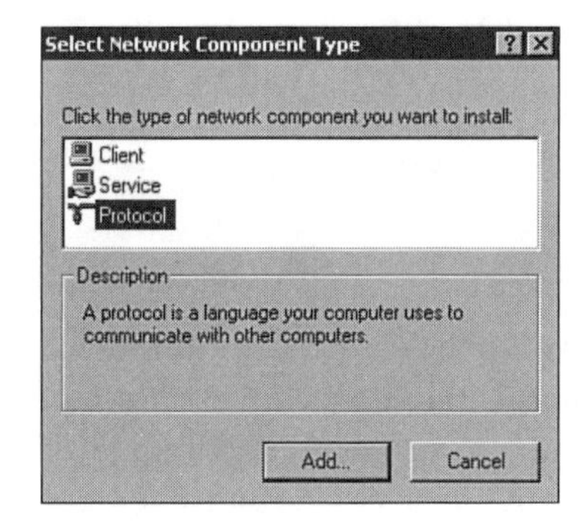

Figure 5.1 Installing additional protocols.

Configuring TCP/IP

As discussed in Chapter 2, "DNS," IP addresses can be assigned dynamically or statically. When TCP/IP is installed, it is automatically configured to use the Dynamic Host Configuration Protocol (DHCP). If you choose the have an IP address assigned dynamically, you can leave the default configuration as is.

Although not normally used, there is a third method of assigning IP addresses known as Automatic Private IP Address (APIPA) . In the event that a DHCP server is not available, a DHCP client will assign itself an IP address in the range of **169.254.0.1–169.254.255.154**. The address is used until a DHCP server becomes available.

However, for many servers, depending on the role configured, it is recommended or even required that you statically configure an IP address. For example, if you install Active Directory on a server with a dynamically assigned IP address, a warning will appear during the installation informing you that the server should be configured with a static IP address. Or if you are installing the DHCP service, the server must first be configured with a static IP address.

TCP/IP can be configured using the Properties window for the Local Area Connection by performing the following steps:

1. Right-click Local Area Connection within the Network and Dial-up Connections applet.
2. From the list of installed components, select Internet Protocol (TCP/IP) and click the Properties button.
3. The Internet Protocol (TCP/IP) Properties window appears, as shown in Figure 5.2. To override the default settings and statically configure an IP address, select Use The Following IP Address. Type a unique IP address, corresponding subnet mask, default gateway, and the IP addresses of the primary and alternate DNS servers.
4. Click OK.

You can configure advanced settings by clicking the Advanced button shown in Figure 5.2. The Advanced TCP/IP Settings window appears, as shown in Figure 5.3. Using the TCP/IP Settings tab, you can assign additional IP addresses to the network connection. For example, a single connection can be assigned a private address for the internal network and a public address for the Internet. The Interface metric box allows you to associate a cost with the route.

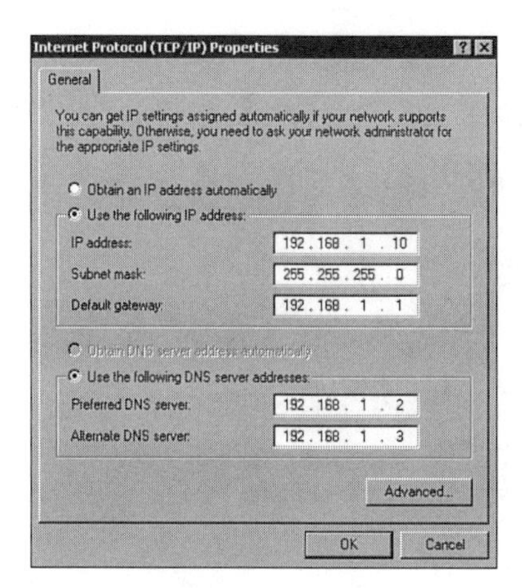

Figure 5.2 Statically configuring an IP address.

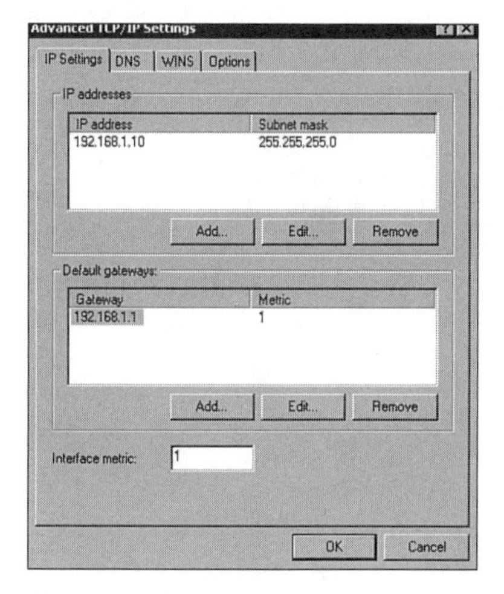

Figure 5.3 Configuring advanced TCP/IP settings.

Testing TCP/IP

Once the necessary settings have been specified, the configuration can be tested using the `ipconfig` and `ping` commands. Using `ipconfig`, you can verify the settings that have been configured. To do so, open the Command Prompt window and type `ipconfig` (using the `/all` parameter brings up more detailed configuration information), as shown in Figure 5.4. Table 5.2 outlines some of the common parameters that can be used with the `ipconfig` command.

```
C:\WINNT\System32\cmd.exe
Windows 2000 IP Configuration

        Host Name . . . . . . . . . . . . : server
        Primary DNS Suffix  . . . . . . . : BAYSIDE.NET
        Node Type . . . . . . . . . . . . : Hybrid
        IP Routing Enabled. . . . . . . . : Yes
        WINS Proxy Enabled. . . . . . . . : No
        DNS Suffix Search List. . . . . . : BAYSIDE.NET

Ethernet adapter Interface1:

        Connection-specific DNS Suffix  . :
        Description . . . . . . . . . . . : AMD PCNET Family PCI Ethernet
r
        Physical Address. . . . . . . . . : 00-50-56-76-5C-F2
        DHCP Enabled. . . . . . . . . . . : No
        IP Address. . . . . . . . . . . . : 192.168.0.4
        Subnet Mask . . . . . . . . . . . : 255.255.255.0
        Default Gateway . . . . . . . . . : 192.168.0.1
        DNS Servers . . . . . . . . . . . : 192.168.0.2
                                            192.168.0.3

C:\>
```

Figure 5.4 Verifying TCP/IP configuration using the **ipconfig** command.

Table 5.2 Parameters Used with the ipconfig Command

Parameter	Description
/all	Displays detailed IP configuration information.
/release	Releases the IP address for the specified adapter.
/renew	Renews the IP address for the specified adapter.
/flushDNS	Purges the entries in the DNS cache.
/registerDNS	Refreshes all leased IP addresses and re-registers DNS names.
/displayDNS	Displays the contents of the DNS cache.

Use the `ping` command to verify connectivity with other hosts on a TCP/IP network. Connectivity on the network is verified by sending Internet Control Message Protocol (ICMP) echo requests and replies. When the `ping` command is issued, the source computer sends echo requests messages to another TCP/IP host. The remote host, if reachable, then responds with four echo replies. The `ping` command is also issued at the command prompt along with the TCP/IP address or domain name of the other TCP/IP host, as follows:

```
C:> ping 124.120.105.110
```

or

```
C:> ping www.bayside.net
```

To determine whether TCP/IP is initialized on the local computer, issue the **ping** command and specify the loopback address of **127.0.0.1**.

The general steps for troubleshooting TCP/IP using the `ping` command are as follows:

1. `ping` the loopback address of `127.0.0.1` to ensure TCP/IP is initialized on the local computer.
2. If successful, `ping` the IP address assigned to the local computer.
3. Next, `ping` the IP address of the default gateway. If this fails, verify that the IP address of the default gateway is correct and that the gateway is operational.
4. Next, `ping` the IP address of a host on a remote network. If this is unsuccessful, verify that the remote host is operational, verify the IP address of the remote host, and verify that all routers and gateways between the local computer and remote computer are operational.

A quick way of verifying TCP/IP connectivity is to complete step 4 in the preceding steps. If you can successfully **ping** the IP address of a remote host, steps 1 through 3 will be successful.

Two other utilities that you can use for TCP/IP troubleshooting are `tracert` and `pathping`. The `tracert` command determines the route that is taken to a specific destination. You may want to use the `tracert` command if you are not able to successfully `ping` the IP address of a remote host. The results of the `tracert` command indicate if there is a problem with a router or gateway between the local computer and the remote destination.

The `pathping` command is basically a combination of the `ping` and `tracert` commands. When the command is issued, packets are sent to each router between the local computer and a remote computer. The results determine which routers and gateways may be causing problems on the network.

Installing the NWLink Protocol

If there are NetWare servers hosting resources on the network, you'll want to install the *NWLink* protocol. This is Microsoft's 32-bit version of Novell's Internetwork Packet Exchange/Sequences Packet Exchange (IPX/SPX) protocol used to communicate with NetWare servers.

NWLink is not installed by default like TCP/IP, but can be installed using the same steps outlined in the section on installing TCP/IP, only choose to install the NWLink IPX/SPX NetBIOS Compatible Transport Protocol instead. Once it's installed, it can be configured using the Properties window of the local area connection.

Configuring NWLink

There are two configuration settings for the NWLink protocol. The first is the *internal network number*; the second is the *frame type*. From the Properties window of the local area connection, select NWLink IPX/SPX/NetBIOS Compatible Transport Protocol (see Figure 5.5).

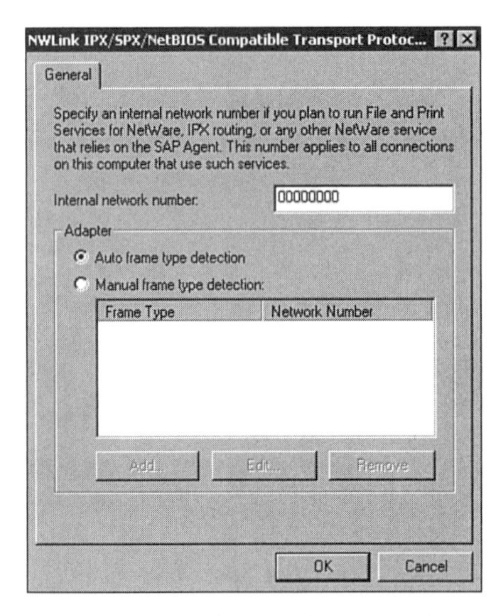

Figure 5.5 Configuring the NWLink protocol.

The internal network number is used for internal routing. By using the internal network number, virtual networks can be created. If there are multiple network adapters, information can be more efficiently routed to the services running on a computer.

The default internal network number is automatically set to all zeros. The following list describes certain instances in which the number must be manually configured:

- ➤ The computer is running File and Print Services for NetWare and there are multiple frame types configured.
- ➤ The Windows 2000 computer is configured as an IPX router.
- ➤ The Windows 2000 computer is running a program that uses NetWare Service Advertising Protocol (SAP).

The *frame type* defines how a computer running Windows 2000 and NWLink formats data being sent on the network (specifically the header and footer information). To communicate with a NetWare server, the computer running Windows 2000 must be using the same frame type.

If there is only one frame type being used on the network, such as 802.2 for example, you can leave the frame type to autodetect. Once NWLink is installed, the frame type will be automatically detected. If there are multiple frame types detected, NWLink will default to 802.2.

You may need to configure the frame type if you have more than one NetWare server on the network using different frame types, because the frame types are not compatible. To manually configure the frame type, select Manual Frame Type Detection and click the Add button from the Properties window for NWLink. When configuring the frame types, keep the following points in mind:

- If there are NetWare 3.12 or later servers running on an Ethernet network, configure the frame type as 802.2.
- If there are running versions of NetWare earlier than 3.12 on an Ethernet network, configure the frame type as 802.3.
- For token-ring networks, the frame type must be set to 802.5.

On Ethernet networks, the standard frame type for Netware 2.2 and 3.11 is 802.3. Starting with Netware 3.12, the default frame type became 802.2.

Communicating with NetWare Servers

Installing the NWLink protocol does not in itself enable a computer to access a NetWare server; additional software must be installed.

Client Service for NetWare (CSNW) enables a computer to directly access resources on a NetWare server. Each client requiring access to resources on the NetWare server must have a user account.

Gateway Service for NetWare (GSNW) enables a Windows 2000 server to act as a gateway for clients when accessing resources on a NetWare server, eliminating the need for clients to be running NetWare client software. Once GSNW is installed on a Windows 2000 server, Microsoft clients can gain access to NetWare resources through the gateway. Installing GSNW reduces administration because the gateway is the only computer that requires a user account on the NetWare server. You don't have to install any additional software on the workstations.

The software you choose to install depends on the network environment. If your network consists of both Windows 2000 and NetWare servers, consider installing CSNW on all clients so they can directly access the NetWare servers. If you intend to migrate the NetWare servers to Windows 2000, consider installing GSNW to decrease administration.

To install CSNW on a Windows 2000 Professional workstation, perform the following steps:

1. Click Start, point to Settings, and click Control Panel.
2. Open the Network and Dial-up Connections applet.
3. Right-click the Local Area Connection and click Properties.
4. From the properties window, click the Install button. Select Client and click Add.
5. Select Client Service for NetWare and click OK. If NWLink is not already present, it will be installed when CSNW is installed.

GSNW is installed on a Windows 2000 server using the preceding process. The difference being when you select to Add a new client, you must install Gateway (and Client) Service for NetWare. During the installation of GSNW, NWLink and CSNW are installed and a Gateway Service for NetWare applet is added to the Control Panel.

The GSNW applet is used to configure the gateway for NetWare connectivity. If you are working within a Novell NDS environment, specify the default tree and context. This identifies the position of the user object within the NDS tree that the GSNW server logs on with. If you are not in an NDS environment, specify the preferred server. The preferred server is the NetWare server you are automatically connected to when you log on.

You must also create a group called `NTGATEWAY` on the NetWare server. Within the group, a user account must be added. This is the user account the GSNW server uses to access resources on the NetWare server.

The final step is to actually enable the gateway. Again, you can do this by using the GSNW applet within the Control Panel. Simply open the applet and click the Gateway button. Select the option to Enable Gateway and type the username and password for the account on the NetWare server. You can then use the Add button to configure the NetWare resources that will be available to clients through the gateway.

Configuring Network Bindings

Most servers have a number of protocols and services installed as well as multiple network adapters. Bindings determine the protocols and services that are available to a particular network adapter card as well as the order in which they are used. For example, a local network may use TCP/IP as its primary communication protocol but require NWLink for occasional access to a NetWare server. Because the server attempts any network connectivity using the first protocol bound to the network adapter card, the most frequently used protocol should be listed first. Another example is installing WINS but unbinding it from the external interface connected to the Internet for security purposes.

Configuring the bindings can also aid in reducing network traffic. If a network rarely uses NWLink except for occasional access to a NetWare server and it is listed first in the binding order, the server will attempt to use this protocol first for any network communication, thereby generating unnecessary network traffic.

To configure the bindings for a network connection, perform the following steps:

1. Within the Network and Dial-up Connections applet, click the Advanced menu and select Advanced Settings (see Figure 5.6).
2. The Connections box lists the available network connections and the order in which they are used by network services.
3. In the Bindings for this connection box, select and deselect the services you want bound to the network interface card and the protocols bound to each of the services installed.
4. Use the up and down arrows to change the binding order of protocols so the most frequently used protocol is listed first.
5. Click OK.

Be prepared to encounter exam questions regarding network bindings. Know what network bindings are and how they can be configured to optimize network traffic and communication.

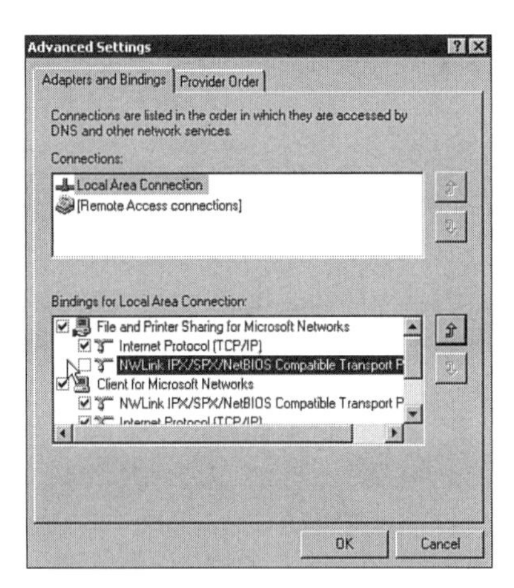

Figure 5.6 Configuring network bindings.

Configuring TCP/IP Packet Filters

For increased security, you can implement IP *packet filters* to control the type of inbound IP traffic allowed to enter your computer and/or network. Inbound traffic can be filtered by destination TCP port, destination UDP port, and by IP protocol type.

Implementing IP Packet Filters

Use the following process to implement IP packet filters:

1. Within the Network and Dial-up Connections applet, right-click the Local Area Connection and select Properties.
2. Select the Internet Protocol (TCP/IP) and click the Properties button.
3. From the Internet Protocol (TCP/IP) Properties window, click the Advanced button and select the Options tab (see Figure 5.7).
4. From the Optional Settings list, select TCP/IP Filtering and click Properties.
5. The TCP/IP Filtering window appears. To enable filtering, select the check box beside the Enable TCP/IP filtering option (see Figure 5.8).

By default, traffic on all TCP and UDP ports are allowed. To specify the type of traffic allowed to reach your computer, select one of the Permit Only options (depending on whether you want to configure TCP, UDP, or protocols) and click Add. If you are configuring TCP and UDP traffic, you will specify the port number (Tables 5.3 and 5.4 summarize some of the common ports used by TCP and UDP). To configure protocols, specify the type of IP protocol to which you want to allow access.

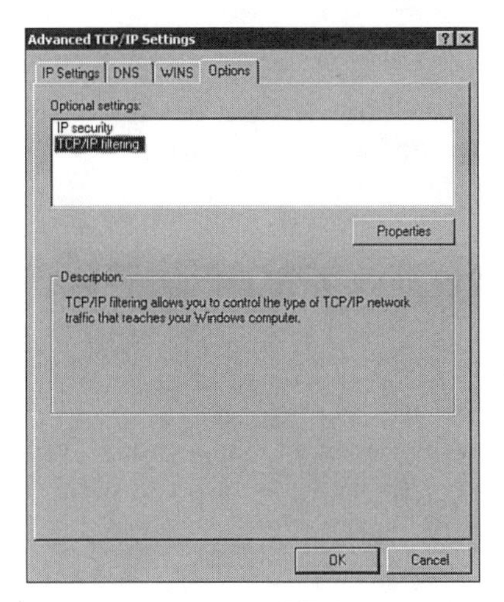

Figure 5.7 Configuring TCP/IP options.

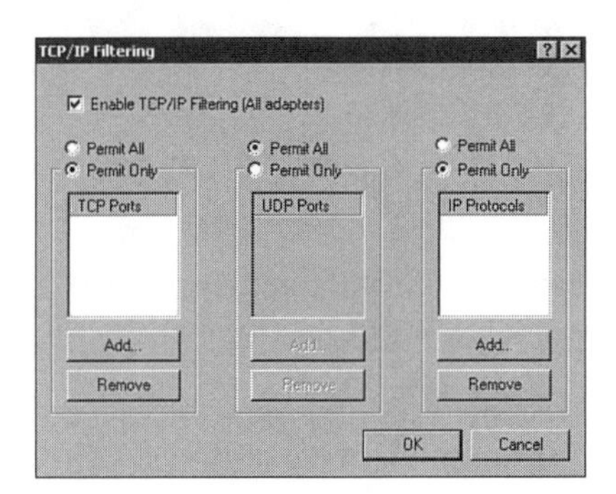

Figure 5.8 Enabling TCP/IP filtering.

Table 5.3 TCP Ports

Port Number	Description
20	FTP-Data
21	FTP-Control
23	Telnet
25	SMTP
80	HTTP
443	HTTPS

Table 5.4 UDP Ports

Port Number	Description
53	DNS Name Resolution
110	POP3
137	NetBIOS name service
143	IMAP

Managing and Monitoring Network Traffic

As networks increase in size (because new services and applications are installed and network shares are created), traffic on a network can greatly increase. For example, adding a service such as DHCP increases traffic through the IP address lease and renewal process.

Remember that methods for optimizing network traffic include configuring the bindings and disabling unnecessary protocols and services.

Using a tool called *Network Monitor*, you can monitor and log network activity and then use the information to manage and optimize traffic. Network Monitor consist of two components:

- *Network Monitor Driver*—The Network Monitor Driver is responsible for capturing the frames coming to and from a network adapter.
- *Network Monitor Tools*—The Network Monitor tools are used to view and analyze the data captured by the Network Monitor Driver.

Installing Network Monitor

Network Monitor is not installed with Windows 2000 by default but can be installed using the following process. Installing Network Monitor automatically installs the Network Monitor Driver.

1. Within the Control Panel, select the Add/Remove Programs applet.
2. Click Add/Remove Windows Components.

3. Within the Windows Component wizard, select Management and Monitoring Tools and click the Details button.
4. Select the Network Monitor Tools check box (see Figure 5.9). Click OK.
5. Click Next. Click OK.

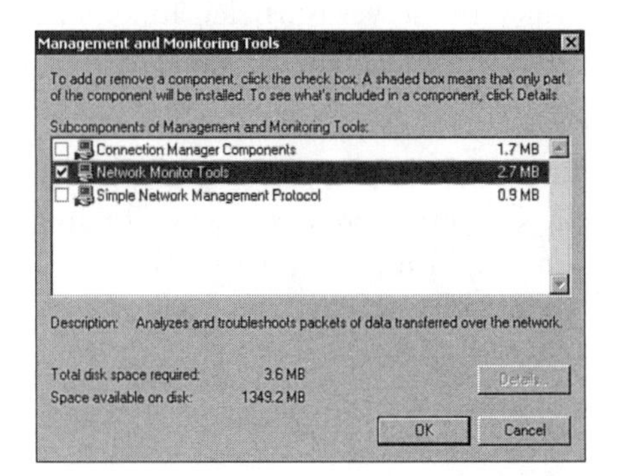

Figure 5.9 Installing the Network Monitor tools.

Network Monitor should only be used by authorized users. To prevent unauthorized users from running it, when Network Monitor starts up, it can detect other instances on the network and display information such as the computer name, where the instance is installed, and the user currently logged onto the computer.

There may be instances when you only want to install the Network Monitor Driver. Installing the driver enables you to capture traffic on a network interface. You will then need to use software such as SMS to view the captured data. This is useful for capturing data from a number of servers and viewing the data from a central location. For example, a computer running Network Monitor Driver can capture the information and forward it to a SMS server. To install the Network Monitor Driver component only, perform the following steps:

1. Within the Network and Dial-up Connections applet, right-click the Local Area Connection and choose Properties from the pop-up menu.
2. From the Properties window for the Local Area Connection, click the Install button.
3. In the list, click Protocol and then click the Add button.
4. Within the Network Protocol window, click the Network Monitor Driver.
5. Click OK.

Using Network Monitor

Network Monitor can display a large amount of information about the frames captured to and from a network adapter card. When Network Monitor is first opened, four panes are displayed within the console. The Graph pane displays the network activity in a bar chart. The Session Stats pane displays information about individual sessions. The Station Stats pane displays statistics about the sessions in which the server is participating. The Total Stats pane displays summary statistics since the capture was started.

To view statistics about network traffic, you must first start a capture. To do so, click the Start option from the Capture menu. To view the captured data, click the Start and View option from the Capture menu. Network Monitor displays all the frame captures during the capture period with a Summary window. To view specific information about a frame, click the frame within the Summary window (see Figure 5.10).

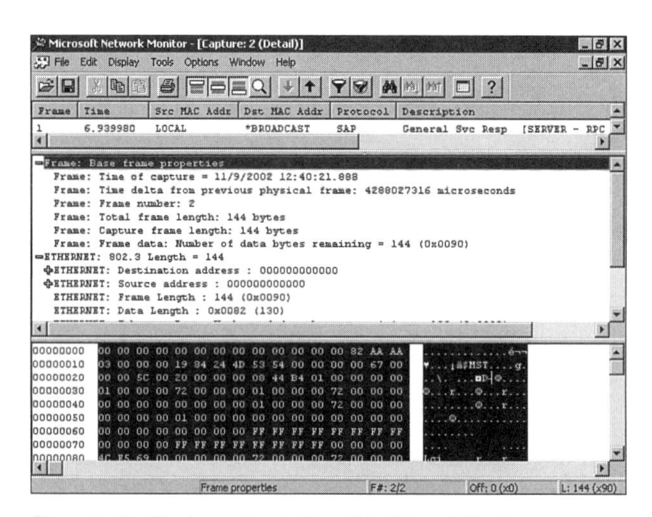

Figure 5.10 Viewing captured data within Network Monitor.

Now when you run Network Monitor, all frames going to and from a computer are captured. If you're looking for specific types of traffic, you can create a capture filter to define which types of frames should be captured. To configure capture filters within Network Monitor, choose the Filter option from the Capture menu (see Figure 5.11).

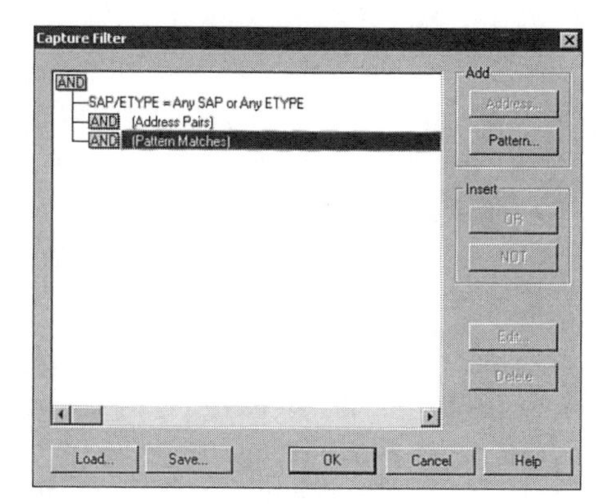

Figure 5.11 Configuring a capture filter.

From the Capture Filter window, you can create filters based on the following criteria:

- *Protocol*—Allows you to specify the protocols to capture or the specific protocol properties.
- *Address Pairs*—Specifies the computer addresses from which frames should be captured.
- *Pattern Matches*—Allows you to configure different variables that captured frames should meet.

The network monitor supplied with Windows 2000 does not run in promiscuous mode. This means that it will intercept packets that are intended either to or from your computer. To get the full version of network monitor, you need SMS.

Configuring and Troubleshooting IPSec

As networks throughout the world become more and more interconnected, network administrators are challenged with ensuring data transferred across a network is secure. This is where the *IP Security (IPSec)* protocol comes into play and allows for authentication of hosts, data integrity, and data encryption.

IPSec is used to protect data that is sent between hosts on a network, which can be remote access, VPN, LAN, and WAN. IPSec ensures that data cannot be viewed or modified by unauthorized users while being sent to its destination. Before data is sent between two hosts, the source computer encrypts the information. It is decrypted at the destination computer. IPSec provides the following benefits:

- Secure end-to-end communication between hosts.
- Secure connections for remote access clients using the Layer 2 Tunneling Protocol (L2TP).
- Secure router-to-router connections.

As you will see when you begin to configure IPSec, different levels of security can be implemented to meet varying needs. IPSec is implemented through IPSec policies. The policies are created and assigned to individual computers or groups of computers (or groups of users). The policies determine the level of security that will be used.

IPSec can use Data Encryption Standard (DES) or Triple DES (3DES) for encryption data. DES uses a 56-bit key, whereas 3DES uses two 56-bit keys.

IPSec consists of several components that work together to provide secure communications between hosts:

- *IPSec Policy Agent*—This component is responsible for retrieving policy information from the local computer or Active Directory.
- *ISAKMP/Oakley Key Management Service*—This component is responsible for establishing a secure channel between hosts and creating the shared key that is used to encrypt the data. It also establishes a security association between hosts before data is transferred. The security association determines the mechanisms that are used to secure data.
- *IPSec Driver*—On the sending computer, this component monitors IP packets. Packets matching a configured filter are secured using the security association and shared key. The IPSec Driver on the receiving computer decrypts the data.

The following steps outline how the different components work together to provide secure communications:

1. When `Computer1` starts, the IPSec policy agent retrieves policy information from the local computer or Active Directory.
2. When `Computer1` attempts to send data to `Computer2`, the IPSec Driver examines the IP packets to determine whether they match the

configured filters. If a match is determined, the IPSec Driver notifies the ISAKMP/OAKLEY.

3. The ISAKMP/OAKLEY service on the two computers is used to establish a security association and a shared key.

4. The IPSec Driver on `Computer1` uses the key and security association to encrypt the data.

5. The IPSec driver on `Computer2` decrypts the information and passes it to the requesting application.

In summary, before any data is transferred between two hosts, the level of security must be negotiated. This includes negotiating an authentication method, a hashing method, and an encryption method.

Configuring IPSec

IPSec can be enabled in one of two ways depending on where you want the policy settings stored. An IPSec policy can be configured for a local computer using the Advanced tab from the TCP/IP Properties window for the Local Area Connection. To enable the policy, select the TCP/IP options tab, click IP Security, and click the Properties button (see Figure 5.12). To enable IPSec, select the Use This IP Security Policy option. Using the drop-down box, select one of the following three security policies:

- *Client (Respond Only)*—This is used for computers that should not secure communications most of the time, but when requested to set up a secure communication, they can respond.
- *Server Secure (Require Security)*—When this option is selected, the server requires all communications to be secure. If a client is not IPSec-aware, the session will not be allowed.
- *Server (Request Security)*—This is used for computers that should secure communications most of the time. In this policy, the computer accepts unsecured traffic, but always attempts to secure additional communications by requesting security from the original sender.

You can also enable IPSec using the Local Security Policy snap-in. The three default policies are listed. Any policy can be enabled for the local computer by right-clicking the policy and choosing the Assign option.

If you are running Active Directory, you can create an IPSec policy that's stored within Active Directory. To view the policies, open the Group Policy snap-in, as shown in Figure 5.13.

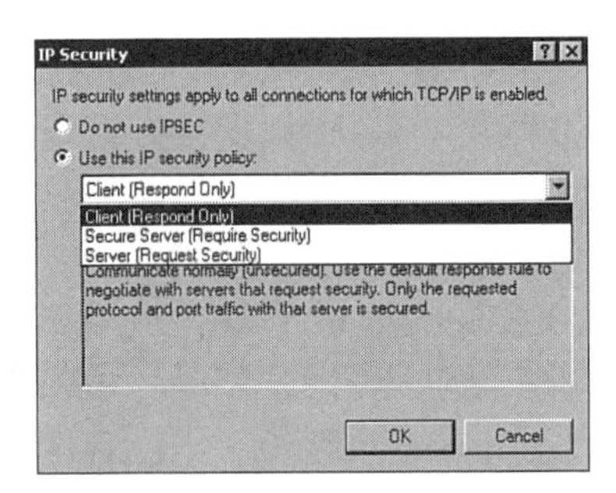

Figure 5.12 Enabling an IPSec policy on a local computer.

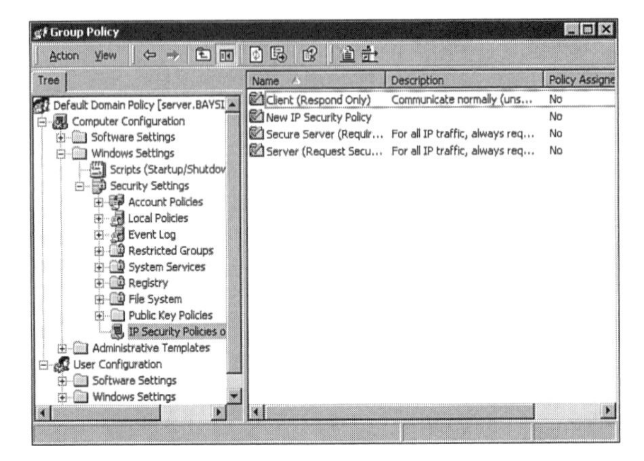

Figure 5.13 IPSec policies within the Group Policy snap-in.

The three policies that exist by default are Client, Server Secure, and Server (the process of creating new IPSec policies is outlined later in the chapter). To assign an IPSec policy to group policy, right-click the policy and click the Assign option.

Configuring IPSec for Transport Mode

IPSec can be used in one of two modes: transport or tunnel mode. Tunnel mode is used for server-to-server or server-to-gateway configurations. The tunnel is the path a packet takes from the source computer to the destination computer. This way, any IP packets sent between the two hosts or between the two subnets, depending on the configuration, are secured.

There are two formats that can be used with tunneling mode: ESP tunnel mode and AH tunnel mode. With Authentication Header (AH) tunnel mode, the data itself is not encrypted. It provides authentication, integrity, and protects the data from modification but it is still readable. With

Encapsulating Security Payload (ESP) tunnel mode, authentication, integrity, and data encryption are provided.

Tunnel mode is not used for remote access VPNs. IPSec/L2TP or PPTP (point-to-Point Tunneling Protocol) is used for VPN connections. Tunnel mode is used for systems that cannot use IPSec/L2TP or PPTP VPNs.

To configure an IPSec tunnel, perform the following steps:

1. From the Properties window of the IPSec policy you want to manage, select the rule you want to edit, and click the Edit button.
2. Select the Tunnel Setting tab.
3. Select "The tunnel endpoint is specified by this IP address" and type the IP address of the tunnel endpoint.
4. Once the tunnel endpoint has been specified, you can configure the tunneling mode using the Filter Action tab (see Figure 5.14). For ESP tunnel mode, select High. For AH tunnel mode, select Medium.

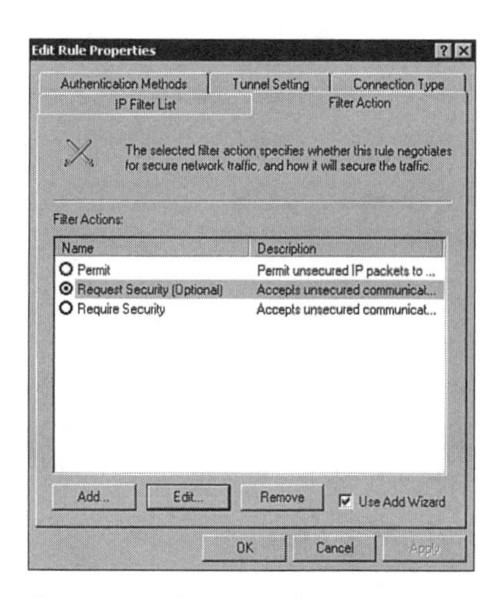

Figure 5.14 Configuring AH and ESP tunnel mode.

Customizing IPSec Policies and Rules

Each of the policies can be edited using the policy's Properties window (see Figure 5.15). IPSec policies consist of several components, including the following:

- *Rules*—IPSec rules determine how and when communication is secured.
- *Filter lists*—Filter lists determine what type of IP packets trigger security negotiations.
- *IPSec Security Methods*—The security methods determine the security requirements of the rule.
- *IPSec Authentication Methods*—Authentication methods determine the ways in which hosts can identify themselves.
- *IPSec Connection Types*—This determines which types of connections, such as remote access or local area connections, to which the rule applies.

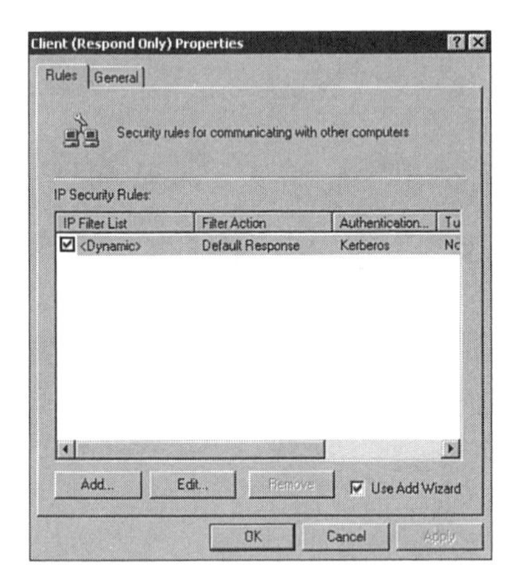

Figure 5.15 Configuring the properties of an IPSec policy.

From the General tab, you can change the name and description for the policy and configure the interval at which the computer will check for policy updates. Using the Advanced button, you can configure the Key Exchange Settings.

When configuring the Key Exchange Settings, you can select the Master Key Perfect Forward Secrecy option. This ensures that no previously used keying material is used to generate new master keys. You can also specify the interval at which authentication and key generation must take place.

The Rules tab lists all the rules that are configured for the policy. Additional rules can be added by clicking the Add button; existing ones can be edited using the Edit button. Clicking the Edit button brings up the Edit Rule Properties window (see Figure 5.16).

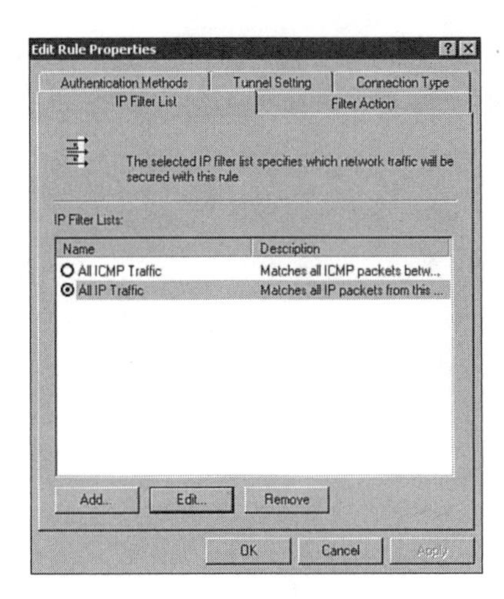

Figure 5.16 Editing IPSec rules.

The Filter Lists tab defines the type of traffic to which the rule will apply. The Filter Action tab defines whether the rule negotiates for secure traffic and how the traffic will be secured. Configuring the filter actions allows you to define the different security methods that can be negotiated. The security algorithms supported by IPSec include MD5 and SHA. The encryption algorithms supported include DES and 3DES.

The Authentication Methods tab allows you to configure the method used to establish trust between the two computers (see Figure 5.17). If there are multiple authentication methods configured for a rule, you can change the order in which they are used. The authentication methods available include

- *Kerberos*—Kerberos 5 is the default authentication method in a Windows 2000 domain. Users running the Kerberos protocol within a trusted domain can authenticate using this method.
- *Certificates*—If there is a trusted certificate authority available, certificates can be used for authentication.
- *Preshared key*—For non-Windows 2000 computers or those not running Kerberos, a preshared key can be used for authentication.

The Connection types tab allows you to define the types of connections to which the rule applies. This allows you to define different rules for different types of connections. Rules can be applied to Local Area Connections, Remote Access connections, or all network connections.

The Tunnel Setting tab allows you to specify a tunnel endpoint when communication will take place between two specific computers.

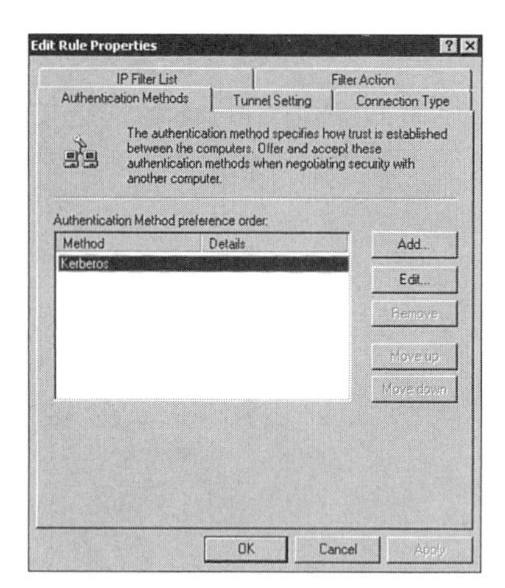

Figure 5.17 Configuring IPSec authentication methods.

You can edit the existing policies or you can create and assign a new policy through the Group Policy snap-in. To create a new policy, right-click IP Security Policies on Active Directory and select Create IP Security Policy. A wizard walks you through the process of creating the initial policy, which you can configure further using the Properties window for the new policy.

Once an IP Security policy has been assigned, you can have the group policy automatically refreshed on a computer by running the **secedit /refreshpolicy machine_policy**.

Managing and Monitoring IPSec

There are a number of tools available that you can use to manage and monitor IPSec. In terms of management, you can use the Group Policy snap-in to create, assign, and configure the IPSec policies or you can use the IP Security Policy Management snap-in. You can also perform a number of other management tasks using the following settings:

- Restore Default Policies
- Import/Export Policies
- Check Policy Integrity
- Manage IP Filter Lists and Filter Actions

When it comes to monitoring IPSec, you can use Network Monitor to capture IPSec packets. You can also use the IPSec Security Monitor utility, which you start from the command prompt to determine whether IPSec communications are secured. It displays the active security associations with other computers as well as several other IP security stats.

Practice Questions

Question 1

Your network is running Windows 2000 but also has two NetWare servers. **SRVNW1** is running NetWare 3.12 and **SRVNW2** is running NetWare 4.11. From **SRVWIN2K1**, you can access resources on **SRVNW2** but not on **SRVNW1**. You normally have no problem accessing resources on Windows 2000 servers. What is causing the problem?

❍ A. **SRVWIN2K1** does not have an IP address.

❍ B. NWLink must be set to autodetect the frame type.

❍ C. The frame type must be manually configured.

❍ D. NWLink is not installed.

Answer C is correct. When NWLink is set to autodetect and there are multiple frame types in use on the network, it defaults to 802.2. However, NetWare servers earlier than 3.3 default to 802.3. Therefore, SRVWIN2K1 will not be able to communicate with the NetWare 3.11 server until the frame type is configured, which means answer B is incorrect. Answer A is incorrect because NWLink does not use IP addresses. Answer D is incorrect because the Windows 2000 server can successfully communicate with SRVNW2.

Question 2

You have just installed Windows 2000 Server. During the installation you accepted the default settings. The server is being placed on an IP network. How can you install TCP/IP?

❍ A. Using the Add/Remove Programs applet in the Control Panel.

❍ B. From the Properties window of the Local Area Connection.

❍ C. Using the System applet within the Control Panel.

❍ D. TCP/IP is installed by default with Windows 2000.

Answer D is correct. Because none of the default settings were changed during the installation of Windows 2000 Server, TCP/IP does not need to be installed. Answers A and C are incorrect because these two applets cannot be used to install TCP/IP. Answer B is incorrect. Although this is the correct way to install the protocol, it does not need to be installed because it is done by default when Windows 2000 is installed.

Question 3

What does the TCP/IP protocol use to determine whether a packet is destined for a host on the local network or a host on a remote network? [Choose all that apply.]

- ❑ A. Subnet mask
- ❑ B. Default gateway
- ❑ C. IP address
- ❑ D. DNS server

Answers A and C are correct. The subnet mask is used to determine whether a packet is destined for a host on the local or remote network. It compares the subnet mask of the local host with the IP address of the destination host and, through a process known as "anding," determines whether the packet is for a local or remote host. Therefore answers B and D are incorrect.

Question 4

Which address class does the IP address 121.107.2.221 belong to?

- ❍ A. Class A
- ❍ B. Class B
- ❍ C. Class C
- ❍ D. Class D

Answer A is correct. Because the first decimal value is between 1 and 126, the IP address belongs to the range of IP addresses within Class A. Therefore, answers B, C, and D are incorrect.

Question 5

You create an OU within Active Directory for a group of computers. Using the Group Policy editor, you create a new IP security policy that applies to the new OU. You configure all the necessary security settings. What is your next step in applying the policy to the OU?

- ❍ A. Restart the computers.
- ❍ B. Assign the policy.
- ❍ C. Enable the policy.
- ❍ D. Replicate the policy to all domain controllers.

Answer B is correct. To apply the policy to the computers within the organizational unit, you must first assign the policy. This can be done by right-clicking the policy and choosing the Assign option. Therefore, answers A, C, and D are incorrect.

Question 6

You are configuring IPSec between two servers in a workgroup. You assign the Client (Respond Only) to each of the servers but notice that IP packets being sent between the two servers are not being secured. What is causing the problem?

- ❍ A. Both are configured with the Client (Respond Only) policy.
- ❍ B. IPSec can only be used with Active Directory.
- ❍ C. One of the servers must be configured as an IPSec client.
- ❍ D. The servers cannot be members of the same workgroup.

Answer A is correct. If both servers are configured with the Client (Respond Only) policy, they will respond only to requests for secure communications. One of the servers must be configured with Server (Request Security). Therefore, answers B, C, and D are incorrect.

Question 7

You are configuring IP security for your network. You want all data to be encrypted but still want clients that do not support IPSec to be able to authenticate with the server. Which of the following policies should you use?

- ❍ A. Secure Server (Require Security)
- ❍ B. Client (Respond Only)
- ❍ C. Client (Require Security)
- ❍ D. Server (Request Security)

Answer D is correct. By assigning the Server (Request Security) policy, the server will always attempt secure communications. Unsecured communications will still be allowed if the client is not IPSec aware. Answer A is incorrect because communications will not be allowed if the client is not IPSec aware. Answer B is incorrect. Assigning the Client (Respond Only) means that the server will only respond to requests for secure communications but will not attempt to secure all communications. Answer C is incorrect because there is no such default IP security policy.

Question 8

You have just installed TCP/IP and have statically configured the settings. You want to make sure the server can communicate with servers and workstations on other subnets. Which of the following can you use to test TCP/IP connectivity?

❍ A. **ipconfig**

❍ B. Network Monitor

❍ C. **ping**

❍ D. ARP

Answer C is correct. TCP/IP connectivity can be tested using the `ping` utility. By pinging the IP address of a host on a remote subnet, you can verify connectivity with that host. Answer A is incorrect because `ipconfig` only verifies the TCP/IP settings configured. Answer B is incorrect because Network Monitor is used to capture and analyze network traffic. Answer D is incorrect because ARP is part of the TCP/IP protocol suite that maps IP addresses to MAC addresses.

Question 9

Which of the following transport layer protocols ensures reliable delivery of packets between two IP hosts?

❍ A. ARP

❍ B. ICMP

❍ C. UDP

❍ D. TCP

Answer D is correct. Transmission Control Protocol (TCP) is a connection-based protocol that operates at the transport layer of the DoD model and ensures reliable delivery between hosts. Answer A is incorrect because ARP is used to map IP addresses to MAC addresses. Answer B is incorrect because ICMP is used for diagnostic purposes. Answer C is incorrect because UDP is connectionless and does not offer reliable delivery of packets.

Question 10

Which of the following tools can be used to monitor IPSec statistics?

- ❍ A. Network Monitor
- ❍ B. IP Security Monitor
- ❍ C. System Monitor
- ❍ D. IP Security Policy Management

Answer B is correct. IP Security Monitor can be used to gather and monitor IPSec statistics. Answer A is incorrect because Network Monitor is used to capture and analyze IP packets. Answer C is incorrect because System Monitor is used to monitor server performance. Answer D is incorrect because IP Security Policy Management is used to create and manage IP Security policies.

Need to Know More?

Search the online version of TechNet and the Windows 2000 Server Resource Kit using keywords such as `IPSec`, `IP Addresses`, and `Network Monitor`.

Minasi, Mark, Christa Anderson, Brian Smith, and Doug Toombs. *Mastering Windows 2000*. Sybex Press, Alameda, CA. ISBN: 0782140432.

Frankel, Sheila. *Demystifying the IPSec Puzzle*. Artech House, 2001. ISBN: 1580530796. This book provides very in-depth technical knowledge about all aspects of IPSec.

WINS

Terms you'll need to understand:

- ✓ WINS replication
- ✓ WINS proxy
- ✓ LMHOSTS file
- ✓ NetBIOS
- ✓ Name resolution
- ✓ Push partner
- ✓ Pull partner
- ✓ Tombstoning
- ✓ Persistent connections

Techniques you'll need to master:

- ✓ Understanding WINS resolution
- ✓ Installing and configuring a WINS server
- ✓ Installing and configuring a WINS client
- ✓ Configuring a WINS proxy
- ✓ Understanding and configuring WINS replication
- ✓ Understanding NetBIOS name resolution
- ✓ Managing and monitoring WINS

Introduction

Windows 2000 no longer requires Network Basic Input/Output System (NetBIOS) names as the primary names for network computers. Windows 2000 Server now uses domain names, which are resolved and managed by the Domain Name Service (DNS). However, previous versions of Windows, and many network applications, still rely on NetBIOS names and Windows Internet Name Service (WINS) servers for name registration and resolution. Because most modern networks still employ legacy clients (such as Windows 95 and Windows 98, as well as legacy servers, such as Windows NT 4.0/NT 3.*x*) it is important to have an understanding of WINS.

This chapter examines NetBIOS name resolution, the methods available for resolving NetBIOS names, and the role a WINS server plays. You'll learn how to install and configure a WINS server as well as how to configure a WINS client. This chapter includes a discussion on WINS replication and introduces the tools available for managing and monitoring a WINS server.

Installing, Configuring, and Troubleshooting WINS

Windows 2000 now uses DNS as its primary namespace. Pre-Windows 2000 operating systems use NetBIOS names to identify and access computers and resources on a network. To locate computers and resources, NetBIOS names must be registered so they can be mapped to a corresponding IP address. This is where WINS comes into play. Keep in mind that in a pure Windows 2000 network, WINS is not required. However, if there are legacy clients and servers on the network that still use NetBIOS, or applications that require NetBIOS name resolution, WINS may be required.

WINS provides a dynamic database to register NetBIOS names and resolve them to IP addresses. Clients dynamically register their NetBIOS names with a WINS server and query a WINS server when they need to resolve a NetBIOS name to an IP address.

In a non-routed environment, NetBIOS names can be registered and resolved using local broadcasts. However, this poses a problem in a routed environment because routers are not normally configured to forward broadcasts between subnets. WINS solves the problem of registering and resolving NetBIOS names in a routed environment. By using WINS, name registration and renewal requests can be directed to a WINS server, which allows the requests to pass routers, thereby allowing name registration and renewal across subnets.

There are a number of other benefits of implementing a WINS server on a network, including

- It provides a dynamic database for registering NetBIOS names and resolving them to IP addresses.
- It centralizes the management of resolving NetBIOS names to IP addresses and eliminates the need for LMHOSTS files.
- It reduces the amount of broadcast traffic on the network. Clients can directly query the WINS server for name registration and resolution instead of performing a broadcast.
- It allows pre-Windows 2000 clients to locate domain controllers that are not on their local subnet.

LMHOSTS files are another method of resolving NetBIOS names to IP addresses. LMHOSTS files are plain text files that consist of entries mapping NetBIOS names (or computer names) to IP addresses. When a computer needs to resolve a NetBIOS name, it can parse the LMHOSTS file located within the Windows directory. The main disadvantage to using LMHOSTS files is that they must be manually updated.

WINS Resolution

WINS clients communicate with a WINS server in any of the following situations:

- NetBIOS name registration
- NetBIOS name renewal
- NetBIOS name release
- NetBIOS name resolution

NetBIOS Name Registration

When a client is configured to use a WINS server, it registers its NetBIOS name with the WINS server that it has been configured to use. A name registration request is sent directly to the WINS server when the client starts and when any network services, such as the workstation service, is started. The WINS server responds with a successful registration message if another host on the network doesn't already register the same name. The WINS server also returns the Time to Live (TTL), which defines how long the name can remain in the WINS database before it must be renewed (the default TTL is six days).

If the WINS server determines that the name a client is attempting to register is already in the database, the WINS server sends a challenge message to the host that currently has the name registered. If the host responds to the challenge, the host requesting to register the NetBIOS name receives a negative response from the WINS server. If the host that currently uses the name does not respond to the challenge, the WINS server sends a successful registration message, thus permitting the new WINS client to register the name.

There may also be instances when a client attempts to register its NetBIOS name when the primary WINS server is unavailable. In this case, the client will attempt to register its name with a secondary WINS server if it has been configured for one. If no response is received, the client can register the name using a local broadcast. Remember that local broadcasts cannot cross routers, so a name that the machine registers in this way might not be unique.

NetBIOS Name Renewal

As IP addresses leased from a Dynamic Host Configuration Protocol (DHCP) server must periodically be renewed. WINS clients must also renew their registered NetBIOS names with the WINS server by sending a refresh request. The refresh request contains the IP address and NetBIOS name of the requesting client. The renewal process occurs as follows:

1. When half of the TTL is reached, the client sends a name refresh request to the WINS server.
2. If the client receives no response from the primary WINS server, it attempts to renew its name at 10-minute intervals for a total of one hour, at which point it attempts to renew with the secondary WINS server.
3. The client continues to contact the primary and secondary WINS servers until its name is renewed.
4. If the client fails to renew its name before the TTL expires, the client releases its NetBIOS name.

NetBIOS Name Releasing

When a WINS client is properly shut down, it sends a name release request containing its IP address and NetBIOS name to the WINS server. This makes the NetBIOS name available for another client on the network.

NetBIOS Name Resolution

When a client is configured for WINS, it automatically sends any NetBIOS name resolution requests to the WINS server. The WINS server uses its database to map the client to its corresponding IP address. When a client needs to resolve a NetBIOS name, the following process occurs:

1. The client checks its local NetBIOS name cache to see if there is an entry for the remote client.
2. If no entry is present, the request is sent to the primary WINS server.
3. If the primary server fails to respond to the request, the WINS client attempts to resolve the name using one of the other WINS servers it has been configured to use.
4. If none of the WINS servers respond, the WINS client attempts to resolve the name using a broadcast on the local network.
5. If the WINS client does not receive a response, it checks the LMHOSTS file. If no entry exists, the WINS client tries to resolve the name using the HOSTS file, and then contacts a DNS server.

Installing WINS

WINS is not installed by default. You can add it as an optional component during the installation of Windows 2000 or you can do so afterward through the Control Panel.

To install WINS, follow these steps:

1. Point to Start, Settings, and click Control Panel.
2. Double-click the Add/Remove Programs applet. Click Add/Remove Windows Components.
3. In the list of components, select Networking Services and click Details.
4. Click Windows Internet Name Service (WINS) and click OK (see Figure 6.1).

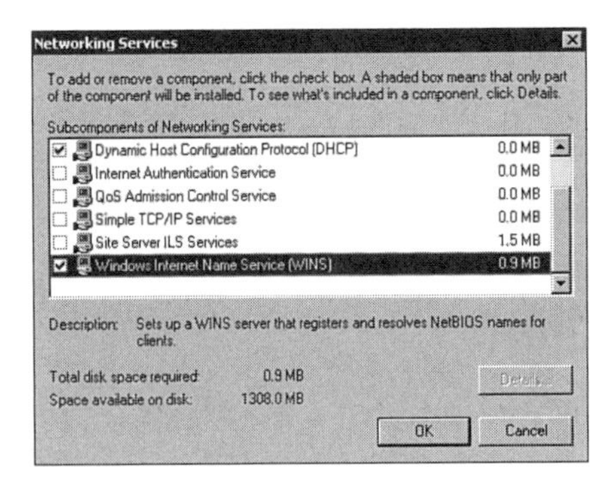

Figure 6.1 Installing WINS through the Add/Remove Programs applet in the Control Panel.

Configuring a WINS Server

Once the WINS service is installed, you can configure its properties using the WINS management console available on the Administrative Tools menu. Once the console is opened, right-clicking the WINS server and selecting Properties brings up its Properties window. Using the General tab, you can configure how often server statistics are updated (you can also disable this option) and specify a location to back up the WINS database.

From the Intervals tab, you can configure the rate at which records are renewed, deleted, and verified (see Figure 6.2). Table 6.1 summarizes the configurable options.

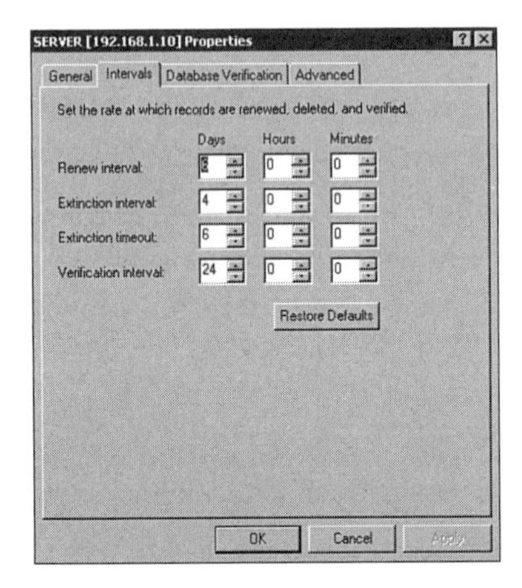

Figure 6.2 Configuring the rate at which records are renewed, deleted, and verified from the WINS Properties window.

Table 6.1 Configuring Settings from the Intervals Tab

Option	Description
Renew interval	Specifies the number of days before a WINS client must renew its registered NetBIOS name.
Extinction interval	Specifies the amount of time before a record marked as released is marked as extinct.
Extinction timeout	Specifies the amount of time before a record marked as extinct is removed from the WINS database.
Verification interval	Specifies the amount of time before a WINS server must verify that any records replicated from a replication partner are still active.

The process of deleting records marked as extinct is known as *scavenging*. Using the Scavenge database option allows an administrator to initiate the scavenging process manually.

The Database Verification tab allows you to configure how often and at what time the WINS server should verify the records within its database.

The Advanced tab has several configurable options (see Figure 6.3). You can enable logging so WINS-related events are written to the Windows event log. You can enable or disable burst handling, which allows you to configure the number of requests to which a WINS server can successfully respond without actually registering the name within the database. You can also specify the location of the WINS database and configure the version number.

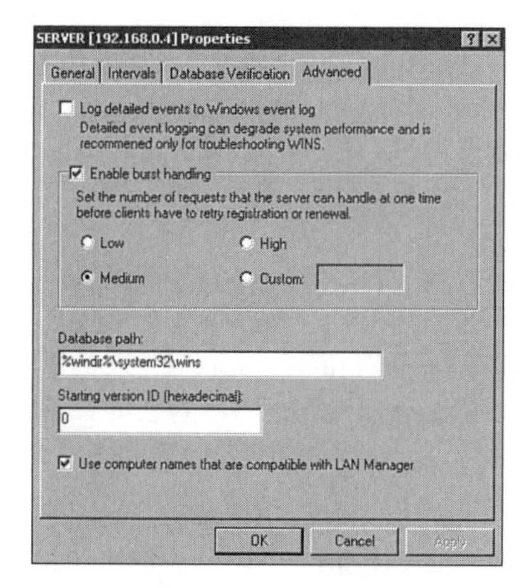

Figure 6.3 Configuring advanced WINS server options.

Making configuration changes to any server can have negative effects. However, you can add a user account to the WINS Users group, which allows a user to view the contents of the WINS database but not to make configuration changes.

Configuring WINS Clients

For clients to dynamically register their NetBIOS names with a WINS server and use the server for name resolution, they must be configured with the IP address of the WINS server. A WINS client can run on any of the following platforms:

- Windows XP
- Windows 2000
- Windows NT 3.51 and higher
- Windows 95
- Windows 98
- Windows for Workgroups 3.11 running MS TCP/IP32
- Microsoft Network Client 3.0 for MS-DOS
- LAN Manager 2.2c for MS-DOS

There are two methods available for configuring clients with the IP address of the WINS server. You can use a DHCP server or you can configure each client manually.

If you opt to use DHCP, Windows 2000 clients require no configuration because they are enabled for DHCP by default. But you must configure the DHCP server to assign the IP address of the WINS server to DHCP clients. To do so, configure the 044 WINS/NBNS Servers and the 046 WINS/NBT Node Type DHCP options (see Figure 6.4). You can do so by configuring the scope options within the DHCP management console (refer to Chapter 3, "DHCP," for instructions on how to configure scope options). The first option specifies the IP address of the WINS server. The second option specifies the node type or methods the client uses to resolve NetBIOS names and in what order it does so.

Clients can also be configured manually by an administrator, which means visiting each workstation and typing the IP address of the WINS server. To manually configure a Windows 2000 client for WINS, perform the following steps:

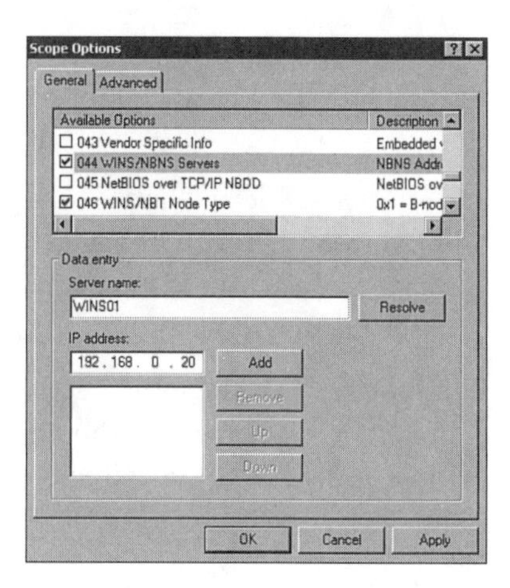

Figure 6.4 Configuring DHCP to support WINS clients.

1. Point to Start, Settings, and click Network and Dial-up Connections.
2. Right-click the Local Area Connection and click Properties.
3. From the list of components, select Internet Protocol (TCP/IP) and click Properties.
4. From the Internet Protocol (TCP/IP) Properties window, select the Advanced button and click the WINS tab (see Figure 6.5).
5. Click the Add button and enter the IP address for the WINS server. Repeat the process for additional WINS servers on the network. Click OK.

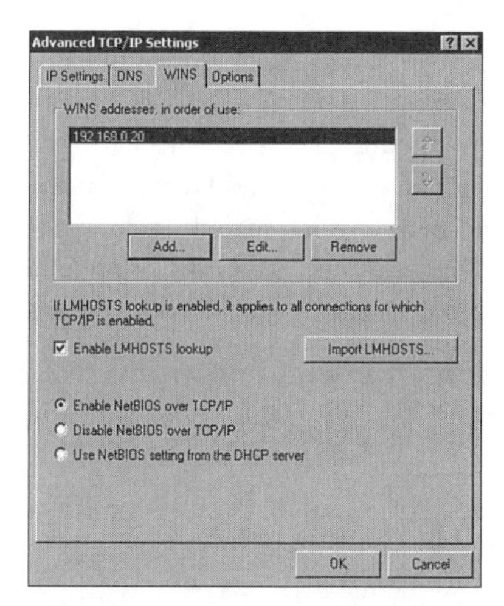

Figure 6.5 Configuring a WINS client.

As you can see from Figure 6.5, there are several other configurable options available on the WINS tab. These options are summarized in the following list:

- *Enable LMHOSTS Lookup*—This option is selected by default and enables the client to use an LMHOSTS file to resolve NetBIOS names to IP addresses. The Import LMHOSTS button allows you to import an existing file into the LMHOSTS file on the client computer.
- *Enable NetBIOS over TCP/IP*—This option specifies that the local area connection uses NetBIOS over TCP/IP and WINS. This setting should be enabled if the computer must communicate using NetBIOS computer names or with pre-Windows 2000 clients.
- *Disable NetBIOS over TCP/IP*—This option disables NetBIOS over TCP/IP and WINS for the local area connection. On a network that runs only Windows 2000, this option can be selected.
- *Use NetBIOS setting from the DHCP server*—Select this option to have the client obtain WINS information from a DHCP server. If the client is configured to receive its IP address from a DHCP server, this option is selected by default.

Windows 2000 now supports up to 12 configurations of WINS. Windows NT 4.0 supports two.

Configuring Static Mappings

In some cases, there may be clients on the network that are unable to dynamically update their NetBIOS name with a WINS server. A UNIX host is an example of a client that cannot register and update its record with a WINS server. In these instances, the administrator can manually add a static mapping to the WINS database. Once a static mapping is created, it does not need to be renewed, nor does it expire. The administrator must manually delete the entry. To configure a static mapping, perform the following steps:

1. Click Start, point to Programs, Administrative Tools, and click WINS.
2. Within the WINS management console, right-click Active Registrations and select New Static Mapping.
3. Within the New Static Mapping dialog box, enter the computer name (NetBIOS name) for the host (see Figure 6.6).
4. If required, type the NetBIOS scope.

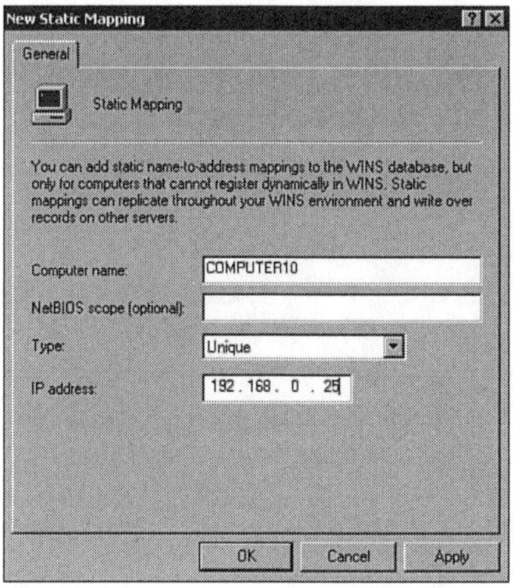

Figure 6.6 Configuring a static mapping.

5. Using the drop-down arrow, select the type of entry you are creating.
6. Enter the IP address of the host and click OK.

Keep in mind that if the client for which you created a static mapping is also a DHCP client, a client reservation is created so the client is leasing the same IP address all the time. If the client leases an IP address that is different from the IP address listed in the WINS database, the name will be resolved incorrectly (to the incorrect IP address) .

WINS Proxy

Clients that do not support WINS resolve NetBIOS names using a broadcast. For routed IP networks, this method of name resolution becomes difficult, if not impossible. In such situations, you can configure what is known as a *WINS proxy agent.*

A WINS proxy agent (sometimes just called a WINS proxy) is a computer on a local subnet that listens for name resolution broadcasts. Once the WINS proxy receives a broadcast, it queries the WINS server on behalf of the non-WINS client and returns the results to the client. In terms of NetBIOS name registration, the WINS proxy also listens for name registration broadcasts on the local subnet. When a non-WINS client attempts to register its NetBIOS name, the WINS proxy queries the WINS server to ensure that the name has not already been registered by another host.

To configure a computer to act as a WINS proxy, you must edit the local Registry. To do so, navigate to the `HKEY_LOCAL_MACHINE\System\CurrentControlSet\Services\NETBT\Parameters` key and change the value of the `EnableProxy` to `1` (see Figure 6.7) .

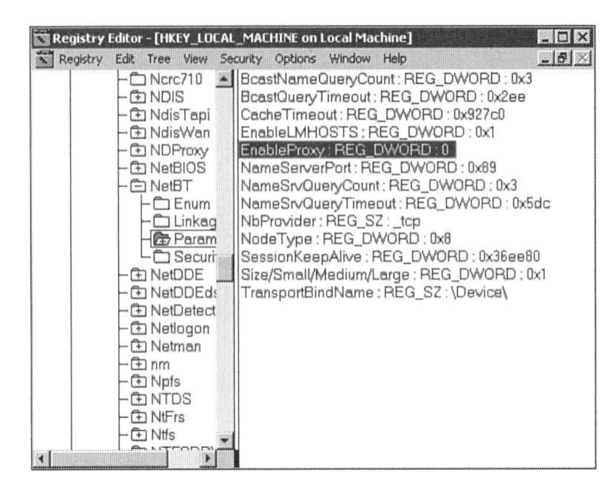

Figure 6.7 Enabling the WINS proxy using the Registry.

Configuring WINS Replication

Consider the following scenario: Two subnets exist on a physical network, each with its own WINS server. Clients on each subnet register their names with their local WINS server. When a host on subnet A attempts to communicate with a host on subnet B, it will be unable to resolve the name to an IP address. This is because the local WINS server will not have an entry in its database for the host on subnet B.

In a WINS environment, replication must be configured between WINS servers to facilitate network communication between hosts on different subnets. WINS servers can be configured as push partners, pull partners, or both, depending on how you want replication to occur. Push partners notify other WINS servers when changes are made to their database; pull partners request database changes from partner WINS servers. To accomplish one-way replication, one of these partnerships (either a push or pull) must be configured.

When considering whether to configure push or pull partners, keep the following points in mind:

- If WINS servers are connected by slow links, configure a pull partner so replication can be scheduled.

➤ If WINS servers are connected by fast links, configure a push partner so replication can occur when changes are made to the database.

WINS servers can be configured for replication using the WINS management console. To configure replication, follow these steps:

1. Within the WINS management console, right-click Replication Partners and select New Replication Partner.
2. Enter the name or IP address of the WINS server you want to add as a replication partner. Click OK.
3. Right-click the WINS server that was added as a replication partner and click Properties.
4. From the Advanced tab within the WINS server's properties window, use the drop-down list to select the replication partner type. Click OK.

If you do not want to manually set up WINS replication partners, you can configure WINS servers to automatically find one another and configure themselves for replication. They do so by multicasting to the IP address of 224.0.1.24. When WINS servers locate each other, they automatically configure themselves as push/pull replication partners. This automatic discovery option can be enabled by right-clicking Replication Partners within the WINS management console and clicking Properties. From the Replication Partners Properties window, select the Advanced tab and choose the Enable automatic partner configuration option (see Figure 6.8) .

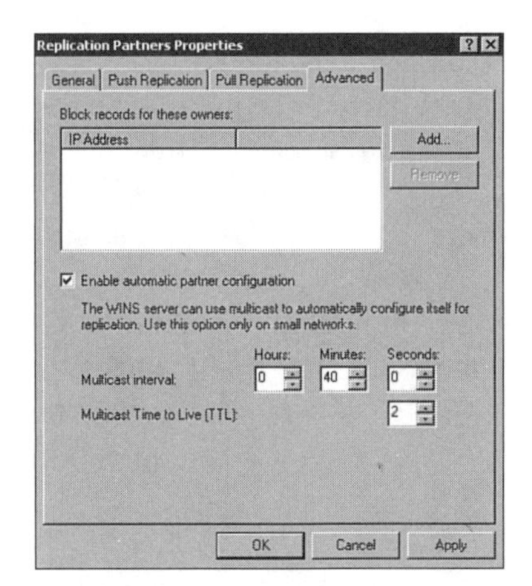

Figure 6.8 Enabling automatic partner configuration.

Configuring NetBIOS Name Resolution

Some clients require NetBIOS names to communicate with other hosts on a network. A NetBIOS name is a 16-character name where the first 15 characters identify a unique host and the 16th character identifies a service or application running on the host, such as the Workstation or Server service.

As with domain names, NetBIOS names must be resolved to an IP address before two hosts can communicate. There are a number of methods available for name resolution and the method employed will depend on the environment.

The three standard ways of resolving NetBIOS names to IP addresses are through a local broadcast, using the local cache, or by using a NetBIOS name server (such as a WINS server). With a local broadcast, a broadcast is sent out on the network requesting the IP address of a specific host. One of the disadvantages of this method is the increase in traffic. All hosts maintain a local cache that can be used for name resolution. Each time a host resolves a NetBIOS name to an IP address, the record is added to the local cache and remains valid for 10 minutes. By default, all clients check their local cache before using any of the other resolution methods available. The third option is to use a NetBIOS name server to resolve names to IP addresses.

In a Microsoft environment, several other methods for resolving names are also available, such as DNS servers, HOSTS files, and LMHOSTS files.

Depending on the requirements of an environment, clients can be configured to use a single method for name resolution or they can use a combination of methods. The exact method a client uses to resolve NetBIOS names is determined by its node type. For example, if a client is configured as an M-Node, it attempts to resolve a NetBIOS name by first performing a local broadcast. If this is unsuccessful, it then tries to resolve the name using a NetBIOS name server. You can check the node type a client is configured for by typing `ipconfig /all` at the command prompt (see Figure 6.9). The node type can be changed via the local Registry. Table 6.2 summarizes the four node types.

Remember that before performing a broadcast or contacting a WINS server, the host attempts to resolve a NetBIOS name using its local cache.

```
C:\WINNT\System32\cmd.exe
Windows 2000 IP Configuration

        Host Name . . . . . . . . . . . . : server
        Primary DNS Suffix  . . . . . . . : BAYSIDE.NET
        Node Type . . . . . . . . . . . . : Hybrid
        IP Routing Enabled. . . . . . . . : Yes
        WINS Proxy Enabled. . . . . . . . : No
        DNS Suffix Search List. . . . . . : BAYSIDE.NET

Ethernet adapter Interface1:

        Connection-specific DNS Suffix  . :
        Description . . . . . . . . . . . : AMD PCNET Family PCI Ethernet
r
        Physical Address. . . . . . . . . : 00-50-56-5F-80-72
        DHCP Enabled. . . . . . . . . . . : No
        IP Address. . . . . . . . . . . . : 192.168.0.4
        Subnet Mask . . . . . . . . . . . : 255.255.255.0
        Default Gateway . . . . . . . . . : 192.168.0.1
        DNS Servers . . . . . . . . . . . : 192.168.0.2
                                            192.168.0.3

C:\>_
```

Figure 6.9 Checking the node type using the ipconfig command from the command prompt.

Be prepared to encounter exam questions pertaining to the NetBIOS node types. Make sure you are familiar with which methods of resolution are used for each type and in what order.

Table 6.2 Node Types

Node Type	Description
B-node	A broadcast is used for NetBIOS name registration and resolution.
P-node	A NetBIOS name server is used for name registration and resolution.
M-node	A broadcast is attempted first for name resolution. If this method fails, a NetBIOS name server is contacted.
H-node	A NetBIOS name server is attempted first for name resolution. If this fails, a broadcast is used.

A Windows 2000 client that is configured as a DHCP client automatically uses H-node for NetBIOS name resolution. This means the client will attempt to resolve NetBIOS names using a WINS server first before using a local broadcast (after checking the local cache). The client resolves names in the following order: local cache, WINS, broadcast, LMHOSTS, HOSTS, and DNS. A useful mnemonic for remembering this order is: *Can We Buy Large Hard Drives?*

LMHOSTS Files

As already mentioned, one of the ways that NetBIOS names can be resolved is through the use of a text file known as an *LMHOSTS file*. One of the benefits of using an LMHOSTS file is that entries from the file can be preloaded into the local cache to facilitate name resolution (because this is the method a client will use to resolve a NetBIOS name). So if a client cannot resolve a NetBIOS name using any of the previous methods, clients can parse the LMHOSTS file to determine whether a record exists.

For clients to resolve names using an LMHOSTS file, they must be configured to do so (refer to the "Configuring WINS Clients" section for more information).

The LMHOSTS file can be found in the `%SYSTEMROOT%\system32\drivers\etc` directory. By default, the file is named LMHOSTS.SAM and must be renamed LMHOSTS before it will work. Figure 6.10 provides an example of the contents of an LMHOSTS file. When configuring records within the file, there are several directives that can be used, as outlined in Table 6.3.

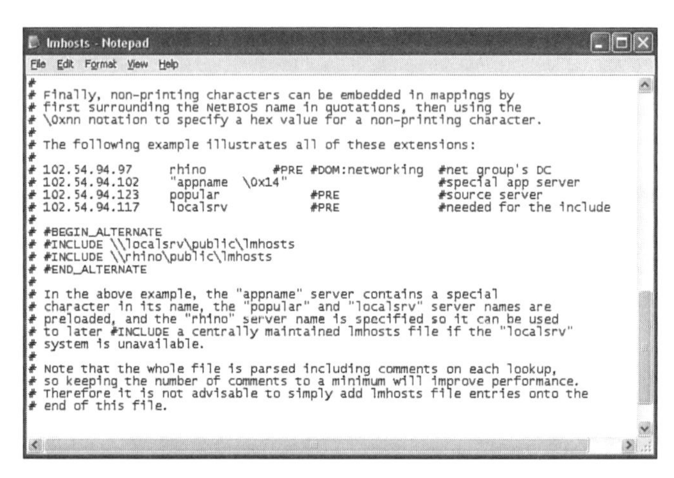

Figure 6.10 A sample LMHOSTS file.

Table 6.3 Predefined LMHOSTS Directives

Predefined Keyword	Description
#Pre	Defines which entries within the file should be loaded into the local cache.
#DOM:domain_name	Indicates the record of a domain controller.
#Begin_Alternate **#End_Alternate**	Specifies a list of other locations for an LMHOSTS file.
#include	Loads entries from a separate LMHOSTS file separate from the default file on the local computer. This option is most often used to specify a centrally located LMHOSTS file.
#MH	Adds multiple entries for a multihomed computer.

Be sure you are familiar with the different directives that can be used within an LMHOSTS file and their purposes.

Forcing WINS Replication

The replication of WINS records between WINS servers normally occurs in any of the following situations:

- When a WINS server starts.
- When the number of changes to the database reaches a certain number.
- At specific intervals configured by an administrator.

Sometimes, however, you might need to update the WINS database immediately. Within the WINS management console, administrators have the option of forcing replication to occur between WINS partners. To force replication between WINS server replication partners, click Replication Partners, right-click the server you want to replicate with, and then select Start Push Replication or Start Pull Replication.

WINS Persistent Connections in Windows 2000

One of the new features introduced in Windows 2000 is persistent connections between WINS replication partners. In previous versions of Windows, WINS servers disconnected from one another when replication was complete. Each time the replication process occurred, a new connection needed to be established, thus requiring more processor cycles. In other words, it's inefficient, especially when the WINS servers are connected with high-speed links. To make the replication process more efficient, administrators could configure replication to occur after a large number of changes occurred to the database, as opposed to having to reestablish a connection for a small number of changes. In any case, replication was slow and it was not uncommon to find inconsistencies in the WINS database.

With persistent connections, WINS servers no longer close connections after replication is complete. Not only does this increase the speed and efficiency of replication, because changes can be sent without having to wait for a connection to be established, but it also provides better consistency within the WINS database.

Managing and Monitoring WINS

Most management and monitoring tasks can be performed within the WINS management console. Most of the maintenance tasks performed will be to the WINS database, such as ensuring it is backed up in the event it becomes corrupt and ensuring the database remains consistent over a period of time.

Backing Up and Restoring the WINS Database

You can configure a WINS server to periodically back up its local database through the WINS management console. From the WINS server Properties window, you can specify a backup location (see Figure 6.11). You can also right-click the WINS server and select the Backup Database option.

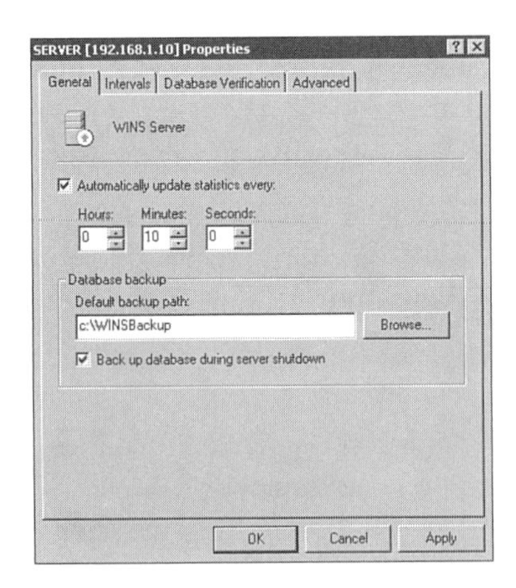

Figure 6.11 Configuring a backup for the WINS database from the WINS management console.

After you specify a backup location, the WINS server creates the `Wins_bak\NewFolder` within the location you specify (see Figure 6.12) and backs up the local database to this location at the intervals you specify. You also have the option of selecting whether the WINS server should perform a backup when the server is shut down.

If you have a backup of the WINS database, you can restore it by right-clicking the WINS server, choosing the Restore Database option, and specifying the location of the backup folder. Keep in mind that before you perform a restore, the WINS service must be stopped. If the WINS service is running, the option to restore the database is not available.

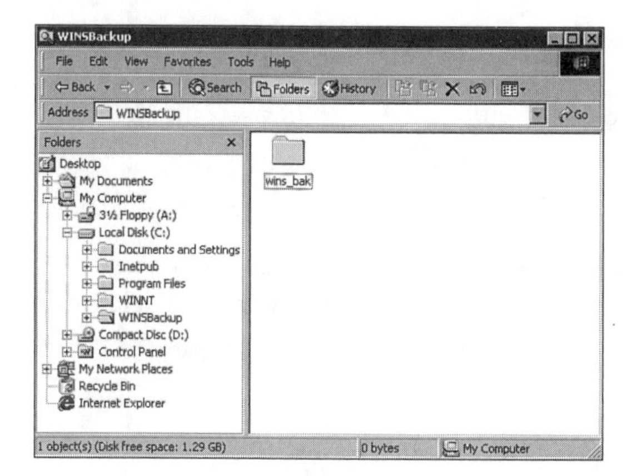

Figure 6.12 The WINS management console creates a Wins_bak folder in the location you specify.

Server Statistics

Viewing the statistics of a WINS server can provide an administrator with a general idea of what is happening. Within the WINS management console, you can right-click the WINS server and select the Display Server Statistics option. Some of the information provided includes when the server was last started, when replication last took place, and the number of name queries resolved.

Tombstoning

Records that are deleted or marked as extinct on one server can cause inconsistencies to the database of its replication partners. For example, a record that was deleted from the database on one server can easily still appear within the database of a replication partner.

Windows 2000 supports a feature known as *tombstoning*. Once a record is marked as tombstoned, it is no longer considered to be active on the local WINS server. The record remains within the local database for replications purposes. When a tombstoned record is replicated, all replication partners mark the record as being tombstoned. The record becomes extinct and is eventually removed from the database.

Records within the WINS database can be manually deleted or tombstoned using the following process:

1. Within the WINS console, right-click the Active Registrations container and click either the Find by Name or Find by Owner option to locate the appropriate record.

2. If you select Find by Name, type the NetBIOS name you are searching for. If you select Find by Owner, specify whether to have all entries in the local WINS database displayed or records from a specific WINS server. Click Find Now.
3. In the Details pane, right-click the appropriate record and click Delete.
4. Within the Delete Record dialog box, select one of the following options: Delete the record only from this server or Replicate deletion of the record to other servers (tombstone) .

Verifying Database Consistency

With multiple WINS servers configured for replication, a WINS database can become inconsistent over a period of time. Using the Verify Database Consistency and Verify Version ID Consistency options, an administrator can periodically perform database consistency checks. Checking the WINS database for inconsistencies forces the local WINS server to check all names replicated from other WINS servers and then to compare them to the local versions on the servers that own the records. The WINS server then updates its local records.

Practice Questions

Question 1

A junior network administrator has recently been hired. Due to his lack of experience, his rights and privileges will be closely monitored for the first few months. You want to allow the new junior administrator to view the contents of the WINS database without being able to make any configuration changes. How should you proceed?

❍ A. Add the user account to the Administrators group.

❍ B. Add the user account to the WINS Administrators group.

❍ C. Add the user account to the WINS Users group.

❍ D. Add the user account to the Enterprise Admins group.

Answer C is correct. By adding a user account to the WINS Users group, the user is given the right to view the contents of the WINS database but is not allowed to make any configuration changes. Answers A and D are incorrect because adding the user to either of these groups gives the user the capability to make configuration changes. Answer B is incorrect because there is no such group as the WINS Administrators group.

Question 2

You have two WINS servers on the network that are configured as replication partners. Each WINS server is located on a different subnet. You want to automatically back up the WINS database on both WINS servers every couple of hours. How should you configure this?

❍ A. Within the WINS console, right-click the WINS server and choose Properties. From the Properties window, select the Backup tab and click the Automatically Backup Database option.

❍ B. Within the WINS console, right-click the WINS server and choose Properties. From the Properties window, select the General tab and specify the backup path.

❍ C. Within the WINS console, right-click the WINS server and choose Properties. From the Properties window, select the General tab and click the Automatically Backup Database option.

❍ D. Within the WINS console, right-click the WINS server and choose Properties. From the Properties window, select the Advanced tab and specify the backup path.

Answer B is correct. Automatic backups can be configured by right-clicking the WINS server and choosing Properties. From the Properties window, click the General tab and specify the backup path. Once the path is specified, the WINS database is automatically backed up every three hours. Therefore, answers A, C, and D are incorrect.

Question 3

A network consists of several subnets. All clients are WINS-enabled and capable of updating their records dynamically. Each of the subnets has its own WINS server. One of the subnets contains two UNIX servers. Hosts on the local subnet can communicate with the UNIX servers; however, hosts on other subnets are unsuccessful. Clients can resolve NetBIOS names for hosts on other subnets. How can you configure WINS, so clients on all subnets can resolve the NetBIOS names of the UNIX servers to IP addresses?

❍ A. On each of the subnets, configure a secondary WINS server on each subnet.

❍ B. Configure the WINS servers as replication partners.

❍ C. Configure the WINS servers to back up their local databases.

❍ D. Configure static mappings for the two UNIX servers.

Answer D is correct. To allow hosts on other subnets to resolve the NetBIOS names of the UNIX servers, static mapping must be configured because the UNIX servers are unable to register their NetBIOS records dynamically. Answers A and C are incorrect because performing these tasks does not allow hosts to resolve the NetBIOS names of the UNIX servers. Answer B is incorrect because if the clients can already resolve the names of hosts on other subnets, replication is already configured between the WINS servers.

Question 4

A routed IP network has a mixture of WINS and non-WINS clients. Three of the seven subnets contain WINS servers. Several users report that they are unable to browse hosts on other subnets. Upon investigating the reports, you discover that the problem is only affecting non-WINS clients. How can the B-node broadcasts be resolved across the network?

❍ A. Configure static mappings for the non-WINS clients.

❍ B. Install a WINS proxy on each subnet that does not have a local WINS server.

❍ C. Configure replication between the three WINS servers.

❍ D. Configure a DHCP relay agent on each subnet.

Answer B is correct. To allow B-node broadcasts to be resolved across the network, a WINS proxy agent must be configured. The WINS proxy listens for B-node broadcasts and contacts the WINS servers on the other subnets to resolve the name resolution request on behalf of the non-WINS client. Therefore, answers A, C, and D are incorrect.

Question 5

Your network consists of two subnets. Due to budget constraints, only one server is configured. You need to configure a WINS proxy on the subnet that does not contain a WINS server. How should you proceed?

- ❍ A. Using the Add/Remove programs applet, install the WINS proxy component.
- ❍ B. Add the WINS proxy component through the Properties for the local area connection.
- ❍ C. Edit the Registry and change the value for the **EnableProxy** parameter to **1**.
- ❍ D. Edit the Registry and change the node type from B-node to M-node.

Answer C is correct. The WINS proxy component can be enabled on a computer through the Registry by changing the value of the `EnableProxy` parameter to `1`. Answers A and B are incorrect because the WINS proxy is not a component that is installed. Answer D is incorrect because changing the node type changes the way in which a client resolves NetBIOS names.

Question 6

Your network experienced a power outage that lasted for several hours. When the outage occurred, the client workstations did not shut down properly. When the power was returned, the WINS server was unable to handle the large number of registration requests. How can you increase the number of registration requests that a WINS server can handle at a given time?

- ❍ A. Configure burst handling.
- ❍ B. Enable persistent connections.
- ❍ C. Configure the refresh interval.
- ❍ D. Initiate manual scavenging of the WINS database.

Answer A is correct. By configuring burst handling, the WINS server can successfully respond to name registration requests before actually registering the name in the WINS database. Answer B is incorrect because persistent connections are used between WINS replication partners. Answer C is incorrect because the refresh interval determines how long a name can be registered by a client before it needs to be renewed. Answer D is incorrect because scavenging removes those entries from the WINS database that have been marked as extinct.

Question 7

A client has been configured to use P-node for name resolution. Which method will the client use first when trying to resolve a NetBIOS name to an IP address?

- ❍ A. NetBIOS name server
- ❍ B. LMHOSTS file
- ❍ C. Broadcast
- ❍ D. Local cache

Answer D is correct. When resolving NetBIOS names to IP addresses, clients always check their local name cache regardless of the node type with which they are configured. Therefore, answers A, B, and C are incorrect.

Question 8

A client has been configured to use H-node for name resolution. After checking the local name cache, which of the following name resolution methods will the client attempt to use next to resolve the NetBIOS name?

- ❍ A. LMHOSTS
- ❍ B. Broadcast
- ❍ C. NetBIOS name server
- ❍ D. DNS

Answer C is correct. After checking the local name cache, a client that is configured to use H-node for name resolution will attempt to resolve the name by contacting a NetBIOS name server. Answer A is incorrect because LMHOSTS files are parsed after the client has tried to resolve the NetBIOS name using one of the other methods. Answer B is incorrect because the client performs a broadcast only if the WINS server is unable to resolve the name. Answer D is incorrect because a DNS server is not contacted until an attempt is made to resolve the name using one of the other methods.

Question 9

You are configuring an LMHOSTS file for use by clients to resolve NetBIOS names to IP addresses. To facilitate the logon process, you want to place entries in the file for domain controllers on the network. Which of the following directives should be included when creating the entries for the domain controllers?

❍ A. **#pre**

❍ B. **#MH**

❍ C. **#include**

❍ D. **#DOM:domain_name**

Answer D is correct. The `#DOM:`*`domain_name`* directive indicates that the record is for a domain controller on the network. Answer A is incorrect because the `#pre` option is used to preload entries into the local cache. Answer B is incorrect because the `#MH` option is used to identify a multihomed computer. Answer C is incorrect because the `#include` option specifies an LMHOSTS file other than the local one that clients should use.

Question 10

Your network consists of a single WINS server. You want all clients to use the WINS server when resolving NetBIOS names. However, in the event that the WINS server is unavailable, you want the clients to use a local broadcast to resolve names. Which of the following node types should clients be configured with?

❍ A. B-node

❍ B. H-node

❍ C. M-node

❍ D. P-node

Answer B is correct. When clients are configured to use H-node, they first attempt to resolve NetBIOS names using a NetBIOS name server, and then perform a local broadcast. Answer A is incorrect because B-node indicates only a broadcast. Answer C is incorrect because M-node indicates a broadcast is performed, and then the NetBIOS name server is queried. Answer D is incorrect because P-node indicates that names are resolved using a NetBIOS name server only.

Need to Know More?

Search the online version of TechNet and the Windows 2000 Server Resource Kit using keywords such as `WINS`, `NetBIOS`, and `Name Resolution`.

Minasi, Mark, Christa Anderson, Brian Smith, and Doug Toombs. *Mastering Windows 2000, 4th Edition*. Sybex Press, Alameda, CA, 2002. ISBN: 0782140432.

IP Routing

Terms you'll need to understand:

- ✓ Routing Information Protocol (RIP)
- ✓ Open Shortest Path First (OSPF)
- ✓ Area Border Router
- ✓ Static routing
- ✓ Dynamic routing
- ✓ Demand-dial routing

Techniques you'll need to master:

- ✓ Understanding the different routing protocols
- ✓ Managing and monitoring border routing and internal routing
- ✓ Implementing demand-dial routing
- ✓ Configuring demand-dial routing
- ✓ Understanding the difference between dynamic and static routing
- ✓ Configuring static routes

Introduction

As networks continue to become interconnected, businesses are always looking for cost effective and practical ways to implement routing. The option is always available to purchase high-end dedicated complex routing solutions; however, with Windows 2000, a simple, efficient, and effective routing solution is built in to the operating system.

The *Routing and Remote Access service* enables a Windows 2000 Server to be turned into a network router and perform other network roles at the same time. This chapter examines how to implement IP routing using Windows 2000.

Installing, Configuring, and Troubleshooting IP Routing

With Routing and Remote Access (RRAS) , a system running Windows 2000 can function as a network router, which routes packets between networks. This setup allows LANs and WANs to be interconnected. The benefit is that the routing technology is built into the operating system, thus providing small and large businesses with a cost effective and secure way of interconnecting their networks. Some of the features included with RRAS in Windows 2000 include:

- Support for both the Routing Information Protocol (RIP) and Open Shortest Path First (OSPF)
- Support for Network Address Translation (NAT), which allows a single public IP address to be shared among clients on the internal network
- Support for demand-dial routing that initiates a connection with a router when outbound traffic is required and terminates the connection when the link is not needed (although the connection can also be configured as persistent)
- Support for both unicast and multicast routing. With unicast routing, a packet is sent to a single host, whereas multicast routing sends a packet to a group of hosts
- Support for virtual private networks (VPNs), which allows remote users or remote offices to securely connect to a network using a public network, such as the Internet, as a transport medium

The following section looks at the fundamental concepts behind IP routing and discusses how to implement, configure, and troubleshoot IP routing using Windows 2000 Server.

Keep in mind that Windows 2000 can also route IPX packets. However, the focus of this chapter is on IP routing.

IP Routing

Because all IP packets have a source and destination IP address, routing is the process of sending a packet from the source address to the destination address. Of course, how the routing of IP packets actually occurs is much more complex.

Because each IP packet has addressing information within the header, routers can use this information to determine where a packet should be sent to reach the destination host. Routers maintain information about the physical network, such as the path to a destination network and the metric associated with the route. (The metric is the number of hops, or the number of routers to cross, between the source and destination network.)

For routers to know the location to which packets must be forwarded, they must also know about their neighboring routers. This information is stored within the *routing table*. When a router receives a packet, it checks the routing table to determine where the packet must be sent to reach the destination host. The information within a routing table can be generated statically or dynamically, as you discover in the next sections.

Static Routing

With *static routing*, an administrator must manually configure the routing table by adding entries that tell the router how to reach other networks. Using the `route` command, an administrator updates the routing table by specifying the network addresses, the subnet masks, and the metrics associated with each route.

When deciding whether to use static routing, keep in mind that it works best for networks that do not change on a regular basis. If the network configuration is constantly changing, the administrative overhead associated with constantly having to update the routing tables greatly increases because the changes must be made on each router. In such cases, it may be more beneficial to implement dynamic routing.

Dynamic Routing

Dynamic routing eliminates the overhead associated with manually updating routing tables. Routers can dynamically build their own routing tables by communicating with other routers on the network.

With dynamic routing, the routing tables are built automatically through router communication. Using a routing communication protocol, routers periodically exchange messages containing location information about routes through the network. This information is used to build and update routing tables.

The major advantage of dynamic routing is that it reduces the administrative overhead associated with manually updating routing tables. For example, if a router goes down, the change is automatically propagated to all routers on the network so they are all aware of the change in the network topology. One of the major disadvantages is the amount of traffic that it generates.

Routing Protocols

For routers to share information and dynamically update their routing tables, a routing protocol must be used. As already mentioned, the two routing protocols supported by Windows 2000 are *Routing Information Protocol (RIP)* and *Open Shortest Path First (OSPF)* . Although both routing protocols are used for dynamic routing, there are some distinct differences between the two.

Routing Information Protocol (RIP)

The Routing Information Protocol (RIP) is designed for small- to medium-sized networks. There are two versions of RIP: RIPv1 and RIPv2. RIPv1 was originally a classful, broadcast-based routing protocol and had no protection; RIPv2 added subnet masking with each route entry, uses multicasts, and provides for a simple authentication scheme. One of the main benefits for choosing RIP is that it's very simple to configure and deploy. One of the major drawbacks associated with this protocol is that it's limited to a maximum hop count of 15. This means any networks more than 15 hop counts away are considered unreachable. Also, as a network increases in size, there can be excessive traffic generated from RIP announcements.

As mentioned earlier, all routes to a destination network are assigned a metric, which defines the distance between the source and destination. RIP uses a *hop count* (the number of routers to cross) to identify the distance between two networks. A value of 1 is added to the hop count for each router between a source and destination network.

When a router is first configured as a RIP router, the only entries in the routing table are for those networks to which it is physically connected. It then begins to send announcements of its availability to notify other routers of the networks it services. RIPv1 sends the announcements as broadcasts whereas RIPv2 can broadcast multicast packets for the announcements.

When changes occur to the network topology, RIPv2 uses triggered updates to communicate the changes to other routers. With triggered updates, the change to the network topology can be propagated immediately.

If you are considering using RIPv1, keep in mind that it does not support multicasting, it does not support any type of security between routers, and it does have known issues with routing loops. Because it may take several minutes for routers to reconfigure themselves after a change in network topology (for example, when an existing router becomes unavailable), routing loops in which routers send data in a circle can occur.

The Windows 2000 implementation of RIP supports the following features:

- The capability to select the version of RIP to implement for incoming and outgoing packets
- Support for routing filters to configure which routes should be accepted or denied
- Password authentication between routers
- Split-horizon to avoid router loops
- Triggered updates to ensure changes to the network topology are propagated immediately

RIPv2 supports multicasting for updating the routing tables. RIPv1 does not support this feature. RIPv1 routers cannot communicate with RIPv2 routers using multicasting for updates.

Open Shortest Path First (OSPF)

OSPF is designed for large internetworks (especially those spanning more than 15 router hops). The disadvantage of OSPF is that it's generally more complex to set up and requires a certain amount of planning.

OSPF is not supported for non-persistent, demand-dial connections.

OSPF uses the Shortest Path First (SPF) algorithm to calculate routes. The shortest path (the route with the lowest cost) is always used first.

Unlike RIP, which only uses announcements to update and share routing information, OSPF maintains a map of the network, known as the *link state database*. This map is synchronized between adjacent routers, or those neighboring OSPF routers. When a change is made to the network topology, the first router to receive the change sends out a change notification. Each router then updates its copy of the link state database and the routing table is recalculated.

One of the main differences between OSPF and RIP is that OSPF divides the network into different areas. Each of the routers maintains information only in the link state database about those areas to which it is connected. Another difference is that OSPF replicates only the changes to the routing table, not the entire table.

An *area* is a group of neighboring networks. The areas are connected to a backbone area. Area border routers connect the different areas to the backbone area.

Configuring RRAS

Routing and Remote Access (RRAS) is installed by default with Windows 2000. Before you can use a Windows 2000 Server as a network router, RRAS must be enabled. To enable RRAS, perform the following steps:

1. Click Start, point to Programs, Administrative Tools, and click Routing and Remote Access.
2. Right-click the server you want to configure and select Configure and Enable Routing and Remote Access. This launches the Routing and Remote Access Server setup wizard. Click Next.
3. From the Common Configurations window, select Network router (see Figure 7.1). Click Next.
4. Verify that all the protocols you want to route are listed. If additional protocols are required, select the No I Need to Add Protocols option. Click Next.
5. From the Demand-dial Connections window (see Figure 7.2), select Yes to set up a demand-dial connection. If you select No, a demand-dial connection can be configured afterward. Click Next.

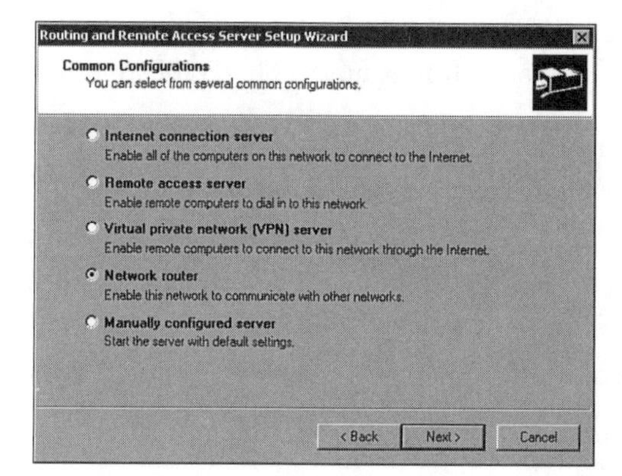

Figure 7.1 Configuring a network router from the Common Configurations window.

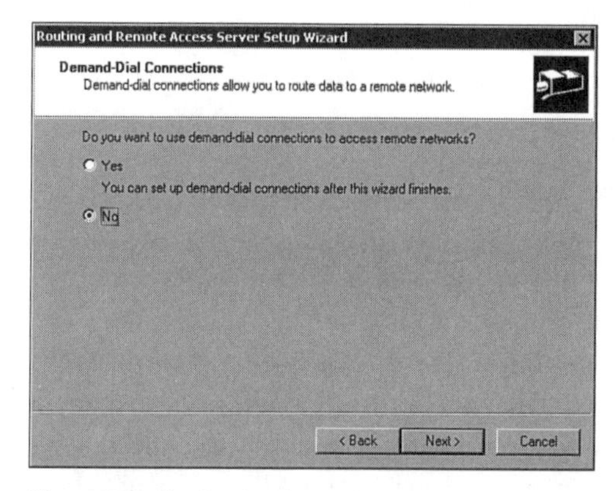

Figure 7.2 Configuring demand-dial routing via the Demand-dial Connections window.

6. If you selected No at the Demand-dial Connections window, click Finish. If you selected Yes, specify how incoming demand-dial connections will be assigned an IP address. If you select From a specified range, click Next and type in the range of IP addresses. Click Finish.

For a server running RRAS to be configured as a network router, you must configure a demand-dial interface (if demand-dialing is required). After demand-dialing is configured, you will assign an IP address to each network interface that will route IP packets, and install and configure one or both of the routing protocols just mentioned.

Configuring IP Routing

Once RRAS has been enabled, some general IP Routing properties can be configured. When you select the General node found under the IP Routing option within the RRAS console, all the known interfaces on the system are displayed. Right-clicking the General node brings up the General Properties window shown in Figure 7.3.

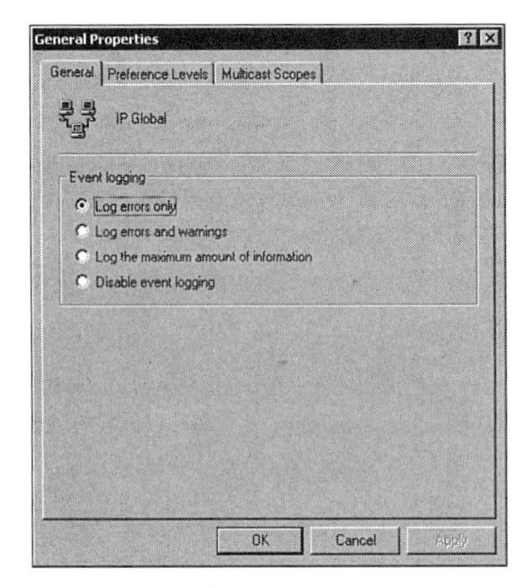

Figure 7.3 Configuring IP routing properties via the General Properties window.

The configuration options are not overly complex. You can enable or disable logging and specify the type of information to log on the General tab. The Preference Levels tab is used to configure the preference level of different routing sources. For example, routes that are statically configured are given preference over dynamic routes. You can change the preference level of a routing source by selecting the source and using the Move Up or Move Down buttons.

Configuring Interfaces

The General node lists all the interfaces available on the system that can be used for IP routing. This includes any LAN interfaces, as well as any demand-dial interfaces. You'll also notice two other ones listed by default: *internal* and *loopback*. Summary information is listed about each interface, including the type of interface (such as dedicated or demand-dial), the IP address, and the status of the interface. To view this summary information, expand the RRAS server, IP Routing, and click the General Node.

As you will see, each interface has its own set of configurable options (see Figure 7.4).

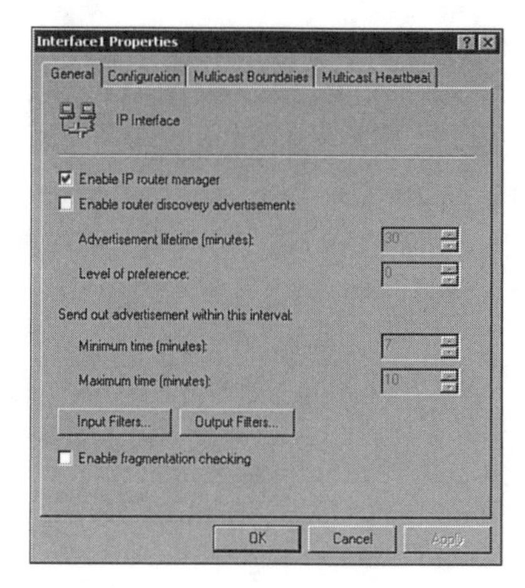

Figure 7.4 Configuring interface properties from an interface's General tab.

Use the General tab to configure any of the following options:

➤ *Enable IP router management*—Select this option to configure the administrative status of the interface.

➤ *Enable router discovery advertisements*—Enables ICMP discovery messages over the interface. The Advertisement lifetime defines how long a discovery advertisement remains valid. The Preference level is used to define the preference level for using the interface as the default gateway.

➤ *Minimum time*—The minimum time allowed (measured in minutes) between router advertisements.

➤ *Maximum time*—The maximum time allowed (measured in minutes) between router advertisements.

➤ *Enable fragmentation checking*—Specifies whether fragmented IP packets are discarded.

The Configuration tab is used to configure the IP address for the interface. An IP address can be obtained from a DHCP server or a static IP address can be configured. The remaining two tabs are used to configure multicasting.

Updating a Windows 2000 Routing Table Using Static Routes

There might be instances when you need to add a static route to your Windows 2000 router. This, of course, has its advantages and disadvantages.

Creating a static route is simple enough to do; however, the routes you configure are not shared between routers.

Static routes specify the network address and subnet mask telling the router how to get to a certain destination. The router uses the information to determine which gateway to forward the packet to so it can get to the destination host.

Static routes can be configured in one of two ways: using the Route command or through the RRAS management console. Using the `Route Add` command, static entries can be added to the local routing table on a router (you can also specify whether they should be persistent routes—meaning they will remain in the routing table when the system reboots—by using the `-p` parameter).

The syntax for the Route Add command is as follows:

```
route add <destination> mask <netmask> <gateway> metric <interface>
```

The second option is to configure a static route within the RRAS management console. To configure a static route using this method, perform the following steps:

1. Within the RRAS management console, expand IP routing.
2. Right-click Static Routes and select New Static Route. The Static Route window appears (see Figure 7.5).
3. Using the drop-down arrow, select the interface that will be used to route IP packets.
4. Type the destination IP address and subnet mask.
5. Type the IP address of the gateway for the RRAS server.
6. Click OK.

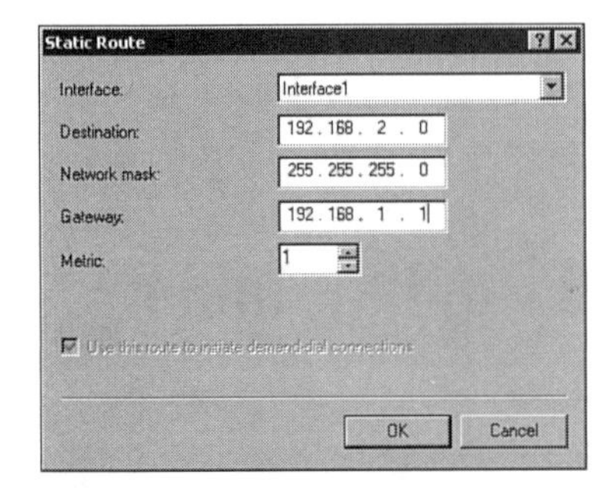

Figure 7.5 Creating a new static route via the Static Route window.

Implementing Demand-Dial Routing

There are two types of demand-dial connections: *on-demand connections* and *persistent connections*. With demand-dial connections, a connection with the remote router is established only when necessary. A connection is established to route information and terminated when the link is not in use. The benefit of this is obviously the cost associated with using a link. With persistent connections, the link does not need to be terminated, even when it is not in use. No additional charges are incurred.

Connections between network routers can be one-way initiated or two-way initiated, meaning a connection can be initiated by only one router or by both the routers.

With one-way initiated connections, one router is designated as the answering router and the other is designated as the calling router, which is responsible for initiating any connections.

Creating a One-Way Demand-Dial Interface

Demand-dial connections can be created within the Routing and Remote Access snap-in. How you configure the connection depends on whether you are configuring a one-way or two-way initiated connection. To create a demand-dial interface on the calling router, perform the following steps:

1. Right-click Routing Interfaces and click New Demand-dial Interface. This launches the Demand-dial Interface wizard. Click Next.
2. Type a name for the interface. Click Next.
3. From the Connection Type window, ensure the option to Connect using a modem, ISDN adapter, or other physical device. Click Next.
4. Enter the phone number of the remote dial-up server or router. Click Next.
5. From the Protocols and Security window (see Figure 7.6), select the necessary options from the list that follows.

    - Route IP packets on this interface
    - Route IPX packets on this interface
    - Add a user account so remote users can dial in
    - Send a plaintext password if that is the only way to connect
    - Use scripting to complete the connection with the remote router

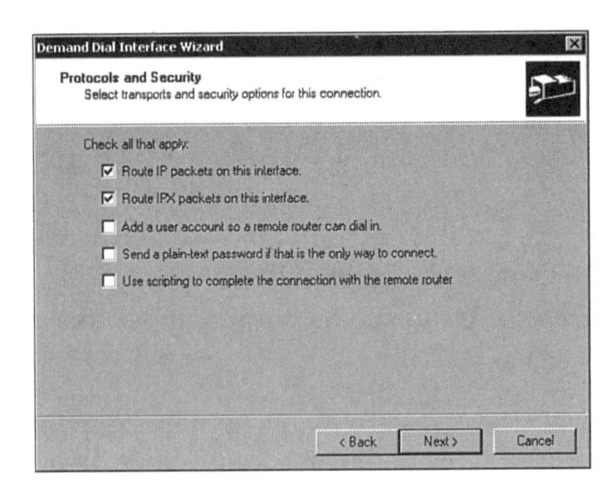

Figure 7.6 Configuring demand-dial protocols and security.

If you are routing IP only packets, make sure Route IPX Packets on This Interface is not selected. Click Next.

6. From the Dial Out Credentials window, specify the username and password that the dial-out router will use to connect to the remote router (see Figure 7.7). Click Next.
7. Click Finish.

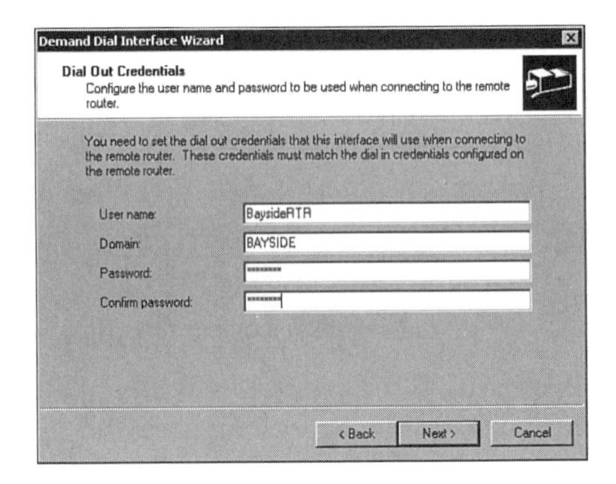

Figure 7.7 Configuring the dial out credentials via the Dial Out Credentials window.

Before you attempt to create a new demand-dial interface, make sure the router is enabled for LAN and demand-dial routing instead of just a LAN router. You can enable this option by right-clicking the RRAS server and choosing Properties. From the General tab, select the LAN and demand-dial routing.

The answering router also needs to be configured for one-way demand-dial connections. A user account must be created on the answering router with dial-in permissions and the appropriate policy permissions. The user account is used to authenticate connections from the calling routers. A static route can then be configured on the user account. Also make sure when creating a user account that the Password Never Expires option is selected and the User Must Change Password at Next Logon option is not selected.

When configuring the calling router, make sure that the dial out credentials match the user account name configured on the answering router.

Creating a Two-Way Demand-Dial Connection

Creating a two-way demand-dial connection is similar to configuring a one-way connection with a few distinct differences. A demand-dial interface is created on each RRAS server using the process outlined previously. You must assign the interface a name, as well as specify the phone number to dial, the device to be used, the protocol and security settings, and the dial-out credentials. A user account must also be configured on each RRAS server with the appropriate remote access permissions. The important thing to keep in mind is that the user account name must be identical to the name assigned to the demand-dial interface of the calling router. Finally, a static route must be configured using the demand-dial interface.

Remember when you are configuring two-way demand-dialing, the user account names on the answering router must be identical to the demand-dial interface names on the calling routers.

Configuring a Demand-Dial Connection

Once a demand-dial connection has been created, you can configure it further using the Properties window for the connection. From the General tab, you can configure the connection device and specify alternative phone numbers to dial. As shown in Figure 7.8, the Options tab is where you configure the connection type: demand-dial or persistent. The dialing policy can also be set by specifying the number of times the calling router will redial if there is no answer and specifying the interval between redial attempts.

The Security tab enables you to configure the security options for the dial-out connection (see Figure 7.9). This includes whether unsecured passwords are permitted, whether the connection requires data encryption, and whether a script will be run after dialing.

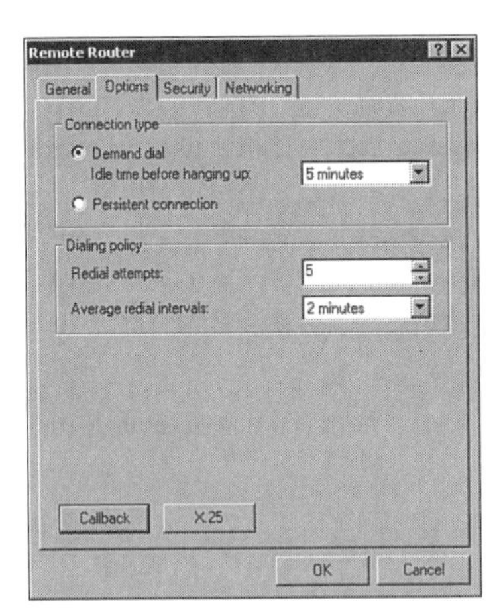

Figure 7.8 Using the Options tab to configure a connection type.

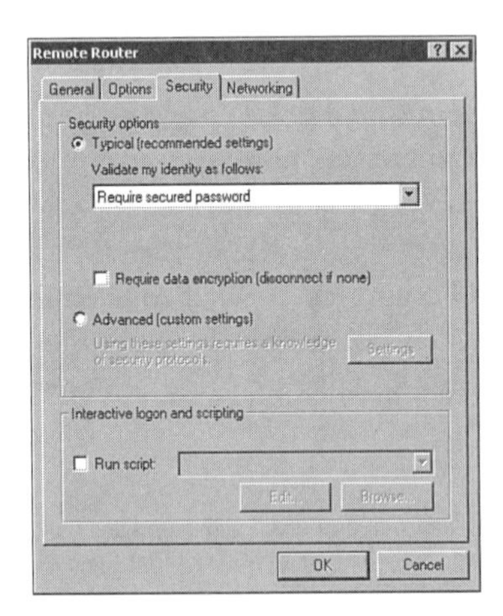

Figure 7.9 Configuring security options via the Security tab.

As shown in Figure 7.10, the Networking tab is used to configure the type of dial-up server that is dialed in to and the different network components that the connection uses.

There are several other configurations that you can make to a demand-dial interface. Demand-dial filtering allows you to control the type of IP traffic that can initiate a connection. You can allow or deny a connection based on the type of IP traffic. For example, you may only want Web and FTP traffic to initiate the demand-dial connection.

Dial-out hours determine the times of day that a connection can be initiated. This allows an administrator to control when the demand-dial connection is used.

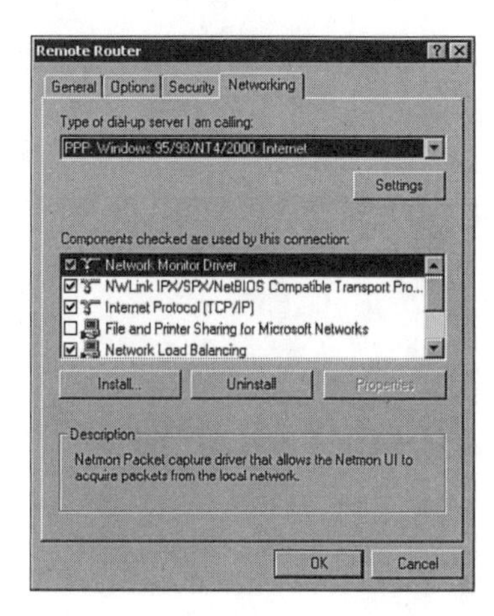

Figure 7.10 Configuring network settings for a demand-dial connection.

Managing and Monitoring IP Routing

Several options exist within the RRAS management console that you can use to manage and monitor IP routing. You can use these options to view the status of an RRAS server, making it much easier to ensure the server continues to perform as expected. The following list summarizes some of the commands available within the console.

- *Show TCP/IP Information*—Right-click the General node under the IP Routing option to access this. It displays information such as the number of IP routes in the routing table, the number of connections on a protocol basis, and the number of IP packets sent and received.
- *Show IP Routing Table*—Use this option to view the entries in the IP routing table. To do so, right-click the Static Routes node found under the IP Routing option.
- *Show Neighbors*—Depending on whether you select the RIP node or OSPF node, this command displays information about the router's neighboring routers.
- *Show Area*—This option, found by right-clicking the OSPF node under the IP Routing option, displays the configured areas and their current states.

- *Show Linkstate Database*—This option, found by right-clicking the OSPF node under the IP Routing option, can be used to view the contents of the link state database.
- *Show Virtual Interface*—This option, found by right-clicking the OSPF node under the IP Routing option, displays a list of all the virtual interfaces for the router.

Managing and Monitoring Border Routing and Internal Routing

Internal routing refers to IP packets being routed in a local internetwork. To manage this type of routing, you need to administer the routing tables and choose the appropriate routing protocol. As mentioned earlier, routing can be static where the routing tables are manually created or dynamically using a routing protocol. Also recall that the two routing protocols supported by Windows 2000 are RIP and OSPF.

Border routing refers to the division of an internetwork into different areas where some routers handle routing within an area and others handle routing between areas. The border routers are responsible for storing routing information to other areas on the internetwork. Because static routing is almost impossible within large internetworks, border routing normally uses one of the supported routing protocols so border routers can discover information from other border routers.

Installing and Configuring Routing Protocols

Once the demand-dial and/or LAN interfaces have been created, the last detail you need to address is to configure the RRAS server as a network router is to configure the appropriate routing protocol interfaces. The following sections explore installing the protocols, and then take a more detailed look at each of the protocol interfaces.

You must first add the routing protocol; you right-click the General node and choose New Routing Protocol. The window that appears lists protocols to choose from (see Figure 7.11). Select RIPv2 or OSPF and click OK.

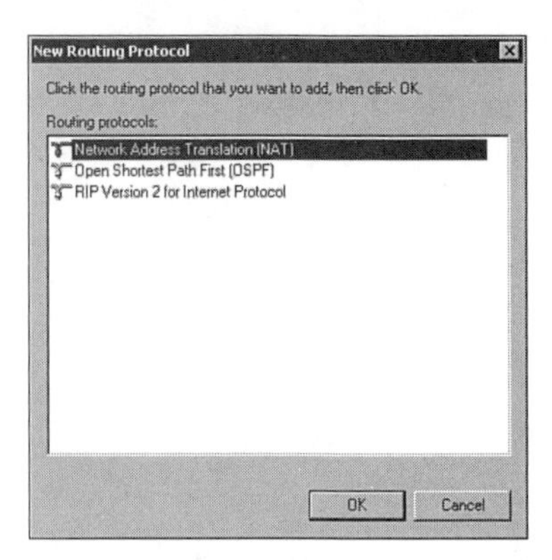

Figure 7.11 Adding a new routing protocol to the General node.

Configuring Routing Protocols

Once RIP or OSPF has been installed, you can configure a general set of properties for each of the protocol types. Because RIP requires little configuration, the Properties window for the protocol has only two tabs, as shown in Figure 7.12.

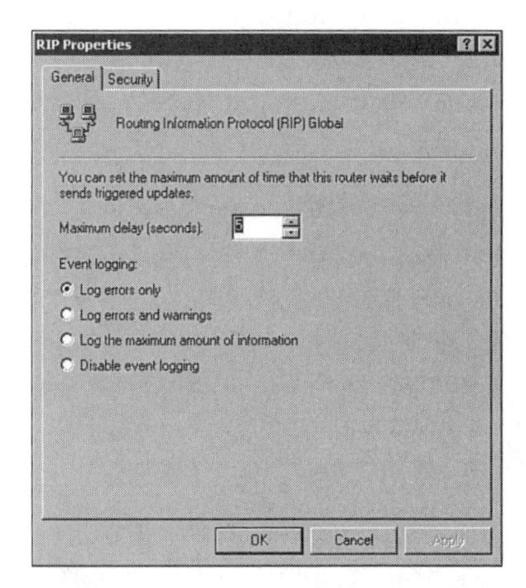

Figure 7.12 Configuring RIP properties.

From the General tab, you can configure the Maximum Delay value, which determines how long a router waits to send an update notification message to other routers on the network. The remaining options allow you to set up event logging for the protocol. The Security tab allows you to configure from which routers the local router can accept announcements.

Because OSPF is slightly more complex than RIP, it requires more detailed configuration and, as a result, has more options in its Properties window (see Figure 7.13).

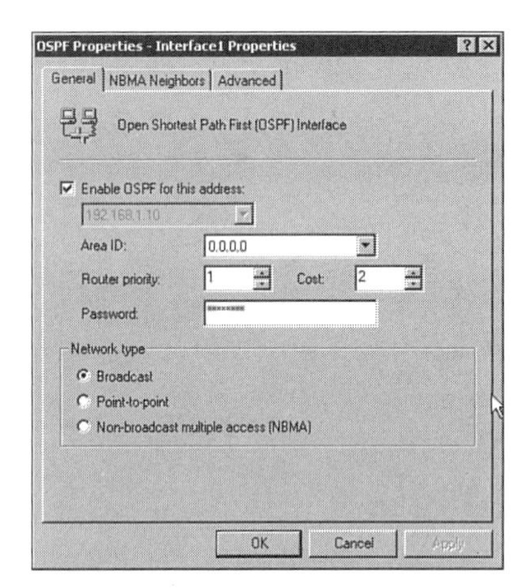

Figure 7.13 Configuring OSPF properties.

From the General tab, the router can be assigned an IP address it can use to identify itself. You can also enable an autonomous system boundary router, which means the router will advertise external routes that it learns from other sources. Using the remaining options, you can enable OSPF event logging.

The Areas tab lists all the areas for the router. With OSPF, areas can be used to subdivide a network in order to reduce the size of the database. Routers within an area maintain database information only for the area in which they belong. Using this tab, areas can be added, deleted, and edited. The Virtual Interface tab lists all the configured virtual interfaces. A virtual interface is a virtual connection between an area border router and a backbone area border router. This logical connection allows the two routers to share information.

If the Enable Autonomous System Boundary Router option is selected, you can use the External Routing tab to control which sources from which routes are accepted or ignored (see Figure 7.14). The Ignore Filters button defines the specific routes that should be accepted or ignored.

Configuring RIP Interface Properties

Every RIP interface has it own properties window from which you can configure a number of options. Within the RRAS console, expand IP Routing, RIP, and then right-click one of the available interfaces and click Properties.

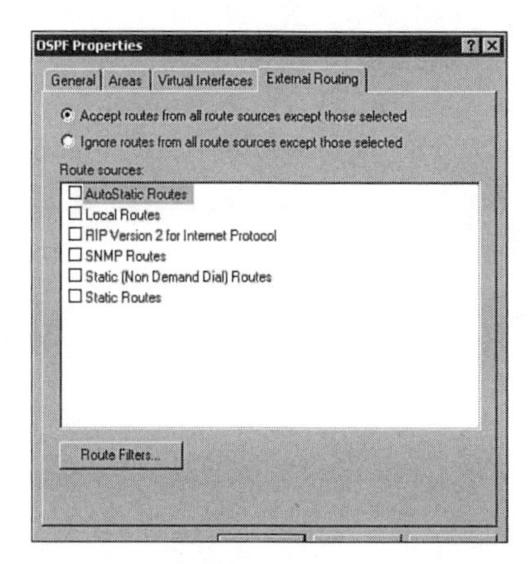

Figure 7.14 Configuring external routing settings to configure accepted and ignored routes.

The General tab allows you to configure the operation mode. You can select auto-static update mode or periodic update mode. With auto-static update, RIP announcements are sent when updates are requested by other routers. Any routes learned while in auto-static update mode are marked as static and remain in the routing table until the administrator manually deletes them. In periodic update mode, announcements are sent out periodically (the Periodic Announcement Interval determines how often). These routes are automatically deleted when the router is stopped and restarted. The outgoing and incoming packet protocol allows you to configure the type of packets, such as RIPv1 or RIPv2, that the router sends out and accepts.

The Activate Authentication and Password options allow you to maintain an added level of security. If authentication is enabled, all outgoing and incoming packets must contain the password specified in the password field. When using authentication, make sure that all neighboring routers are configured with an identical password.

From the Security tab, an administrator can configure RIP route filters. The router can be configured to send and accept all routes, send and accept routes only from the ranges specified, or to accept and send all routes except for those specified.

The Neighbors tab is used to configure how the router interacts with other RIP routers. The Advanced tab (see Figure 7.15) has several configurable options, which are summarized in Table 7.1.

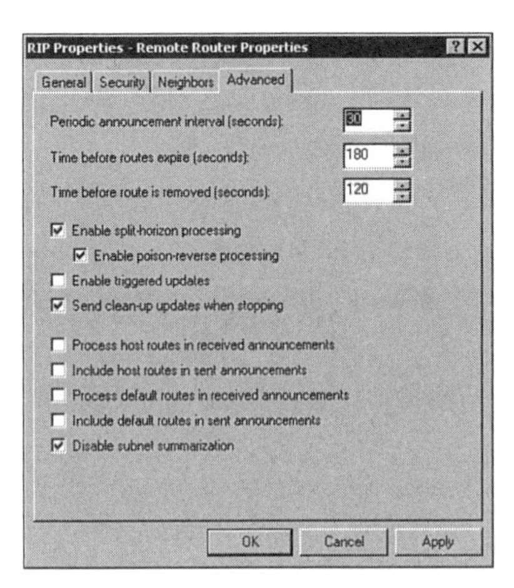

Figure 7.15 Configuring Advanced options for a RIP interface.

Table 7.1 RIP Advanced Options

Option	Description
Periodic announcement interval	Controls the interval at whichperiodic update announcementsare made.
Time before route expires	Determines how long a route remains in the routing table before it expires.
Time before route is removed	Determines how long an expired route remains in the routing table before being removed.
Enable split horizon processing	Ensures routing loops do not occur as the routes learned from a router are not in turn rebroadcast to that network.
Enable triggered updates	Controls whether changes in the routing table are immediately sent out.
Send clean up updates when stopped	Controls whether the router sends an announcement when it is stopped notifying other routers that the routes it was responsible for are no longer available.
Process host routes in received announcements	Controls whether host routes received in RIP announcements are accepted or denied.
Include host routes in send announcements	Controls whether host routes are included in RIP announcements.
Process default routes in received announcements	Controls whether default routes received in RIP announcements are accepted or denied.
Process default routes in send announcements	Controls whether default routes are included in RIP announcements.
Disable subnet summarization	This option is only available for RIPv2. It controls whether subnets are advertised to routers on different subnets.

Demand-dial interfaces are configured by default for auto-static update whereas LAN interfaces are configured for periodic update mode.

Configuring OSPF Interface Properties

If OSPF has been installed, each of the OSPF interfaces can be configured using its Properties window, just as RIP interfaces can be configured. An OSPF interface can be added on the same way as a RIP interface. Simply right-click OSPF under the General node and click New Interface. Select the interface that the protocol will run on and click OK. Figure 7.16 Shows the OSPF properties window that will appear.

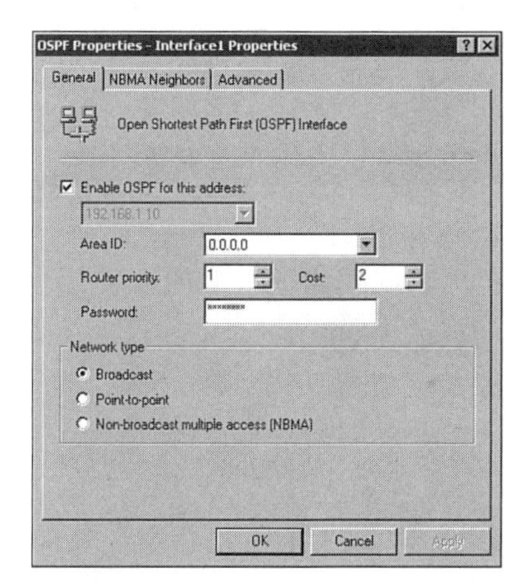

Figure 7.16 Configuring an OSPF interface via the Properties window.

From the General tab, OSPF can be enabled and the area ID, router priority, cost, and password can be configured. The Network Type options allow you to configure whether the OSPF is a broadcast interface, point-to-point interface, or a non-broadcast multiple access interface.

The NBMA Neighbors tab allows you to specify the IP address of neighboring routers and associate a priority with the neighbor. Figure 7.17 shows the options available on the Advanced tab, which are summarized in Table 7.2.

NBMA stands for *non-broadcast multiple access.* If you are on an NBMA network, a frame relay network that does not support broadcasts, the NMBA option on the General tab needs to be selected. You also need to configure the IP addresses of OSPF neighbors using the NMBA Neighbors tab.

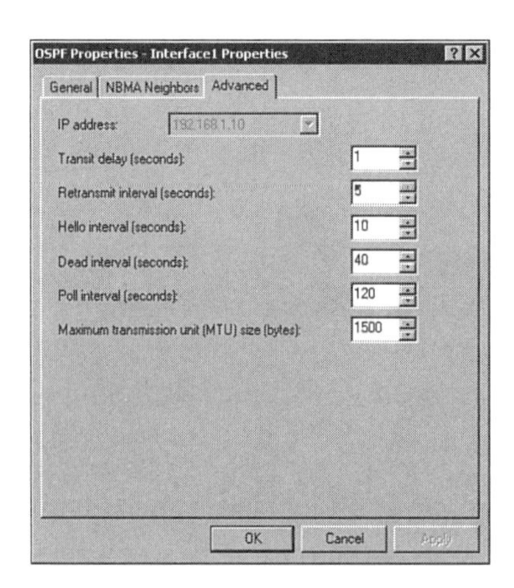

Figure 7.17 Configuring advanced OSPF options via the Advanced tab.

Table 7.2 OSPF Advanced Options

Option	Description
Transit delay	An estimation of the number of seconds for a link state update to be transmitted over the network.
Retransmit interval	The number of seconds between link state advertisement retransmissions.
Hello interval	Determines how often hello packets are sent out to discover other routers.
Dead interval	Determines the number of seconds until a neighboring router determines this router to be down.
Poll interval	Determines the number of seconds between poll intervals sent to a dead neighbor.
Maximum transmission unit (MTU) size (bytes)	Specifies the maximum byte size of an OSPF IP packet.

Practice Questions

Question 1

You are creating a two-way demand-dial connection between two Win2K RRAS servers. When creating the user account on the answering router, what must you remember?

- ❍ A. Any user account name can be used.
- ❍ B. The user account name should match the demand-dial interface name of the answering router.
- ❍ C. The user account name should match the demand-dial interface name of the calling router.
- ❍ D. The user account name must match the computer name of the answering router.

Answer C is correct. When creating demand-dial connections, the user account name created on the answering router must match the demand-dial interface name on the calling router. Therefore, answers A, B, and D are incorrect.

Question 2

The routers on your internal LAN are Windows 2000 RRAS Servers running RIPv2. The network address range is 192.168.10.0 to 192.168.30.0. How can you prevent the routers from adding routes that fall within a certain network range?

- ❍ A. Create IP packet filters
- ❍ B. Create RIP route filters
- ❍ C. Create network filters
- ❍ D. Create IP route filters

Answer B is correct. To control the routes that a router accepts and adds to the routing table, RIP route filters can be created. Answer A is incorrect because IP filters are used to filter IP traffic based on protocol type and port number. Answers D and C are incorrect because there are no such options.

Question 3

Users in a branch office need occasional access to data located in the corporate office by means of a demand-dial connection. You want the connection to be established only during the day—not after 6p.m. or before 6a.m. How should you proceed?

- ❍ A. Using the Dial-out hours, highlight 6p.m.–6a.m. Sunday to Saturday and click Permitted.
- ❍ B. Using the Dial-out hours, highlight 12a.m.–6a.m. and 6p.m.–12p.m. Sunday to Saturday and click Denied.
- ❍ C. Using the Dial-out hours, highlight 6p.m.–6a.m. Sunday to Saturday and click Denied.
- ❍ D. Using the Dial-out hours, highlight 12a.m.–6a.m. and 6p.m.–12p.m. Sunday to Saturday and click Permitted.

Answer B is correct. To limit when the demand-dial connection is available, the dial-out hours can be set. To limit the hours of use between 6a.m. and 6p.m., highlight 6p.m.–12p.m. and 12a.m.–6a.m. and select Denied. This means the demand-dial connection is not available during these hours. Answers A and C are incorrect because the hours that need to be denied cannot be set in a single selection. Answer D is incorrect because the configuration would make the demand-dial connection available between the hours of 6p.m. to 6a.m.

Question 4

You are creating a user account on an answering router that will be used to authenticate a calling router. When configuring the password, which of the following options should be enabled or disabled? [Choose all that apply.]

- ❑ A. Disable the User Must Change Password at Next Logon option.
- ❑ B. Disable the User Cannot Change Password option.
- ❑ C. Enable the Password Never Expires option.
- ❑ D. Disable the Password Never Expires option.
- ❑ E. Enable the User Must Change Password at Next Logon option.

Answers A and C are correct. When configuring the password options for the user account, deselect the User Must Change Password at Next Logon option and select the Password Never Expires option. Answers B, D, and E are incorrect because configuring these options as such may result in the calling router not being able to authenticate with the answering router.

Question 5

Your internetwork consists of seven subnets. All subnets are connected using Windows 2000 RRAS servers. Non-persistent demand-dial connections have been configured. You do not want to be burdened with updating the routing tables and want any changes made to the network topology propagated immediately. Which of the following should you implement?

❍ A. Static routes

❍ B. ICMP

❍ C. OSPF

❍ D. RIPv2

Answer D is correct. To have changes propagated throughout the network when changes occur and to reduce the administrative overhead associated with updating the routing tables, a routing protocol is required. Because OSPF cannot be used with non-persistent connections, RIPv2 must be used (or RIPv1). Therefore, answers A and C are incorrect. Answer B is incorrect because ICMP is not a routing protocol.

Question 6

There are five subnets on your internetwork. You are configuring Windows 2000 RRAS servers to route between the subnets. Your goal is to do this while minimizing the administrative overhead associated with maintaining the routing tables and minimize the amount of traffic generated between routers when updating routing tables. Which of the following should you do?

❍ A. Configure static routes on all routers.

❍ B. Implement OSPF.

❍ C. Implement RIPv1.

❍ D. Implement RIPv2.

Answer B is correct. OSPF is the best choice in this situation because it does not generate as much traffic when updating the routing tables as RIPv1 and RIPv2 do. Therefore, answers C and D are incorrect. Answer A is incorrect because configuring static routes would greatly increase the administrative overhead associated with maintaining the routing tables.

Question 7

Which of the following routing protocols can be used with non-persistent demand-dial connections? [Choose all that apply.]

- ❑ A. RIPv2
- ❑ B. RIPv1
- ❑ C. OSPF
- ❑ D. ARP

Answers A and B are correct. Both RIPv1 and RIPv2 can be used with non-persistent demand-dial connections. Answer C is incorrect because OSPF can only be used with persistent demand-dial connections. Answer D is incorrect because ARP is not a routing protocol.

Question 8

Which of the following commands would add a static route to a routing table?

- ❍ A. **route -p 192.168.126.0 mask 255.255.255.0 192.168.125.1 metric 2**
- ❍ B. **route add 192.168.126.0 mask 255.255.255.0 192.168.125.1 metric 2**
- ❍ C. **route add 192.168.126.0 255.255.255.0 192.168.125.1 metric 2**
- ❍ D. **route add 192.168.126.0 mask 255.255.255.0 gateway 192.168.125.1 metric 2**

Answer B is correct. The correct syntax when adding new static routes using the `route` command is `route add <network> mask <subnetmask> <gateway> metric`. Therefore answers A, C, and D are incorrect.

Question 9

A demand-dial connection has been configured between subnet A and subnet B. Router A on subnet A will be configured as the calling router thereby providing users access to resources on subnet B. Router B will be the answering router. Which of the following steps needs to be completed when configuring static routing? [Choose all that apply.]

- ❑ A. Configure a static route on Router A.
- ❑ B. Configure a static route for the user account on Router B.
- ❑ C. Configure a static route on Router B.
- ❑ D. Configure a static route for the user account on Router A.

Answers A and B are correct. A static route must be created on the calling router (Router A), telling it where to send packets destined for a specific network. A static router must also be configured for the user account on Router B used by the calling router. Answer C is incorrect because it is only a one-way demand-dial connection. Answer D is incorrect because a user account is required only on the answering router for a one-way demand-dial connection.

Question 10

You have several subnets on the network. You add two new Windows 2000 RRAS servers that will perform routing along with the existing servers. You recall that RIPv1 and RIPv2 routers can interoperate so you configure the new routers with RIPv2. Upon examination, you discover that the RIPv2 routers are communicating with one another but not with any of the existing RIPv1 routers. What is causing the problem?

- ❍ A. RIPv1 and RIPv2 routers do not interoperate.
- ❍ B. The RIPv2 routers are configured to use multicasting.
- ❍ C. The RIPv1 routers are configured to use multicasting.
- ❍ D. The RIPv2 routers are configured to use broadcasts.

Answer B is correct. Because RIPv1 does not support multicasting, any RIPv1 routers cannot communicate with RIPv2 routers configured for multicasting. Answer A is incorrect because RIPv1 and RIPv2 routers can communicate. Answer C is incorrect because RIPv1 does not support multicasting. Answer D is incorrect because the RIPv2 routers must be configured to use broadcasts to communicate with the RIPv1 routers.

Need to Know More?

Search the online version of TechNet and the Windows 2000 Server Resource Kit using keywords such as `IP Routing`, `RIP`, and `OSPF`.

Minasi, Mark, Christa Anderson, Brian Smith, and Doug Toombs. *Mastering Windows 2000*. Sybex Press, Alameda, CA. ISBN: 0782140432.

Charles, Kackie. *Windows 2000 Routing and Remote Access Services*. New Riders Publishing. 2000, Indianapolis, IN. ISBN: 0735709513

Network Address Translation and Internet Connection Sharing

Terms you'll need to understand:

✓ Network Address Translation (NAT)
✓ NAT editor
✓ Internet Connection Sharing (ICS)
✓ DHCP Allocator

Techniques you'll need to master:

✓ Understanding the services provided through ICS and NAT
✓ Understanding the differences between ICS and NAT
✓ Installing and configuring ICS
✓ Configuring an ICS client
✓ Installing NAT
✓ Configuring NAT properties
✓ Configuring NAT interfaces

Introduction

Over the past few years, the Internet has become increasingly popular in both business and home environments. As a result, there is now a shortage of IP addresses. Network Address Translation (NAT) eliminates the need for all computers on the network to have a public IP address. Instead, it allows multiple computers to access the Internet by sharing a single public IP address.

Two technologies included with Windows 2000, *Internet Connection Sharing* and *Network Address Translation*, provide small businesses and home offices with a cost-effective, relatively simple way of connecting to the Internet. Internet Connection Sharing (ICS) allows a single Internet connection to be shared among multiple computers. Network Address Translation (NAT) offers a similar solution to ICS, but includes additional features that may make it a more suitable choice than ICS in certain environments. This chapter looks at the services provided by ICS and NAT, as well as the distinct differences between the two technologies. You will also look at how to install and configure both ICS and NAT.

Installing Internet Connection Sharing

Internet Connection Sharing (ICS) was introduced in Windows 98 and is included as a feature of Windows 2000. ICS allows multiple computers on a local area network to simultaneously access the Internet using a single Internet connection. This technology provides home offices and small businesses with Internet connectivity without added cost because only one Internet connection is necessary for the entire LAN. ICS can be enabled on a Windows 2000 Professional workstation or Windows 2000 Server.

To connect multiple computers on a local area network to the Internet, at least one computer must have an Internet connection and have ICS enabled. Enabling ICS is as simple as checking a single box (this is basically the extent of configuring ICS). Once ICS is enabled, the following services are provided:

- *Network Address Translation*—This component is responsible for mapping the private IP address of internal clients to a single public IP address.
- *DHCP Allocator*—Provides a simplified version of the DHCP service. The DHCP Allocator assigns internal clients IP addresses in the range of `192.168.0.0/24`. The range assigned to clients is not configurable.

- *DNS Proxy*—This component resolves DNS names to IP addresses for clients. It passes name resolution requests to the Internet-based DNS server configured in the TCP/IP properties of the external interface of the ICS computer.
- *Auto-dial*—An ICS connection point can automatically dial when a client on the LAN attempts to access the Internet.

Before you enable ICS on a computer, keep the following points in mind:

- ICS should not be enabled on a network with other Windows 2000 domain controllers, DNS servers, DHCP servers, gateways, or other computers using static IP addresses. ICS assigns internal clients addresses from a non-configurable range that could interfere or conflict with the existing address scheme.
- Once ICS is enabled, the IP address of the internal interface is changed to `192.168.0.1`.
- Computers on the internal network must be configured to automatically obtain an IP address. The DHCP Allocator service assigns the clients an IP address.
- For ICS to function with an ISDN or modem, on-demand dialing must be enabled.

ICS should be used only when the computer with the shared connection is the only gateway on the network and no other server on the network is providing IP addressing to clients.

Enabling ICS

To enable ICS on a Windows 2000 computer, perform the following steps:

1. Click Start, point to Settings, and click Control Panel.
2. Double-click the Network and Dial-up Connections applet.
3. Right-click the connection for which you want to enable ICS and select Properties.
4. Select the Sharing tab from the Properties window.
5. Click the option to Enable Internet Connection Sharing for this connection (see Figure 8.1).

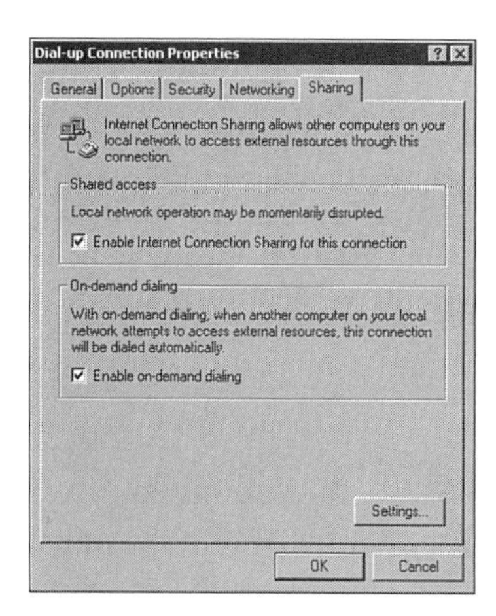

Figure 8.1 Enabling Internet Connection Sharing from the Network and Dial-up Connections applet.

6. Select the box beside Enable On-Demand Dialing to have the computer auto-dial a connection when an internal client attempts to access the Internet.

Configuring ICS

After an administrator has enabled ICS, clients on the network can use their Web browsers and email applications as though they have their own direct Internet connection.

You might need to further configure ICS for applications and services to function; for example, when internal clients want to use the shared connection to play Internet-based games or hold videoconferences using NetMeeting. These types of services and applications require an incoming connection with an internal workstation. Also, if you are hosting Web services on the internal network, ICS must be configured to provide Internet users with access to the service.

Applications and services can be configured for ICS using the Settings button located on the Sharing properties sheet. Click the Settings button to display the Internet Connection Sharing Settings window (see Figure 8.2).

From the Applications tab, you can configure which applications are available to users on the internal network sharing the Internet connection. By default, no applications are listed. Click the Add button to configure an application and provide the following information (see Figure 8.3):

- *Name of application*—Type a descriptive name for the application.

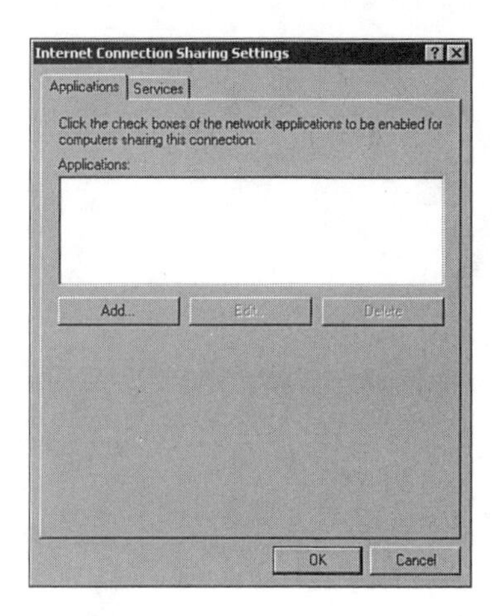

Figure 8.2 To configure ICS settings, you must add applications to be supported.

➤ *Remote server port number*—Type the port number of the remote server where the application resides. Select TCP or UDP.

➤ *Incoming response ports*—Type the TCP or UDP (or both) ports that the application connects to on the ICS computer.

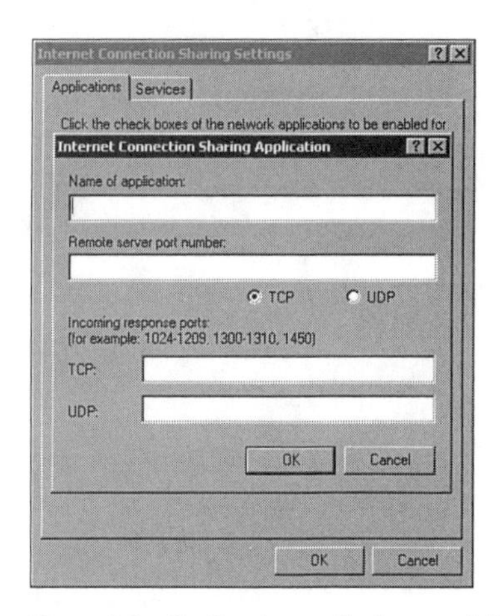

Figure 8.3 Configuring applications available through ICS.

The Services tab lists all the services available for ICS (see Figure 8.4). To provide users on a remote network with access to a specific service, simply check the box beside the service. The window that appears allows you to specify the name or IP address of the computer on the network hosting the service.

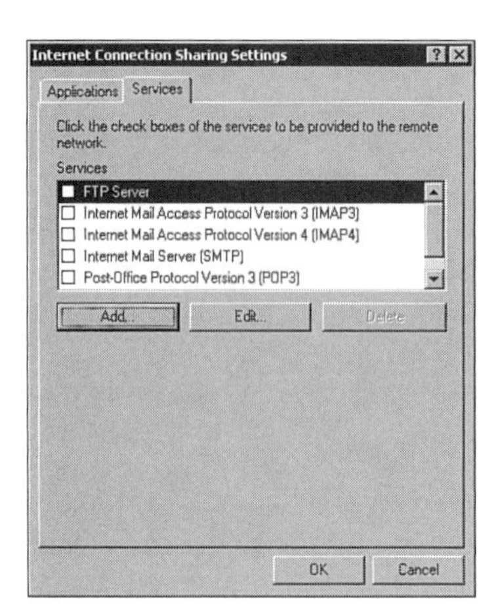

Figure 8.4 Configuring services for ICS.

If you require additional services, click the Add button and provide the following information (see Figure 8.5):

- *Name of service*—Type a descriptive name for the service.
- *Service port number*—Specify the port number of the computer on which the service resides. Select UDP or TCP.
- *Name or address of server computer on private network*—Type the name or IP address of the computer on the internal network hosting the service.

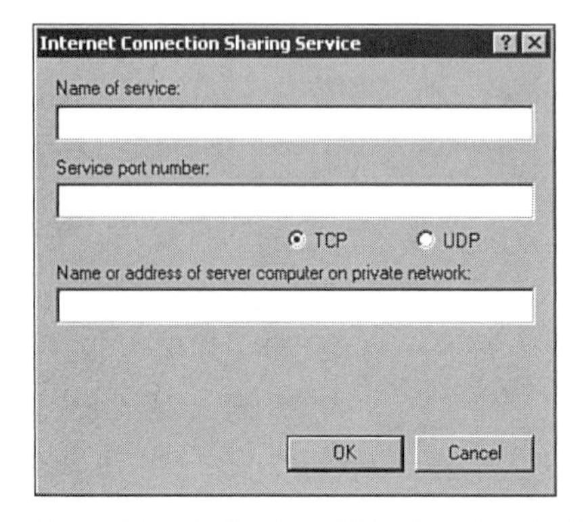

Figure 8.5 Configuring additional services for ICS.

Configuring ICS Clients

Configuring a client to use a shared Internet connection is a relatively straightforward process. You simply configure the TCP/IP properties for the local area connection to automatically obtain an IP address. Also, using the Connection tab from the Properties window for Internet Explorer, make sure that the Never Dial a Connection option is selected and the following options on the Local Area Connection Settings window (see Figure 8.6) are deselected:

- Automatically detect settings
- Use automatic configuration script
- Use a proxy server

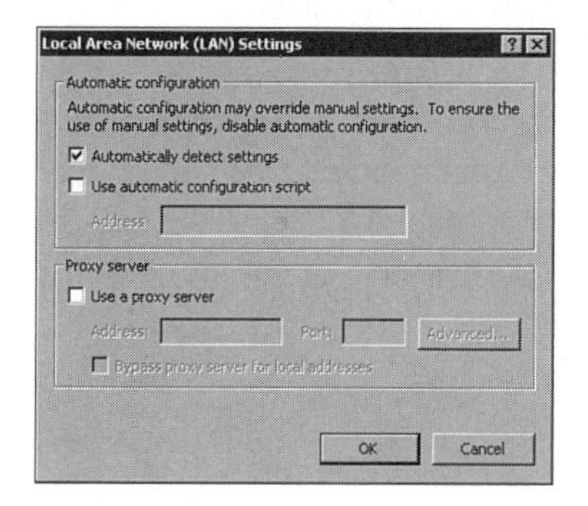

Figure 8.6 Configuring the properties of Internet Explorer on an ICS client.

Installing NAT

Network Address Translation (NAT) allows multiple computers to share a single Internet connection using a single IP address. The benefits of this include the capability to connect multiple computers to the Internet using a single Internet connection. This in turn also helps to solve the increasing shortage of public IP addresses.

Network Address Translation

As the name implies, one of the things NAT does is provide IP address translation services. The system configured with NAT has an external and internal network interface. Because a public IP address is required to access the Internet, the external network interface of the NAT server is configured with an Internet routable IP address. The internal network interface is assigned the IP address of `192.168.0.1` by default and internal clients can be assigned an IP address from one of the private IP address ranges.

All internal requests are routed through the NAT server and appear as though they originated from the same public IP address. The NAT server basically acts on behalf of internal clients. When internal clients access the Internet, NAT receives the request and translates the private IP address and the port numbers before forwarding the request to the Internet. The IP address and port number of the internal client is mapped to the external port number on which the request is made.

When NAT receives a request, it modifies the source IP address, the source port, and the checksum. If additional information must be translated, a NAT editor can be installed. Windows 2000 includes NAT editors for the following protocols: FTP, PPTP, ICMP, and NetBIOS over TCP/IP.

All internal requests are mapped to an external request (the internal IP address is mapped to the IP address assigned to the public interface) and the information is kept in a table that is stored in memory. When the response to a request is returned to the NAT server, it uses the mappings stored within the table to determine the internal client to which the response should be returned.

Static and Dynamic Mappings

Before you discover the NAT process in more depth in the next section, you need to be aware of one of the key benefits of NAT. This benefit is that NAT can use *static* or *dynamic mappings*. Dynamic mappings are created when an internal client initiates communication to an Internet location. Static mappings are manually created so that traffic initiated from the Internet can be mapped to a specific server and port on the private network.

When an internal request is received, NAT can create a dynamic mapping and store the information in the mapping table. Or static mappings can be created. This allows you to specify that certain traffic always be routed to a certain location. For example, all external traffic destined for port 80 on the public interface of the NAT server can be routed to a specific internal Web server.

How Does NAT Work?

The following steps outline the process that occurs when a request is received on the internal interface of the NAT server:

1. NAT first checks whether a static mapping exists that matches the request.
2. If no static mapping is found, a dynamic mapping is created. If the NAT server is configured with a single public IP address, a port

mapping is created. If the NAT server is configured with multiple public IP addresses, the private IP address is mapped to a public IP address.

3. If a NAT editor is required for the request, NAT performs the necessary modifications to the IP datagram.
4. The IP datagram is modified to reflect the mapping and the information is stored in the mapping table.
5. The request is forwarded to the public interface.
6. When the results are returned to the NAT server, it uses the information in the mapping table to route the information back to the appropriate client.

For inbound traffic initiated on the Internet, the process is slightly different. This is for security purposes to protect computers on the local area network from Internet attacks. When an inbound request is received, NAT checks to see if a static mapping exists that matches the request. If there is no mapping, the request is dropped.

Enabling NAT

NAT can be enabled in one of two ways depending on the existing configuration. If Routing and Remote Access is not enabled, NAT can be enabled using the Routing and Remote Access Server Setup wizard.

To enable NAT using the wizard, follow these steps:

1. Click Start, point to Programs, Administrative Tools, and click Routing and Remote Access.
2. Right-click your server and click Configure and Enable Routing and Remote Access. This launches the Routing and Remote Access Server Setup wizard. Click Next.
3. From the list of common configurations, select Internet connection server. Click Next.
4. Select the option to Set Up a Router with the Network Address Translation (NAT) Routing Protocol (see Figure 8.7). Click Next.
5. Select the public interface used to connect to the Internet. If necessary, create a new demand-dial connection. Click Next.
6. Click Finish.

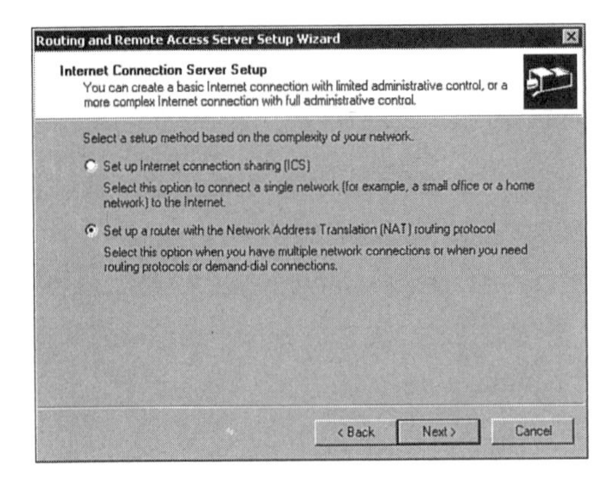

Figure 8.7 Enabling Network Address Translation.

In some cases, Routing and Remote Access may already be enabled on your system. If this is the case, you can use the following process to manually enable and configure NAT. Before you begin, make sure the internal interface is assigned an IP address of `192.168.0.1` and a subnet mask of `255.255.255.0` (this address can be changed if necessary). The ISP will provide the DNS settings you configure. The external interface will be configured with an IP address from your ISP. If necessary, create a new demand-dial interface within the Routing and Remote Access console (refer to Chapter 7 for step-by-step instructions).

To manually enable NAT, follow these steps:

1. Within the Routing and Remote Access console, expand IP Routing. Right-click General and select New Routing Protocol.
2. From the New Routing Protocol window, select Network Address Translation (NAT) (see Figure 8.8). Click OK.

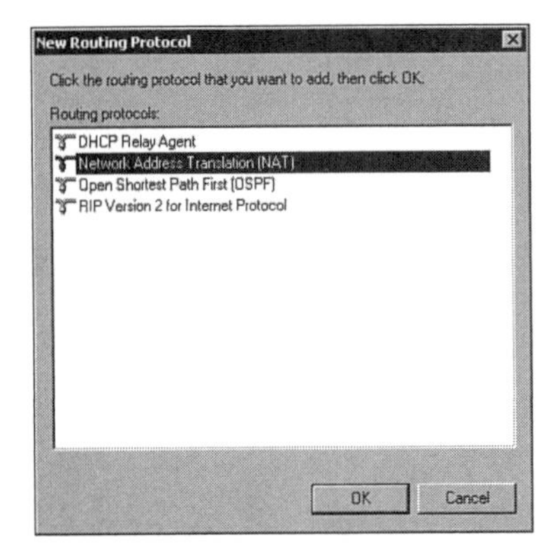

Figure 8.8 Adding the Network Address Translation protocol.

3. Select Network Address Translation. The available interfaces will be displayed.

4. To add additional interfaces, right-click Network Address Translation and select New Interface.

5. From the New Interface for Network Address Translation window, select the appropriate interface and click OK (see Figure 8.9). The Network Address Translation Properties window appears.

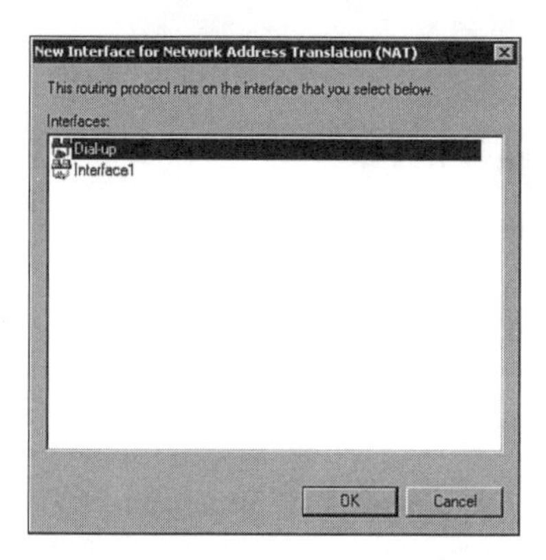

Figure 8.9 Adding a new NAT interface.

6. From the General tab, ensure that Public Interface Connected to the Internet is selected as well as the option to Translate TCP/UDP Headers (see Figure 8.10). Click OK.

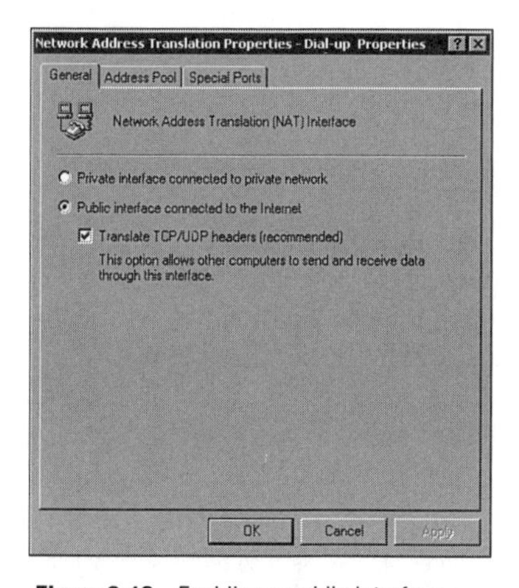

Figure 8.10 Enabling a public interface.

7. To configure the private NAT interface, repeat the process outlined in step 5. When the Network Address Translation properties window appears, select the Private Interface Connected to Private Network option. Click OK.

To configure a computer to use a NAT server, the default gateway on the client must be pointing to the IP address assigned to the internal interface of the NAT server.

Configuring NAT Properties

Once NAT is installed, it can be configured within the Routing and Remote Access console. This section looks at how to configure network addressing and name resolution with NAT.

Network Addressing with NAT

Because clients on an IP-based network all require a unique IP address, NAT offers two ways in which NAT clients can be assigned an IP address. You can use a DHCP server on the local area network or the DHCP Allocator component of NAT.

The *DHCP Allocator* is a simplified version of DHCP. You can use it to assign internal clients an IP address, subnet mask, and default gateway (it does not support any optional components). Keep in mind when deciding which method to use that the DHCP Allocator supports only a single scope. So if more functionality is required, consider using DHCP server.

To configure Network Addressing with NAT, right-click Network Address Translation within the RRAS console and click Properties. From the Properties window, select the Address Assignment tab (see Figure 8.11).

To enable the DHCP allocator, select the option to Automatically Assign IP Addresses by Using DHCP. Type the network address and subnet mask. Clicking the Exclude button allows you to exclude certain IP addresses within the network address range. These addresses will not be assigned to clients. If you plan to use a DHCP server on the local area network for IP address assignment, simply deselect the option to Automatically Assign IP Addresses by Using DHCP.

When using NAT, remember that the IP address range assigned to clients is configurable. If you change the default IP address assigned to the internal interface of the NAT server from **192.168.0.1** to a different network ID, make sure the change is also reflected in the range of IP addresses being assigned by the DHCP Allocator.

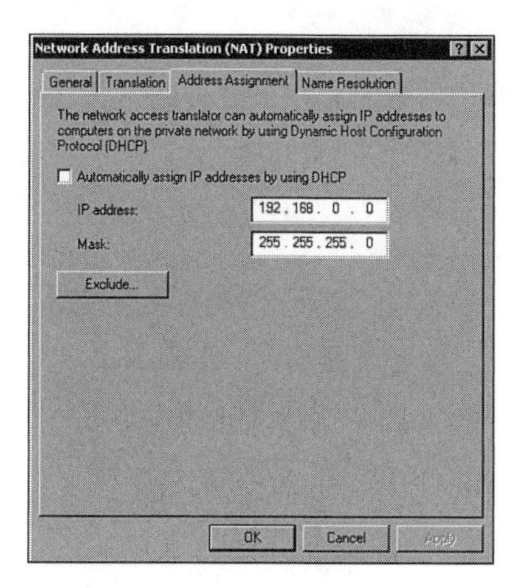

Figure 8.11 Configuring network addressing with NAT.

Name Resolution with NAT

Once NAT is configured, that server essentially acts as a DNS Proxy for the internal clients. It receives name resolution requests, forwards the requests to an Internet based DNS server, and returns the results to the client.

Using the Name Resolution tab from the Network Address Translation properties window, you can configure NAT to perform DNS queries on behalf of internal clients (see Figure 8.12).

To enable name resolution for internal clients, under Resolve IP Addresses for, select the Clients Using Domain Name System (DNS) option. If NAT uses a demand-dial connection to the Internet, select Connect to the Public Network when a name needs to be resolved. Using the drop-down arrow, select the appropriate interface.

Configuring Translation

As already mentioned, all mappings are stored within mapping tables. Using the Translation tab, you can configure how long the TCP and UDP mappings should remain in the table. The default length of time for a TCP mapping to remain in the table is 1440 minutes (24 hours) and UDP mappings are removed after 1 minute (see Figure 8.13).

Using the Applications button, you can configure the applications available for Internet Connection Sharing. Refer to the section on ICS for configuring applications.

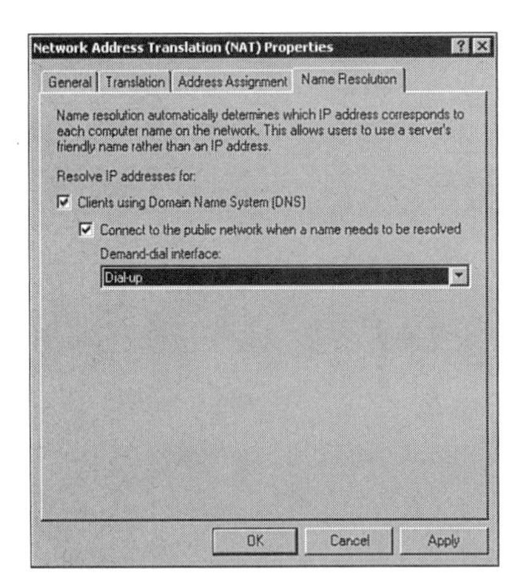

Figure 8.12 Configuring name resolution.

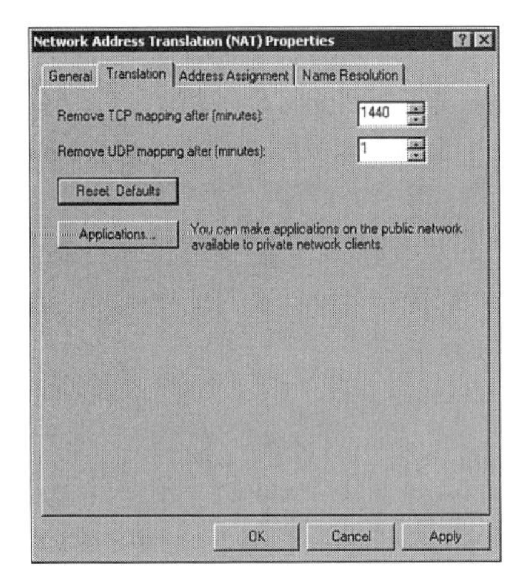

Figure 8.13 Configuring how long mappings remain in the mappings table.

Configuring NAT Interfaces

Once NAT interfaces have been added, they can also be configured through their properties window. Keep in mind that the interface designated as private has a different set of property tabs than the public interface.

Configuring the Public Interface

As shown in Figure 8.10, the properties window for the public connection has three property sheets. From the General tab you can enable an interface as private or public.

Unlike ICS, NAT supports multiple public IP addresses. If you have been assigned only a single IP address from the ISP, nothing needs to be configured. If you have been allocated multiple IP addresses, the public interface must be configured with the range assigned by the ISP. Using the Address Pool tab shown in Figure 8.14, you can identify the range of addresses allocated to the NAT server.

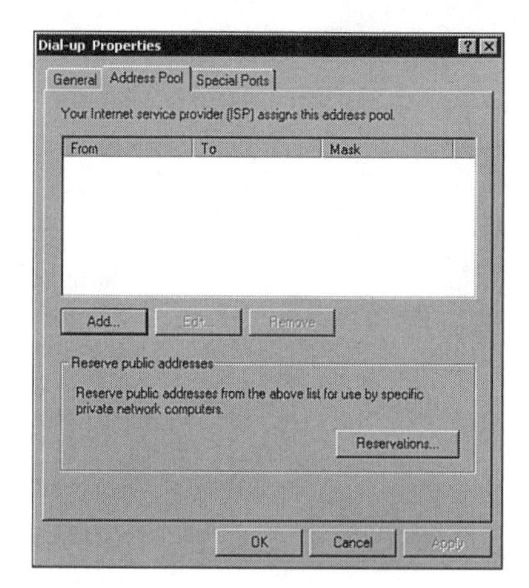

Figure 8.14 Configuring the public address pool.

In some cases, you may need to reserve one of the IP addresses from the public address pool for an internal computer. Clicking on the Reservations button (refer to Figure 8.14), brings up the Add Reservation window, as shown in Figure 8.15. From this window, you can map a public IP address to an internal computer. If the computer needs to be accessible to Internet users, select the option to Allow Incoming Sessions to the Address; for example, if there is a Web server on the local area network that needs to be accessible to users on the Internet.

Configuring Inbound Traffic

NAT is normally used to allow internal clients access to external resources. Once NAT is configured, clients can use their Web browsers, such as Internet Explorer, and email programs, such as Outlook Express, to create connections with external computers. Inbound traffic is accepted on the external interface as long as an internal client initiated the traffic. This is the default behavior of NAT.

However, there may be instances in which you want to make internal resources available to users on the Internet; for example, if you are running Web or FTP services on the local area network. For inbound connections to be permitted, you configure the computer on the local area network that will be made accessible to Internet users with a static IP address. Make sure that the IP address is excluded from the range being assigned by the DHCP server to avoid address conflicts.

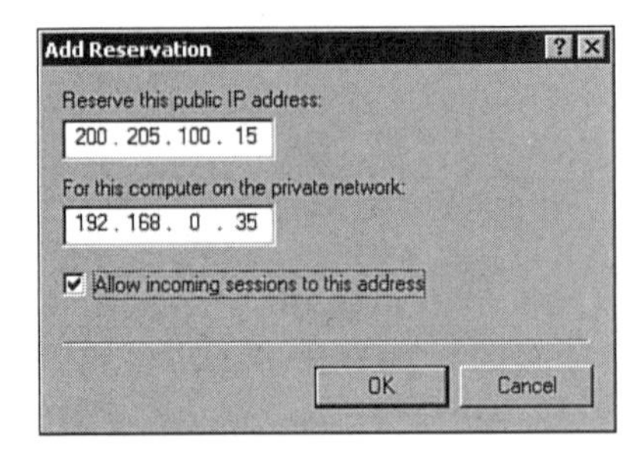

Figure 8.15 Reserving a public IP address for an internal client.

Once the computer has been assigned a static IP address, you can use the Special Ports tab, shown in Figure 8.16, to create a static mapping.

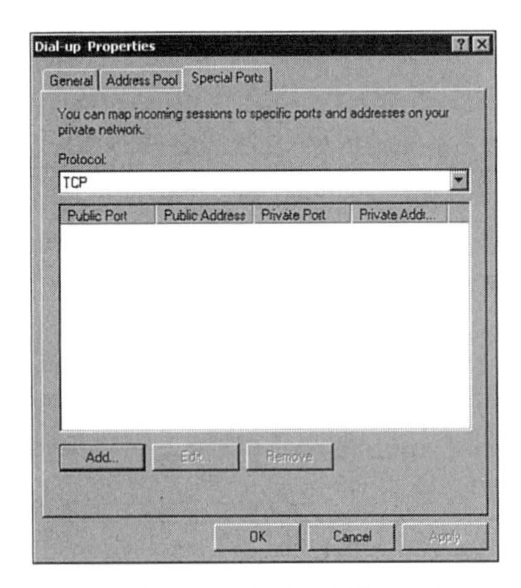

Figure 8.16 Using the Special Ports tab to configure static IP addresses.

The static mapping will map a public IP address and port number to the private IP address and port number of the internal computer. Click the Add button to designate which IP address and port number any traffic received on the public interface (or a specific IP address) should be routed to (see Figure 8.17). The incoming port identifies the port number for incoming traffic. The private address and outgoing port fields identify the private IP address of the internal computer and the port number to which traffic should be sent.

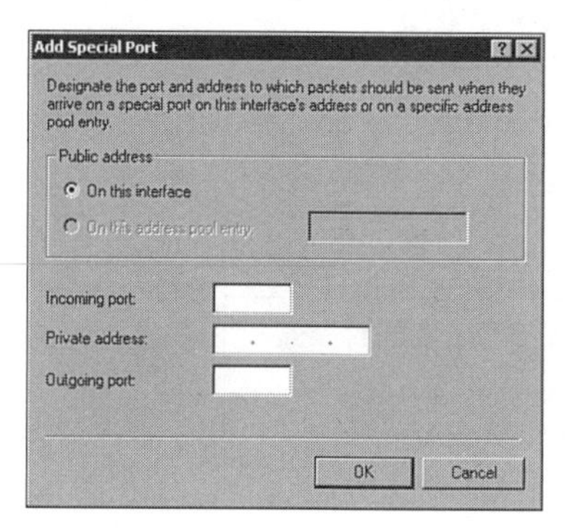

Figure 8.17 Configuring a static mapping.

Before Internet clients can access resources on the local area network, you must assign a static IP address to the internal client and configure a special port mapping.

Comparing NAT and ICS

As you have discovered throughout this chapter, NAT and ICS are two solutions included with Windows 2000 that provide home offices and small businesses a cost-effective method for connecting multiple computers to the Internet using a single connection. Although they provide similar services, there are distinct differences between the two, making each better suited for specific environments. Table 8.1 summarizes the key differences between NAT and ICS.

Table 8.1 Differences Between NAT and ICS

NAT	ICS
Configurable IP address range	Fixed IP address range
Requires manual configuration	Enabled through a single check box
Supports multiple public IP addresses	Supports a single public IP address
Supports multiple internal interfaces	Supports a single internal interface

Be sure you are familiar with the differences between ICS and NAT.

Practice Questions

Question 1

Which of the following statements are true regarding Internet Connection Sharing?

❍ A. ICS is available only on computers running Windows 2000 Server.

❍ B. ICS assigns internal clients IP addresses from a fixed range.

❍ C. ICS supports multiple public IP addresses.

❍ D. ICS is enabled through Routing and Remote Access.

Answer B is correct. ICS includes the DHCP allocator that assigns clients on the local area network IP addresses from the range of `192.168.0.1` to `192.168.0.254`. This is a fixed range and therefore cannot be changed. Answer A is incorrect because ICS can be enabled on Windows 2000 Professional, Windows 2000 Server, as well as Windows 98 and Windows Me. Answer C is incorrect because ICS only supports using a single public IP address. Answer D is incorrect because ICS is enabled through the properties for the Internet connection.

Question 2

You have recently moved your small office into a new location. The network now consists of five computers with no plans for expansion. You perform all network administrative tasks, although your experience and knowledge is very limited. There is currently one Internet connection. Which of the following is the best solution for Internet connectivity?

❍ A. Enable ICS on one of the computers.

❍ B. Configure each computer with its own Internet connection.

❍ C. Enable NAT on one of the computers.

❍ D. Enable RIP on one of the computers.

Answer A is correct. The best solution for the scenario is ICS because ICS requires little or no configuration. Answer B is incorrect. Although it is a possible solution, it would add unnecessary costs. Answer C is incorrect. Although NAT could be used, ICS would be a better choice for someone who has limited experience. Answer D is incorrect because RIP is a routing protocol used to dynamically update routing tables.

Question 3

Which of the following components are included with ICS? [Choose all that apply.]

- ❑ A. NAT
- ❑ B. DHCP Allocator
- ❑ C. DNS Proxy
- ❑ D. Groups-based access control

Answers A, B, and C are correct. ICS includes the following components: Network Address Translation, DHCP Allocator, and the DNS Proxy. Answer D is incorrect because ICS cannot control access to the Internet through groups. All computers enabled as DHCP clients on the internal network can access the Internet through the ICS enabled computer.

Question 4

A friend has recently purchased a new computer for his home office. His existing computer has a dial-up connection to the Internet. He wants to share the existing connection between both computers. He calls you and asks how he can enable ICS. Which of the following statements are correct?

- ❍ A. Add the NAT protocol through Routing and Remote Access.
- ❍ B. Enable ICS through the properties of the RRAS server.
- ❍ C. Enable ICS through using the properties of the Internet connection.
- ❍ D. Add the ICS component through the Add/Remove Programs applet.

Answer C is correct. ICS can be enabled through the Properties of TCP/IP for the Internet connection. Therefore, answers A, B, and D are incorrect.

Question 5

You have just finished installing the NAT protocol on a Windows 2000 Server. The internal network has 15 Windows 2000 Professional clients. The Windows 2000 Server has the only Internet connection. Its local interface is assigned the IP address of **192.168.0.1**. Both the private and public interfaces have been added. What should you do next to ensure the server can perform translations?

- ❍ A. Configure a special port.
- ❍ B. Create an IP address reservation.
- ❍ C. Enable TCP and UDP header translation.
- ❍ D. Configure an IP address pool.

Answer C is correct. Once the public and private interfaces have been configured, you enable TCP/UDP header translation on the public interface to ensure proper translation of IP datagrams. Answer A is incorrect because special ports are configured to make internal resources accessible to external clients. Answer B is incorrect because an IP address reservation is configured to reserve one of the public IP addresses for an internal computer. Answer D is incorrect because an address pool is configured when a NAT server has been assigned multiple public IP addresses.

Question 6

Your NAT server has been assigned three public IP addresses: **205.200.2.10**, **205.200.2.11**, and **200.205.2.12**. There is a Web server on the internal network that should be accessible to Internet clients using the same public IP address. How should you proceed?

- ❍ A. Configure a reservation.
- ❍ B. Create a DHCP exclusion.
- ❍ C. Configure a special port.
- ❍ D. Enable TCP/UDP header translation.

Answer A is correct. By creating a reservation, one of the public IP addresses can be mapped to a computer on the local area network. This makes the computer accessible to Internet clients using the same public IP address. Answer B is incorrect because a DHCP exclusion ensures a computer is always assigned the same IP address. Answer C is incorrect because a special port maps specific incoming requests to an internal IP address and specific port. Answer D is incorrect because enabling TCP/UDP translation only allows NAT to change portions of the IP Datagram for outgoing requests.

Question 7

You have been assigned a single public IP address from your ISP. All clients on the local area network access the Internet through a single Internet connection. You want to make the Web server on the internal network accessible to external users. How should you proceed?

- ❍ A. Configure a special port.
- ❍ B. Create a reservation.
- ❍ C. Enable TCP/UDP headers.
- ❍ D. Configure the Web server with its own connection.

Answer A is correct. By creating a special port, incoming traffic for a specific port on the public interface can be routed to a specific port on an internal computer, such as a Web server. Answer B is incorrect because the NAT server is configured with only a single public IP address. Answer C is incorrect because this option enables NAT to translate IP datagrams. Answer C is incorrect. Although it is a feasible option, it would be more cost effective to use the built-in features of NAT.

Question 8

Your NAT server has been assigned a pool of public IP addresses. How can you configure the public interface with the range of IP addresses allocated by your ISP?

- ❍ A. Configure multiple IP addresses through the properties of TCP/IP.
- ❍ B. Use the Address Assignment tab within the Network Address Translation properties window.
- ❍ C. Use the Address Pool tab within the Network Address Translation properties window.
- ❍ D. Use the Address Pool tab within the properties window for the public connection.

Answer D is correct. To configure the a range of public IP addresses assigned by an ISP, use the Address Pool tab from the public interfaces Properties window. Therefore, answer C is incorrect. Answers A and B are incorrect because the Address Assignment tab is used to configure whether the DHCP Allocator is used to assign IP addresses.

Question 9

You have a small home office that is connected to the Internet with a dial-up connection. You enable ICS to enable the remaining computers to access the Internet via this connection. You want the internal computers to be assigned an IP address in the range of **192.168.1.1** to **192.168.2.10**. How should you proceed?

- ❍ A. Use the Address Assignment tab from the TCP/IP properties window to change the IP address range.
- ❍ B. Use the Address Assignment tab from the Network Address Translation properties window to change the IP address range.
- ❍ C. Use the Registry Editor to change the IP address range.
- ❍ D. This cannot be configured.

Answer D is correct. ICS includes a DHCP Allocator. The range of IP addresses assigned to clients is a fixed range and therefore cannot be configured. Therefore answers A, B, and C are incorrect.

Question 10

You are the part-time network administrator for a small office that has a single Windows 2000 Server and 20 Windows 2000 Professional workstations. The Windows 2000 Server has the only Internet connection. Currently, the network uses the private IP address range of **192.168.2.1** to **192.168.2.20**. All other workstations now need Internet access. You have been assigned this task with the following requirements:

- The single connection should be shared between all computers.
- The solution should impose no additional costs.
- The existing IP address scheme should remain the same.
- The internal Web server should be accessible to Internet users.

You propose the following:

- Enable ICS on the Windows 2000 Server.
- Enable HTTP port 80 so it is accessible to Internet users.

Which of the following needs are met by your proposed solution? [Choose all that appy.]

- ❑ A. All workstations can share a single Internet connection.
- ❑ B. The solution imposes no additional costs.
- ❑ C. The internal IP address scheme will not change.
- ❑ D. The internal Web server will be accessible to Internet users.

Answers A, B, and D are correct. By implementing ICS, a single Internet connection can be shared by multiple computers. This solution does not impose any additional costs. By enabling HTTP port 80, an internal Web server can be made accessible to Internet users. Answer C is incorrect because ICS automatically assigns computers an IP address from the network address of `192.168.0.0`. Because this range is not configurable, the internal computers will be assigned new IP addresses.

Need to Know More?

Search the online version of TechNet and the Windows 2000 Server Resource Kit using keywords such as `ICS` and `NAT`.

Minasi, Mark, Christa Anderson, Brian Smith, and Doug Toombs. *Mastering Windows 2000.* Sybex Press, Alameda, CA. ISBN: 0782140432.

Microsoft Corporation. *Microsoft Windows 2000 Server Resource Kit.* Microsoft Press. ISBN: 1572318058. This book provides in-depth information about all aspects of Windows 2000 server, including Network Address Translation.

Certificate Services

Terms you'll need to understand:

✓ Encrypting File System (EFS)
✓ Digital certificates
✓ Certificate Authority (CA)
✓ Enterprise Certificate Authority
✓ Standalone Certificate Authority
✓ Certificate Revocation List (CRL)

Techniques you'll need to master:

✓ Understanding the requirements for the different CA types
✓ Installing Certificate Services
✓ Configuring a Certificate Authority
✓ Understanding the certificate enrollment process
✓ Understanding the different methods of requesting certificates
✓ Revoking certificates
✓ Removing the Encrypting File System keys

Introduction

As security becomes more important in today's network environments, there needs to be a secure method of passing information between hosts. One of the most common ways of doing this is through the use of digital certificates.

Organizations have the option of using a commercial company to issue digital certificates. They can also use Certificate Services, included with Windows 2000. Certificate Services enables the creation of a Public Key Infrastructure (PKI), which allows data to be encrypted, and computers and users to be verified and authenticated. Certificate Services establishes a system of trust.

This chapter covers the fundamentals behind certificates, including how to install, configure, and manage Certificate Services.

Understanding Certificate Authorities

When implementing certificates for security purposes, organizations can opt to use a commercial certificate provider or it can use a tool called *Certificate Services*, which is included with Windows 2000. In either case, before implementing any certificate infrastructure, it is important to understand certificates and certificate authorities.

Certificates

A *certificate* is a digital statement from a trusted authority used for verification purposes. The certificate is used to validate the entity bound to a *public key*. In other words, the certificate confirms that the holder of the key is who he claims to be. The entity issued a certificate can be a person, computer, organization, or a device, such as a router.

Certificates are similar to driver's licenses. A driver's license is issued to an individual from a trusted authority, such as a government agency, and can be used as proof of identity. Because it is a piece of identification issued from a trusted authority, we believe that the person holding the license is indeed who they claim to be. This is the purpose of certificates. Because they are issued from a trusted authority, we trust that the person or entity is who they claim to be.

PKI and Public/Private Keys

A Public Key Infrastructure (PKI) is a system that employs the use of digital certificates, public and private keys, and certificate authorities to secure communications. The digital certificates provide a way of verifying an individual's identity. The public and private keys are used to secure data that is exchanged. The certificate authorities are responsible for generating the key pair and issuing the digital certificates.

Public and private keys ensure data being sent between parties is secure. They also ensure that the entity sending the data is who they claim to be. Once a key pair is generated, the private key is given to the individual who made the request. The public key is made available to others as part of the digital certificate. When a message is encrypted using a public key, only the individual holding the corresponding public key can decrypt it. For example, if Sean wants to send Doug a secure message, he can locate Doug's public key and use it to encrypt the message (remember the public keys are made available to other parties, not the private keys). Once the message is encrypted, only Doug can decrypt it using his private key. Likewise, if Sean wanted to authenticate himself to Doug, he could encrypt a digital certificate using his own private key. Doug can then use Sean's public key to decrypt it.

For an entity to be part of a *PKI*, it must have a *public* and *private key* as well as a certificate. Before a certificate can be issued, a key pair must be generated. The key pair is usually generated by the Cryptographic Service Provider (CSP). The CSP provides the encryption and signature algorithms and determines the algorithms and key lengths used with a certificate. Once the key pair is generated, a request can be submitted to a Certificate Authority (CA). Depending on how CAs are implemented, this request may be sent to a third-party certificate service or to a CA on the internal network (CAs are discussed in the following section). The request for a certificate includes the public key of the requestor as well as any other required information, such as name and email address. If the certificate is issued it will include the following information:

- The entity's name
- Information about the entity, such as email address
- The entity's public key
- An expiration date for the certificate
- Details about the certificate authority that issued the certificate
- Digital signature

Some of the reasons for implementing certificates include:

- Implementing the Encrypting File System (EFS)
- Using IPSec to secure communications
- Signing and encrypting email messages
- Smart Card Logons
- SSL and TLS communications

Certificate Authorities

A *Certificate Authority (CA)* is an entity that has been assigned to issue certificates to users, computers, and organizations. There are two options when using CAs. You can use a third-party CA, such as VeriSign (`www.verisign.com`), or you can create your own CA using Certificate Services.

Certificate requests are submitted to a CA to verify the requestor. In other words, the CA verifies that the person requesting a digital certificate is indeed who they claim to be. This verification is an important step in the information security process. By having a trusted third party, such as VeriSign, identify and legitimize the requestor, entities wanting to transfer data to the requestor can rest assured that they are dealing with a trustworthy and secure party.

Not only is the CA responsible for issuing digital certificates, it is also responsible for revoking them. The CAs publish a list of all revoked certificates to identify which entities no longer have the trusted credentials given by the CA (revoking certificates is discussed later in this chapter).

Because a CA is responsible for sensitive information, it's important that security measures are in place to protect it. First of all, the CA should be physically protected, meaning it should be placed in a secure location accessible only by administrators. Because the CA's private key is the basis for trust in the certification process, this too must be secured.

The CA's private key is used to sign all issued certificates. For example, if Mike receives a digitally signed message from Dana, he can verify her identity by using the CA's public key to decrypt the signature (that was signed using a private key). If the CAs signature is valid, and the information contained within the certificate is valid, Mike can be assured that the message is in fact from Dana.

The cryptographic hardware module can provide tamper-resistant key storage and protect the CA's private key. Finally, you must also consider the possibility of losing a CA. This can obviously cause a number of problems. Certificate Services supports backing up the certificate instance so it can be restored in the event of failure.

Certificate Authority Hierarchies

CAs are organized into hierarchies, similar to the way in which Windows 2000 domains are organized. The top level of the hierarchy consists of a root CA, or root authority, which is responsible for issuing certificates to other CAs. All other CAs then branch off the root, thus creating a parent-child relationship. These CAs are also referred to as subordinate, or child, CAs. Child CAs are certified by their parent CA. A CA hierarchy essentially creates a model of trust. Each child CA trusts its parent CA with the trust path leading back to the root authority.

There are a number of benefits to creating a hierarchy of certificate authorities. Multiple CAs enable you to designate specific CAs to be responsible for issuing specific types of certificates. Depending on the structure of the organization, it can allow each department or geographical location the ability to maintain its own CA. It also offers another level of security because users and computers are not in contact with the root CA to get their certificates. Instead they are issued a certificate by one of the subordinate CAs. Additionally, it gives administrators the ability of taking the root CA offline.

Certificate Authority Classes

Windows 2000 supports two classes of Certificate Authorities: *Enterprise CAs* and *Standalone CAs*. The type of CA you implement depends on to whom you are issuing certificates. For example, a standalone CA would be implemented to issue certificates to entities such as partners or clients outside of your organization. An Enterprise CA would be implemented to issue certificates to entities within the organization. The differences between the two types are outlined in the following sections.

Enterprise Certificate Authorities

An *Enterprise CA* provides certificates to users and computers within an organization. An Enterprise CA is automatically registered in Active Directory and trusted by all computers in that AD domain.

Enterprise CAs have the following features:

- They require a domain controller with Active Directory.
- Information is stored within Active Directory.
- They are used to issue certificates to entities within an organization.

If you encounter an exam question in which domain user accounts are used to verify the identity of a requester, you will be implementing an Enterprise CA.

Standalone Certificate Authorities

In an environment without Active Directory, you can implement Certificate Services using a Standalone CA. Standalone CAs are also implemented if certificates are being issued to entities outside the organization, for example, to business partners or vendors. Standalone CAs have the following characteristics:

- Active Directory is not required.
- Information is stored within a local database.
- This type of CA is normally configured when certificates must be issued to extranet or Internet users.
- Requestors must provide all information needed to complete their certificate. This is unlike an Enterprise CA, which can retrieve the required information from Active Directory.
- All certificate requests are set to pending until the identity of the requestor is verified.

If Active Directory is installed, you have the option of using Enterprise or Standalone CAs. If Active Directory is not present, only Standalone CAs can be implemented.

Certificate Authority Types

Now that you are familiar with the two general classes of CAs, let's take a look at the different CAs that can exist within a certificate hierarchy. The four types of CAs supported by Windows 2000 are as follows:

- Enterprise Root CAs
- Subordinate CAs
- Standalone Root CAs
- Standalone Subordinate CAs

The following sections help you become more familiar with each of these CA types.

Enterprise Root CAs

At the top level of an enterprise certificate authority hierarchy is the Enterprise Root CA. Once the CA is configured, it is automatically registered within Active Directory and trusted by all computers within the domain.

In a CA hierarchy, the Enterprise Root CA is usually responsible for issuing certificates to subordinate CAs, which then issue the certificates to users and computers on the network. The Enterprise Root CA can also issue certificates directly to users and computers if required.

Enterprise CAs have the following requirements:

- Active Directory
- DNS
- The user configuring the Enterprise CA must be a member of the Enterprise Admins group

Remember that a single domain can have multiple Enterprise Root CAs. However, any given CA hierarchy can consist only of a single Enterprise Root CA.

Enterprise Subordinate CAs

In a certificate hierarchy, an Enterprise Subordinate CA exists under an Enterprise CA. Enterprise Subordinate CAs are usually created for a specific purpose, such as issuing certificates to a particular part of an organization. To configure an Enterprise Subordinate CA, an Enterprise Root CA must be present. This can be an Enterprise Root CA on the local network or a third-party root CA.

If you want to have your certificates trusted by people outside the local organization, you can configure the root CA to be from a third-party, such as VeriSign, instead of using a root CA on the internal network.

If a child domain is added to an existing domain tree that already has a CA in place, the default permissions in the new domain will not allow the CA to publish certificates. To solve this problem, the CA must be added to the Cert Publishers group in the new domain.

Standalone Root CAs

If Active Directory is not installed, a Standalone CA is the only type of CA that can be configured. It requires only administrative privileges on the local computer. If your organization needs to issue certificates to entities outside of the organization, a Standalone CA should be implemented All certificate requests are then held as pending until an administrator approves them.

Standalone Subordinate CAs

A Standalone Subordinate CA is very similar to an Enterprise Standalone CA, except it does not require Active Directory. To successfully install a Standalone Subordinate CA, there must already be a root CA in place. Again, this can be a root CA within the organization or from a third party. Also, keep in mind the administrative privileges requirement on the local server.

Installing and Configuring Certificate Services

Certificate Services can be installed during the installation of Windows 2000 or later using the Add/Remove Programs applet within the Control Panel. If you are installing a root CA, a certificate is automatically generated during the installation process and signed with the server's public and private keys. The process is slightly different if you are installing a subordinate CA. Instead of generating a self-signed certificate, a certificate request must be submitted to a root CA for authorization. Before the subordinate CA can be used, the certificate must be issued and installed by the root.

To install Certificate Services, follow these steps:

1. Click Start, point to Settings, and click Control Panel.
2. Double-click the Add/Remove Programs applet.
3. Click Add/Remove Windows Components. From the list of components, select Certificate Services. As shown in Figure 9.1, a window appears warning you that once the service is installed, the computer name and current domain membership cannot be changed. Click Yes to confirm and click Next.
4. Select the type of Certificate Authority you want to configure (see Figure 9.2). If the server is not a member of an Active Directory domain, you will have only the options to configure a Standalone Root CA or a Standalone Subordinate CA. Click Next.

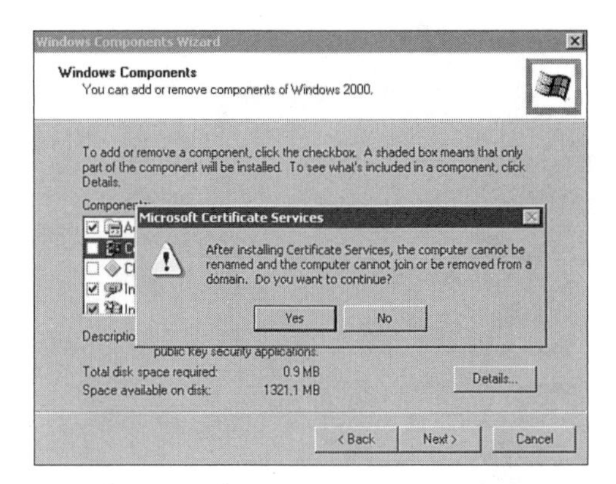

Figure 9.1 Microsoft Certificate Services warning message.

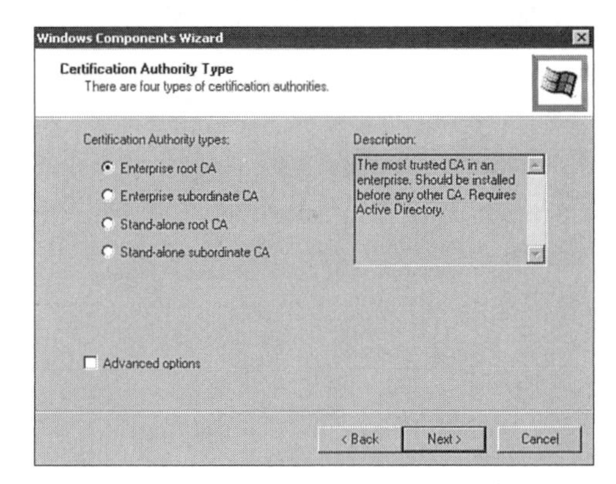

Figure 9.2 Selecting the Certificate Authority type.

5. If you selected the Advanced Options, the Public and Private key Pair window appears, as shown in Figure 9.3. The options are summarized in Table 9.1. Click Next.

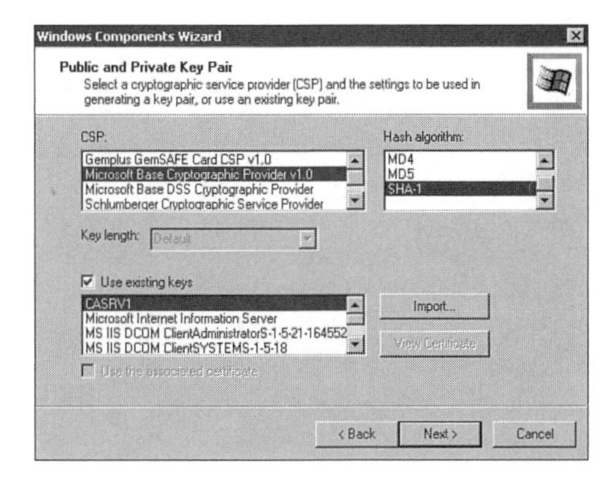

Figure 9.3 Configuring public and private key pair settings.

6. From the CA Identifying Information window shown in Figure 9.4, type the appropriate information. Click Next.

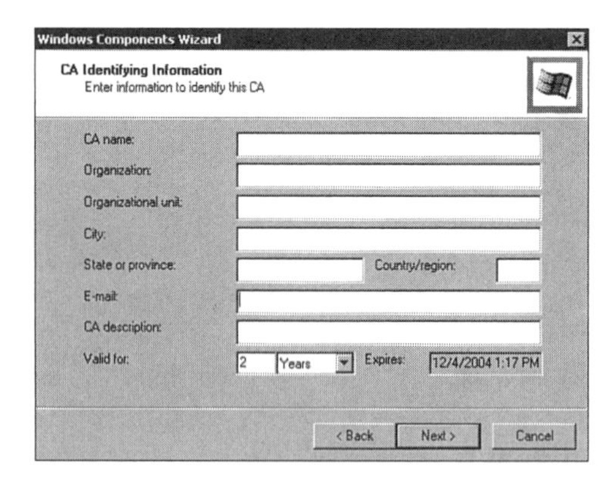

Figure 9.4 CA Identifying Information.

7. Specify the location of the configuration data, database, and logs. You can specify a shared folder for the configuration information if Active Directory is not used. Click Next.
8. A warning message appears stating that IIS must be stopped before proceeding. Click OK.
9. Click Finish.

Table 9.1 CA Identifying Information

Field	Description
CSP	Select the cryptographic service provider used to generate the public and private keys.
Hash Algorithm	The algorithm used to produce a hash value.
Key Length	Specifies the length of the keys.
Use Existing Keys	Select this option to use an existing key pair instead of generating a new one.

Be prepared to encounter exam questions pertaining to renaming or changing the domain membership of a CA. Remember that once certificate services is installed, the computer cannot be renamed nor can its domain membership be changed.

Configuring Certificate Services

After Certificate Services are installed, you can use the Certificate Authority to perform most management tasks and to configure the CA. You can open the Certificate Authority snap-in from the Administrative Tools menu. As shown in Figure 9.5, each CA has a set of configurable options available through its Properties window. The General tab provides some basic information about the CA, such as the name assigned to it, the CSP, and the hash algorithm. These settings were initially configured during the installation of Certificate Services.

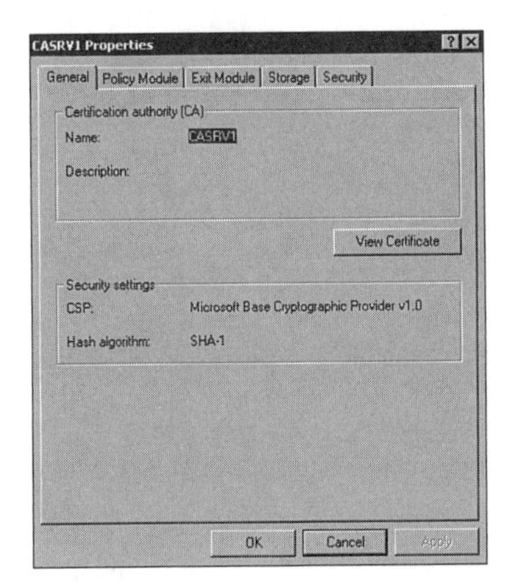

Figure 9.5 Configuring the properties for a CA.

Policy modules enable an administrator to control the behavior of a certificate authority and determine the action that a CA will take when it receives a certificate request. These modules determine whether certificate requests should be issued, denied, or marked as pending when they are received. By selecting the Configure button from the Policy Module tab, you can change the default behavior when a request is received (see Figure 9.6). Keep in mind that the policy module cannot be changed for an enterprise CA because it uses Active Directory to determine the identity of requestors and whether they have permission to request the certificate type. However, on a Standalone CA, the policy module can be changed. The certificate requests will most often be set to pending.

The exit module is used to control any post processing of issued certificates, such as publishing them to Active Directory or to a file system. By selecting the Configure button from the Exit Module tab, you can configure a certificate authority to publish issued certificates to Active Directory and/or a file system (see Figure 9.7). It also determines where the Certificate Revocation List is published.

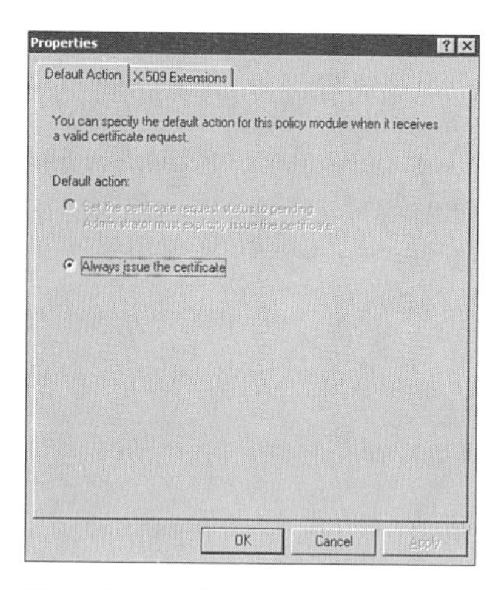

Figure 9.6 Configuring the policy module.

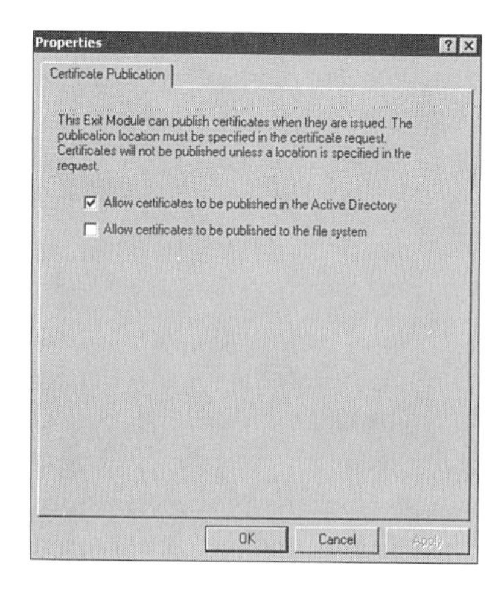

Figure 9.7 Configuring the exit module.

As shown in Figure 9.8, the Storage tab provides information about where the Configuration data is stored. This data can be stored in Active Directory or on a shared folder; it is configured during the installation of Certificate Services. Remember, with an Enterprise CA, the configuration information is stored in Active Directory by default, whereas on a Standalone CA, the information is stored locally.

The Security tab allows you to configure CA access privileges. By default, Authenticated Users are assigned the `enroll and read` permission. These permissions are enabled for all users who are logged on to the domain to request certificates allowing them to request certificates from the CA. The local Administrators group, Domain Admins, and Enterprise Admins group are also granted the `Manage` permission, which gives them full control of the CA. If the default permissions do not meet your requirements, you can use the Security tab shown in Figure 9.9 to modify them.

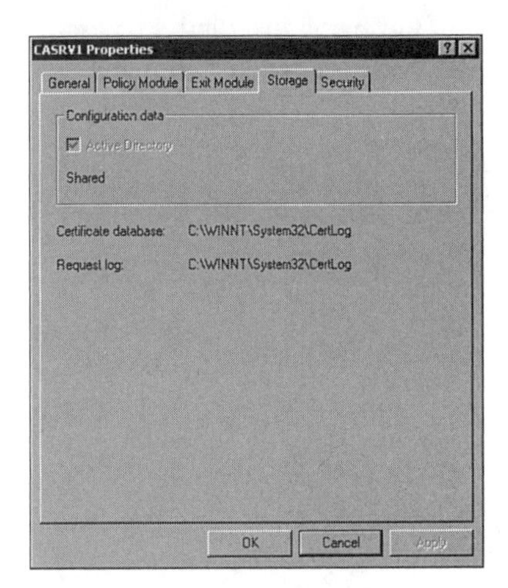

Figure 9.8 Viewing the Configuration data storage location.

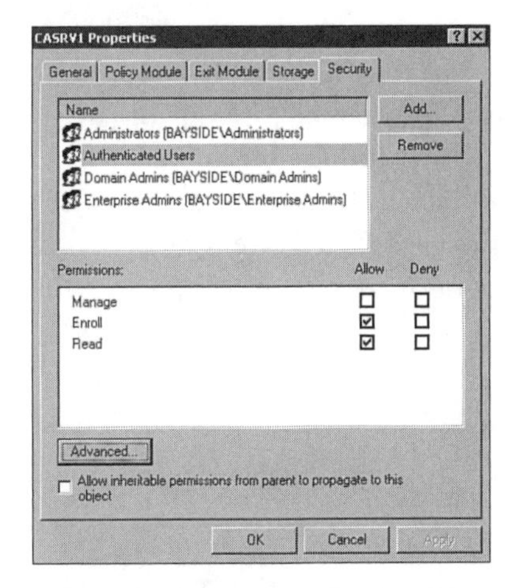

Figure 9.9 Configuring security for a CA.

Certificate Templates

Certificate templates outline a certificate based on its intended use. They contain preset configurations for common types of certificates and outline the intended use of the certificate. The preset configurations are used to issue certificates, thereby simplifying the process of requesting and issuing certificates. When a user attempts to request a certificate from a CA, the user might be able to choose from a number of certificate templates, depending on the configured permissions.

Several certificate templates are included with Windows 2000. The templates that are available depend on the type of CA being installed. For example, when an Enterprise CA is configured, the following templates are installed:

- Administrator
- Domain Controller
- Computer
- Basic EFS
- EFS Recovery Agent
- User
- Subordinate Certification Authority
- Web Server

The templates listed within the Policy Settings container are the default templates that the CA can issue. Other templates can be added within the Certificate Authority Manager if necessary. For example, if your organization deploys SmartCards, you can add the SmartCard Logon and SmartCard User certificates to the Policy Settings container. To do so, right-click the Policy Settings container, point to New, and click Certificate to issue. From the Select Certificate Template window shown in Figure 9.10, select the template you want to add and click OK.

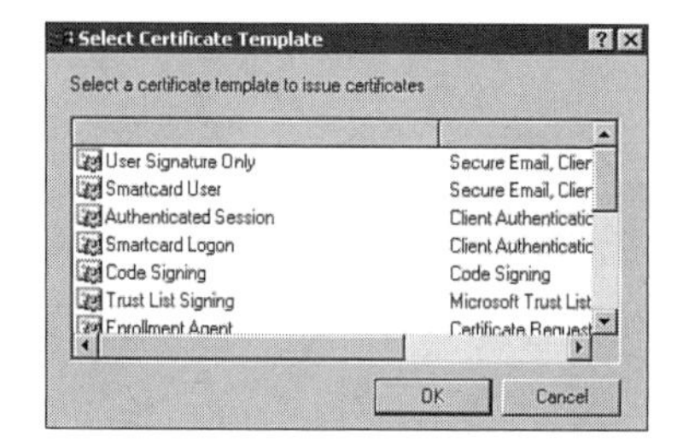

Figure 9.10 Configuring additional templates.

A template's ACL (access control list) controls which users can enroll for that type of certificate. The ACL determines the type of access a user has to an object. Each template has default permissions that can be edited if necessary. Certificate requests are granted only for those users and computers who have been assigned the `enroll` permission.

To edit the ACL of a certificate template, follow these steps:

1. Click Start, point to Programs, Administrative Tools, and click Active Directory Sites and Services.
2. Click the View menu and select the Show Services Node option.
3. Expand the Services container and expand Public key Services.
4. Click the Certificate Templates folder.
5. Right-click the appropriate template, click Properties, and select the Security tab shown in Figure 9.11.
6. Ensure the appropriate users or groups have the Enroll permission to request the certificate type.

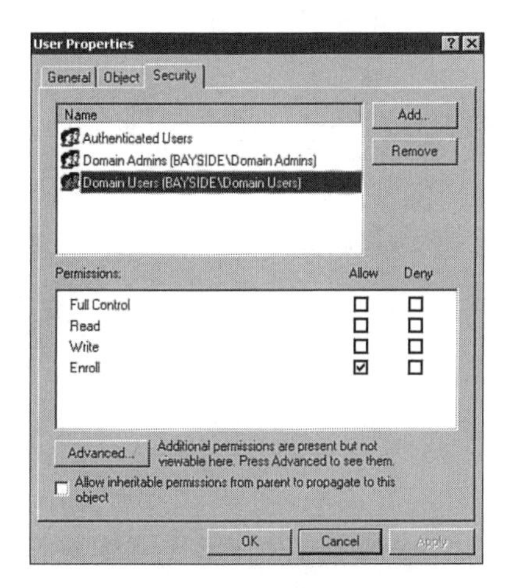

Figure 9.11 Configuring certificate template security.

Issuing and Revoking Certificates

Certificate authorities are responsible for issuing and revoking certificates for users, computers, devices, and even other CAs. Before a certificate can be issued, a request must be generated. Once a certificate has been issued to a requestor, it can be revoked at any time by an administrator. The following section looks at the certificate enrollment process, the different methods for generating a certificate request, and how certificates can be revoked.

Certificate Enrollment

The first step in obtaining a certificate is to submit a certificate request. The process is referred to as *certificate enrollment*.

The following steps outline the basic process that occurs during certificate enrollment:

1. Before a request for certificate can be generated, the requestor generates or is assigned a public and private key pair.
2. The requestor must gather the information required by the CA to verify its identity and issue a certificate.
3. The requestor sends the information to the CA along with its public key.
4. The CA verifies the information based on its policy rules to determine whether a certificate should be issued.
5. The CA creates a digital statement containing the requestor's information and signs it using its private key.
6. The certificate is sent to the requestor and loaded onto the requestor's computer.

There are several ways in which a certificate request can be generated. This includes:

- Certificate Request wizard enrollment
- Web-based enrollment
- Automated enrollment

If an enterprise CA is available, the Certificate Request wizard can be used to generate a certificate request. The wizard can be found within the Certificates snap-in. Administrators can use the snap-in to manage their user account, computer account, or local services. Regular users can use the snap-in to manage their own account certificates. When requesting a certificate, you must choose the appropriate certificate template. The ACLs for the templates determine which users and computers can enroll for the different certificates.

Using the Certificate Services Enrollment pages, clients can also enroll for a certificate. The Certificate Enrollment Web Pages are installed on the computer running Certificate Services (although the pages can be added to other systems). As shown in Figure 9.12, the enrollment page is accessible from the following URL: `http://server_name/certsrv/default.asp`.

If you have to support browsers other than Internet Explorer for Web-based enrollment, you must change the authentication method on the **CertSrv** virtual directory to Basic Authentication.

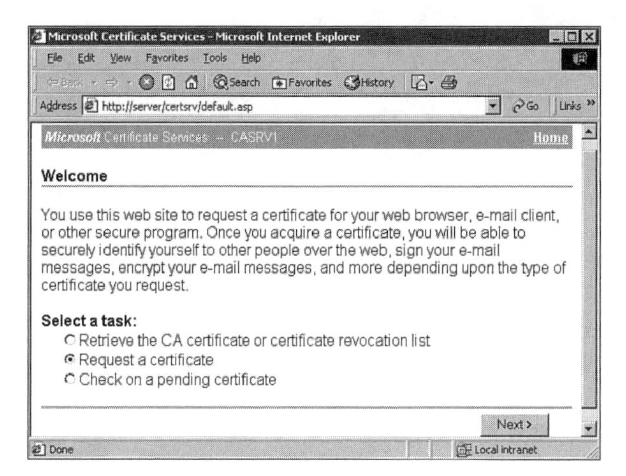

Figure 9.12 Using Web-based certificate enrollment.

Because standalone CAs do not use Active Directory, certificate enrollment must be performed using the Certificate Services Enrollment pages.

The third option is to use automated enrollment, which relies on the Windows 2000 Group Policy. When automated enrollment is configured, the specified certificates are automatically issued to all computers and users within the scope of the policy. Again, this enrollment method is supported only when an Enterprise CA is available. Using automated enrollment is further discussed in the following section.

Using Public Key Group Policy

One of the benefits of configuring the Public Key Group Policy is that you can automate the enrollment of computer certificates. You can use the Group Policy snap-in to configure a Public Key Policy for sites, domains, organizational units, and local computers.

To configure automated certificate enrollment, follow these steps:

1. From the Start menu, click Run. Type `mmc` and click OK.
2. Click Console and click Add/Remove Snap-in. Click Add and select Group Policy. Click Add.

3. Click Finish. Click Close.
4. Navigate to the Computer Configuration container, expand Security Settings, and click Public Key Policy, as shown in Figure 9.13.

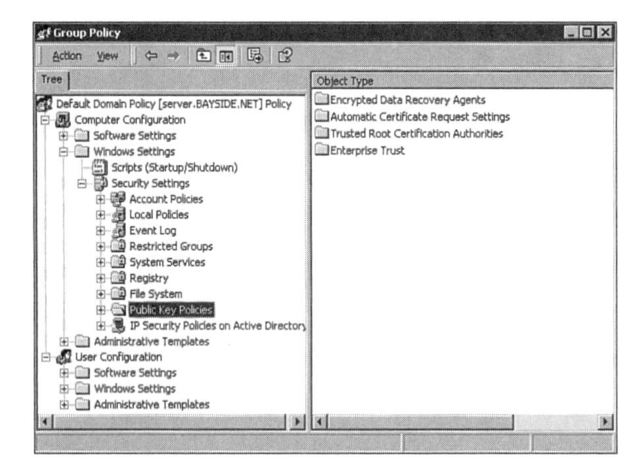

Figure 9.13 Public Key Group Policy.

5. Right-click Automatic Certificate Request, point to New, and click Automatic Certificate Request. This launches the Automatic Certificate Request Setup Wizard. Click Next.
6. Select the Certificate type. Click Next. For a certificate template to be issued, the computer must have the Enroll permission for the template.
7. Select the CAs that can process the requests. Click Next.
8. Click Finish.

Once the automatic certificate request has been created, the certificate templates are issued the next time a computer within the scope of the policy is restarted or logs onto the domain.

Revoking Certificates

One of the tasks associated with managing certificates is revoking them. At some point you may find it necessary to revoke an issued certificate. For example, if an employee leaves an organization, his or her certificate must be revoked.

Once a certificate is marked as revoked, it is moved to the *Certificate Revocation List (CRL)*. (You learn more about the CRL in a moment.) The revoked certificate appears on the CRL the next time it is published. All revoked certificates appear on the list so others can verify valid certificates. An Administrator can use the Certificate Authority snap-in to revoke a certificate.

To revoke a certificate, follow these steps:

1. Click Start, point to Programs, Administrative Tools, and click Certificate Authority.
2. Expand the Certificate Authority and click the Issued Certificates container.
3. Right-click the appropriate certificate, point to All Tasks, and click Revoke Certificate.
4. As shown in Figure 9.14, the Certificate Revocation box appears. Select the reason for revoking the certificate and click Yes.
5. The certificate should now appear in the Revoked Certificates container.

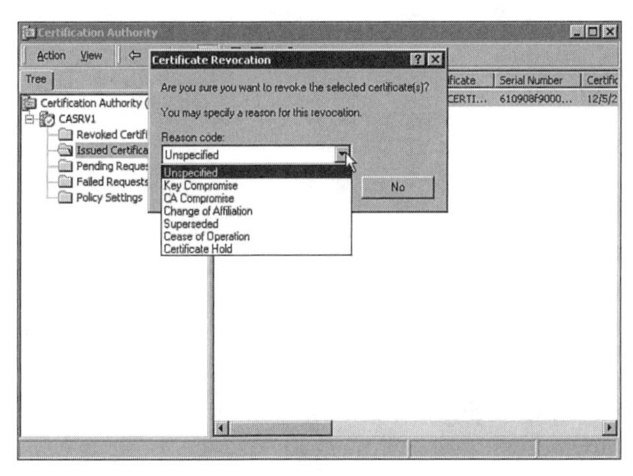

Figure 9.14 Revoking a certificate.

Before you revoke a certificate, keep in mind that once it is revoked it cannot be made valid again. The user must be issued a new certificate to replace the revoked one.

When a certificate is revoked, you must specify a reason code. If the revocation is questionable, meaning there is a chance that the certificate may need to be reinstated, select the reason code called *Certificate Hold*. This is the only reason code that allows you to unrevoke the certificate.

Certificate Revocation List

Periodically, Windows 2000 Certificate Services publishes a *Certificate Revocation List (CRL)*. This list is used to inform other entities which certificates have been revoked and are therefore no longer valid.

The CRL is automatically published once every week, although an administrator can configure the interval for a different time period. For example, if you expect the number of certificate revocations per week to be high, you may want to decrease the Publication interval so it occurs more frequently. This can be done through the Certificate Authority snap-in by right-clicking the Revoked Certificate folder and choosing Properties. In the resulting property box, you can make your adjustments to the time cycle for the CRL's publication (see Figure 9.15).

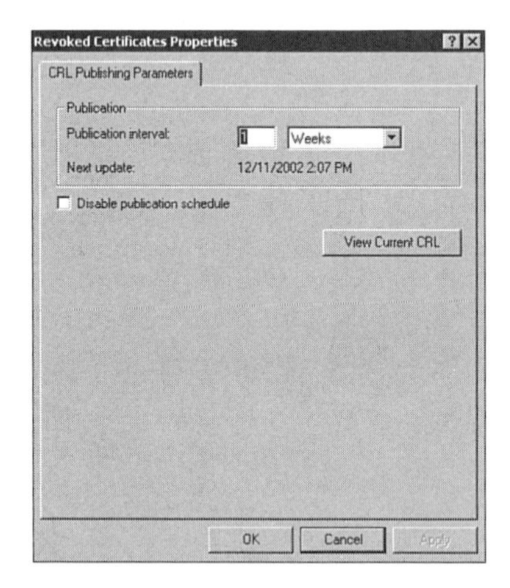

Figure 9.15 Configuring the CRL publication interval.

Although the CRL is published by default once a week, you can manually publish a CRL if you revoke a certificate between publication intervals and need to immediately notify other entities of the change. To do so, right-click the Revoked Certificates folder within the Certificate Authority snap-in, choose All Tasks and choose Publish. The CRL is published in the `<systemroot>\system32\CertSrv\CertEnroll` folder, as well as in Active Directory if the CRL is published by an Enterprise CA. Manually publishing a CRL does not interfere with the regular publication interval.

To provide a higher level of security to ensure the root CA is not compromised, you can configure it as an offline CA, meaning it will be disconnected from the network. To do so, the server that will become the offline root CA must be running IIS and must be a member server within an Active Directory domain. Once the new root CA is installed, the default location of the Certificate Revocation list must be changed to a location on the network that is accessible to users.

Removing the Encrypting File System Keys

One of the new features included with Windows 2000 and NTFS v5 is the *Encrypting File System (EFS)*. This allows files to be stored in an encrypted format so the contents can be viewed only by the individual who encrypted them. EFS encrypts files that are stored on a hard drive using encryption keys.

To increase the security of EFS, the encryption keys can be removed from the local computer and stored elsewhere, such as a network location or some other media type.

To remove the Encrypting file system keys from the local machine, follow these steps:

1. Open the Run command and type `mmc`.
2. Add the Certificate snap-in.
3. Expand Certificates, Personal, and click Certificates.
4. As long as a file has been encrypted previously, a certificate should be listed with the Intended Purpose designated as Encrypting File System, as shown in Figure 9.16.

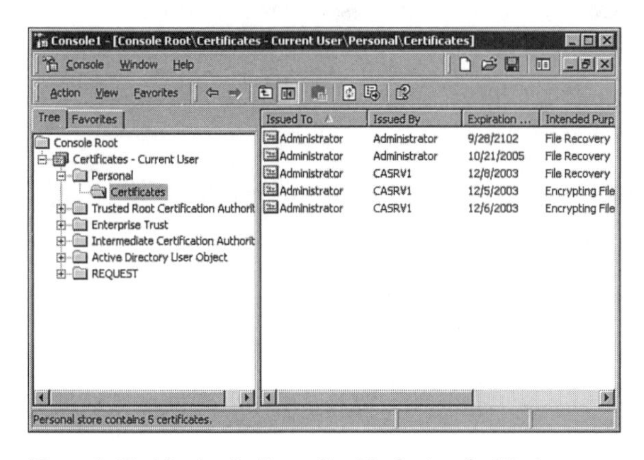

Figure 9.16 Viewing the Encrypting File System Certificate.

5. Right-click the certificate, point to All Tasks, and select Export. This launches the Certificate Export Wizard. Click Next.
6. Select the option to export the private key with the certificate. Click Next.

7. Select the file format in which you want the certificate to be exported. Click Next.
8. Type a password used to protect the private key. Click Next.
9. Specify the name of the file to export. Click Next.
10. Click Finish.

Once complete, the information will be stored within the file you specified. Remove the file from the local computer and store it in a secure network location or on another media type such as a floppy.

An administrator can also disallow users to encrypt files. You do this by modifying the appropriate group policy within Active Directory Users and Computers.

To disable EFS for all domain users, follow these steps:

1. Click Start, point to Programs, Administrative Tools, and click Active Directory Users and Computers.
2. Right-click the domain node and choose Properties.
3. Click the Group Policy tab, select the appropriate policy and click Edit.
4. From the Encrypted Data Recovery Agents container, expand Computer Configuration, Windows Settings, Security Settings, and Public Key Policies.
5. Right-click the container and click Delete. Click Yes to delete the policy.
6. Right-click Encrypted Data Recovery Agents and click Initialize Empty Policy.

Practice Questions

Question 1

Your organization consists of a single Windows 2000 domain. You have been asked to implement Certificate Services within the existing network infrastructure. Certificate Services must integrate with Active Directory. Which of the following should you implement?

- ❍ A. Enterprise CA
- ❍ B. Enterprise Subordinate CA
- ❍ C. Standalone CA
- ❍ D. Standalone Subordinate CA

Answer A is correct. If the Certificate Authority is required to integrate with Active Directory, an Enterprise CA must be configured. Because there is no other CA installed, an Enterprise Root CA must be configured. Answer B is incorrect. To install an Enterprise Subordinate CA, a root CA must be available. However, if a commercial CA was configured as the parent CA, this option would be possible. Answers C and D are incorrect because Standalone CAs do not use Active Directory.

Question 2

Your network currently consists of an enterprise CA. There is a Web server on the internal network that provides services to external business partners. You want to expand the current setup to provide Certificate Services to these users. Which of the following should you implement?

- ❍ A. Enterprise Root CA
- ❍ B. Enterprise Subordinate CA
- ❍ C. Standalone Root CA
- ❍ D. Standalone Subordinate CA

Answer D is correct. Standalone CAs should be implemented when certificates are being issued to users outside of the organization. In this case, Internet users are assured of the Web server's identity, so a standalone subordinate CA should be configured with a commercial CA as the parent. Therefore, answer C is incorrect. Answers A and B are incorrect because Enterprise CAs are used to issue certificates to users within an organization.

Question 3

You have been asked to implement Certificate Services on the network. How can you install the service on a Windows 2000 server?

- ❍ A. Network and Dial-up Connections applet
- ❍ B. Add/Remove Programs applet
- ❍ C. Certificate Services applet
- ❍ D. Administrative Tools applet

Answer B is correct. Certificate Services can be installed using the Add/Remove Programs applet within the Control Panel. Therefore, answers A, C, and D are incorrect.

Question 4

Your organization is implementing Certificate Services. You have been asked to outline the process involved in installing and configuring the service. In your proposal, you outline the requirements of an Enterprise CA. Which of the following should be included in the list of requirements?

- ❍ A. Windows 2000 Advanced Server
- ❍ B. Active Directory
- ❍ C. Internet Information Services
- ❍ D. WINS

Answer B is correct. One of the requirements of an enterprise CA is that an Active Directory domain controller be available. Enterprise CAs use Active Directory to verify the identity of users and computers and store configuration data. Answer A is incorrect. Although Certificate Services can only be installed on one of the Windows 2000 server platforms, it does not require Windows 2000 Advanced Server. Answer C is incorrect because Internet Information Services is not required to install an Enterprise CA. (If you want to use Web-based enrollment, IIS needs to be installed.) Answer D is incorrect because Enterprise CAs require DNS not WINS.

Question 5

Due to reorganization within the company, three employees have been terminated. You revoke the certificates of the three users. When you check the CRL, the certificates are not listed. What is the problem?

❍ A. Revoked certificates must be manually added to the CRL.

❍ B. Revoked certificates are not placed on the CRL.

❍ C. The pending revocation interval has not yet expired.

❍ D. The publishing interval has not yet expired.

Answer D is correct. By default, after a certificate is revoked it will appear on the CRL after the publishing interval expires. The default publishing interval is once a week. Answers A and B are incorrect because all revoked certificates are automatically added to the CRL. Answer C is incorrect because there is no such thing as the pending revocation interval.

Question 6

Your network consists of two domains. A certificate hierarchy is already in place. **SRVCA1** is the Enterprise CA. **SRVCA2** and **SRVCA3** are both configured as Enterprise Subordinate CAs. Due to expansion, a third domain is added to the forest. However, **SRVCA2** and **SRVCA3** are unable to publish any certificates for users in the new domain. How would you fix this problem?

❍ A. Add the Enterprise Subordinates to the Enterprise Admins group

❍ B. Add the Enterprise Subordinates to the Cert Publishers group

❍ C. Add the Enterprise Subordinates to the Domain Admins group

❍ D. Add the Enterprise CA to the Enterprise Admins group

Answer B is correct. For the subordinate CAs to publish certificates, they must be added to the Cert Publishers group in the new domain. Therefore, answers A, C, and D are incorrect.

Question 7

Which of the following is required to implement an Enterprise CA?

❍ A. All users must have accounts within Active Directory.

❍ B. There are no Active Directory requirements.

❍ C. All computers must have accounts within Active Directory.

❍ D. All user and computers must have accounts within Active Directory.

Answer D is correct. An Enterprise CA uses Active Directory to verify the identity of users and computers so all users and computers must have an account within Active Directory. Therefore, answers A, B, and C are incorrect.

Question 8

There are a number of Macintosh clients on your Windows 2000 network. They don't use Internet Explorer as their browser. Users report that they are unable to request certificates using the Web-based enrollment. How should you proceed?

❍ A. Give the Macintosh clients permission to the appropriate certificate templates.

❍ B. Upgrade their browsers to Internet Explorer.

❍ C. Within IIS, configure Basic Authentication to the **CertSrv** virtual directory.

❍ D. Install the Certificate Services client on the workstations.

Answer C is correct. To allow Macintosh clients to use Web-based certificate enrollment, the authentication method on the virtual directory must be set to basic. Therefore, answers A, B, and D are incorrect.

Question 9

Your company's Windows 2000 Web server is hosted on the Internet. The Web developers in the company often develop applications for external clients that download ActiveX controls to the clients' browser. However, with the default settings in Internet Explorer, clients are unable to automatically download the ActiveX controls. How can the problem be fixed?

❍ A. Install an Enterprise CA. Create a new policy setting that allows Web developers to request code signing certificates.

❍ B. Install an Enterprise Subordinate CA with a commercial CA as the parent. Configure a new policy setting that allows Web developers to request code signing certificates.

❍ C. Install an Enterprise Subordinate CA with an internal CA as the parent. Configure a new policy setting that allows developers to request code signing certificates.

❍ D. Install an Enterprise CA. Configure a commercial CA as the parent. Configure a new policy setting that allows developers to request code signing certificates.

Answer B is correct. Because certificates are being assigned to internal users, and Enterprise CA is configured. To assure customers of the Web server's identity, the parent of the Subordinate Enterprise CA should be a commercial CA.

Question 10

Your company has a Web server that is used by customers. It is currently not a member of the company's domain nor will it be. The Web server is now going to be used for customer transactions. For utmost security, the transactions should be encrypted and customers should be assured of the Web server's identity. What type of CA should you configure?

❍ A. Enterprise CA

❍ B. Enterprise Subordinate CA

❍ C. Standalone CA

❍ D. Standalone Subordinate CA

Answer D is correct. Because certificates aren't being assigned to users within the organization, a standalone CA should be used. To assure customers of the Web server's identity, a Standalone Subordinate CA should be configured and assigned a certificate from a commercial CA. Therefore, answers A, B, and C are incorrect.

Need to Know More?

Search the online version of TechNet and the Windows 2000 Server Resource Kit using keywords such as `Certificate Services` and `Certificate Authorities`.

Minasi, Mark, Christa Anderson, Brian Smith, and Doug Toombs. *Mastering Windows 2000*. Sybex Press, Alameda, CA. ISBN: 0782140432.

Microsoft Press. *Windows 2000 Server Resource Kit*. Microsoft Press. 2000. ISBN: 1572318058.

Practice Test 1

Question 1

Your network consists of a single WINS server. To reduce network traffic, you want clients to resolve NetBIOS names using the WINS server. Broadcasts should be used only if the WINS server is unavailable. Which of the following node types should you use to configure clients?

❍ A. P-node

❍ B. B-node

❍ C. H-node

❍ D. M-node

Question 2

For increased security, you want to use the callback function. You configure the user account properties and define the numbers from which users can dial in to the remote access server. For callback to work, which of the following options, shown in this figure should you select?

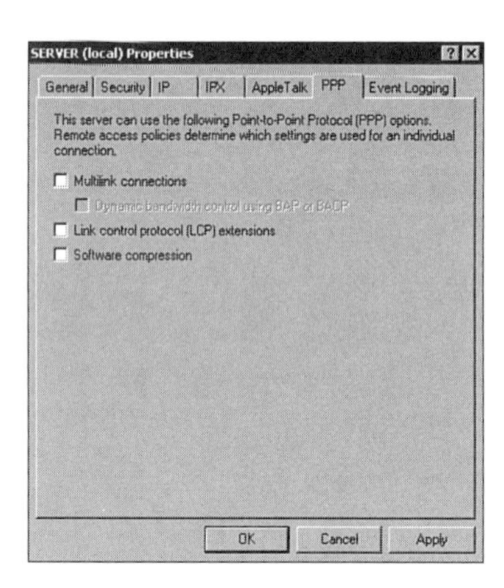

❍ A. Multilink Connections

❍ B. Dynamic Bandwidth control using BAP or BACP

❍ C. Link Control Protocol (LCP) Extensions

❍ D. Software Compression

Question 3

Which of the following DNS server types support dynamic updates? [Choose all that apply.]

- ❑ A. Windows 2000
- ❑ B. Windows NT 4.0
- ❑ C. BIND 4.9.6
- ❑ D. BIND 8.1.3

Question 4

Massa trucking has opened a new branch office. You have been asked to configure a two-way demand-dial connection between the head office and the branch office. You configure the following:

- Branch Office
- Interface: **HeadOffice**
- User Account: **Branch_Office**
- Calling Number: **18315551212**
- Head Office
- Interface: **BranchOffice**
- User Account: **Head_Office**
- Calling Number: **14084441212**

When you test your configuration, neither of the routers can establish a connection. What is causing the problem?

- ❍ A. The demand-dial interface names must be identical.
- ❍ B. The user account names on each router must be identical.
- ❍ C. The interface name on the calling router must be identical to the user account name on the answering router.
- ❍ D. Each router must have completely different user account and demand-dial interface names.

Question 5

Your company is planning on upgrading from Windows NT 4.0 to Windows 2000. Your boss wants to use static IP addresses when the workstations are upgraded to Windows 2000 Professional to avoid the havoc wreaked when a temporary administrator brought a DHCP server online with incorrect scope information. You assure your boss that new features included with Windows 2000 DHCP will prevent this from occurring in the future. On which systems should DHCP be installed when the workstations and server are upgraded to Windows 2000? [Choose all that apply.]

- ❑ A. Windows 2000 Domain Controllers
- ❑ B. Windows 2000 Professional Workstations
- ❑ C. Windows 2000 Member Servers
- ❑ D. Windows 2000 Standalone Servers

Question 6

Your company wants to install a Web server to be used for customer transactions. For security purposes, the Web server will not be a member of the domain. All transactions should be encrypted. Internet customers need to be assured of the Web server's identity. What type of CA should you configure?

- ❍ A. Enterprise root CA
- ❍ B. Enterprise subordinate CA
- ❍ C. Standalone root CA
- ❍ D. Standalone subordinate CA

Question 7

Windows 2000 includes NAT editors for which of the following protocols? [Choose all that apply.]

- ❑ A. FTP
- ❑ B. L2TP
- ❑ C. PPTP
- ❑ D. ICMP
- ❑ E. IGMP
- ❑ F. NetBIOS over TCP/IP
- ❑ G. IPSec

Question 8

TCP/IP filtering can be used to permit or deny traffic based on which of the following criteria? [Choose all that apply.]

- ❑ A. IP protocol
- ❑ B. IP address
- ❑ C. UDP port
- ❑ D. TCP port

Question 9

Your organization hopes to provide remote access capabilities to clients within the next few months. Your senior network administrator has asked you to configure one of the Windows 2000 servers in the test lab as a remote access server to test the proposed configuration. What is the first step you need to complete?

- ❍ A. Install the Routing and Remote Access Service
- ❍ B. Enable Routing and Remote Access
- ❍ C. Configure a remote access policy
- ❍ D. Configure a remote access profile

Question 10

You have been hired to perform an assessment of the Bayside network. The network consists of approximately 25 users and a single server running the DHCP server service. While performing your assessment, you notice the number of IP address lease requests is very high, especially because the number of IP addresses exceeds the number of clients. Where should you begin looking to determine why this is occurring?

- ❍ A. Check the Event Viewer for any DHCP related messages.
- ❍ B. Verify that the lease duration isn't configured with a low value.
- ❍ C. Run System Monitor to view the performance of the server.
- ❍ D. Run Network Monitor to capture DHCP related traffic.

Question 11

You are configuring an LMHOSTS file that you plan to import to the client workstations on the network. You want certain records within the LMHOSTS file to be placed in the local cache to facilitate name resolution. When creating LMHOSTS file entries, which of the following directives should you use to have the records added to the local cache?

❍ A. **#Pre**

❍ B. **#Load**

❍ C. **#MH**

❍ D. **#Include**

Question 12

Bayside has seven offices located in different parts of the U.S. There is one central office that hosts the primary DNS server. All office locations have their own DNS servers configured as secondary servers. The offices are currently connected with slow links with no plans to upgrade them. The annual budget allows for the addition of a second DNS server at each of the locations. However, you do not want any more traffic generated from zone transfers on the WAN or the local networks. What type of DNS servers should you configure?

❍ A. Standard primary servers

❍ B. Standard secondary servers

❍ C. Master name servers

❍ D. Caching-only servers

Question 13

The IP address of **131.107.2.10** belongs to which of the following address classes?

❍ A. Class A

❍ B. Class B

❍ C. Class C

❍ D. Class D

Question 14

You have been asked to configure Certificate Services for your organization. The organization currently consists of a single Windows 2000 domain. Certificate Services must integrate with Active Directory. Which of the following should you implement?

❍ A. Enterprise root CA

❍ B. Enterprise subordinate CA

❍ C. Standalone root CA

❍ D. Standalone subordinate CA

Question 15

You are establishing a nonpersistent demand-dial connection between a branch office and the corporate head office. You plan to use a routing protocol so the routing table does not need to be manually updated. Which of the following protocols can you use? [Choose all that apply.]

❑ A. RIPv1

❑ B. RIPv2

❑ C. OSPF

❑ D. ICMP

Question 16

Your home network consists of a Windows 2000 standalone server (**Server1**) and five Windows 2000 Professional workstations. **Server1** currently has the only Internet connection. You want to enable ICS on **Server1**. How should you proceed?

❍ A. Within the Network and Dial-up Connections applet, right-click the Internet connection and choose Properties. Click the Networking tab and select the option to Enable Internet Connection Sharing for this connection.

❍ B. Within the Routing and Remote Access console, right-click the demand-dial interface and choose Properties. Click the Sharing tab and select the option to Enable Internet Connection Sharing for this connection.

❍ C. Within the Network and Dial-up Connections applet, right-click the Internet connection and choose Properties. Click the Sharing tab and select the option to Enable Internet Connection Sharing for this connection.

❍ D. Within the Routing and Remote Access console, right-click the LAN interface and choose Properties. Click the Sharing tab and select the option to Enable Internet Connection Sharing for this connection.

Question 17

You want to back up the database on the local WINS server. However, you do not want to start the backups manually. Instead, you'd rather have them run automatically every few hours. How should you proceed?

❍ A. From the WINS server's properties window, select the Advanced tab and specify the backup path.

❍ B. Within the WINS management console, configure replication to occur every three hours.

❍ C. From the WINS server's properties window, select the General tab and specify the backup path.

❍ D. From the WINS server's properties window, select the Interval tab and configure the backup to run every few hours.

Question 18

Sean is trying to resolve the IP address of **Wrk01** using the **nslookup** command from **Wrk02**, but is unsuccessful. He can successfully resolve other hostnames on the network using this command. What could be causing the problem?

❍ A. There is no **A** record for **Wrk01**.

❍ B. There is no **A** record for **Wrk02**.

❍ C. There is no **PTR** record for **Wrk01**.

❍ D. There is no **PTR** record for **Wrk02**.

Question 19

Your network consists of two subnets: SubnetA and SubnetB. Each has its own DHCP server. You configure the scope on DHCP1 for SubnetA. Users are all leasing an IP address but report that they cannot access any resources outside of their own subnet. How can you most easily solve the problem?

❍ A. Activate the scope on DHCP1.

❍ B. Configure the default gateway on each workstation.

❍ C. Configure the 003 router option on DHCP1.

❍ D. Configure the 006 DNS server option on DHCP1.

Question 20

You need to install a standalone CA that will be subordinate to a commercial CA. Your server is running Windows 2000. How can you install Certificate Services? [Choose all that apply.]

❑ A. Using the Network and Dial-up Connections applet

❑ B. During the installation of Windows 2000

❑ C. Using the Add/Remove Programs applet

❑ D. Using the Certificate Services applet

Question 21

Which of the following components is responsible for negotiating security between IPSec-enabled hosts?

❍ A. IP Security Policy Management

❍ B. ISAKMP/OAKLEY

❍ C. IPSec Driver

❍ D. IPSec Policy Agent

Question 22

You are configuring NAT for the first time on your Windows 2000 Server. Routing and Remote Access has not been configured. You use the wizard to enable RRAS and configure NAT. When the wizard presents you with the list of common configurations, which one should you select when configuring NAT?

❍ A. Internet connection server

❍ B. Remote access server

❍ C. Network router

❍ D. Network address translator

❍ E. Virtual private network (VPN) server

Question 23

Several users in the programming department work from home offices. Remote access is configured for this group of users. Multilink is enabled to provide them with more bandwidth. Which of the following protocols allows lines to be dynamically added or dropped?

❍ A. LCP

❍ B. PPP

❍ C. BAP

❍ D. EAP

Question 24

You are working as part of a team that has been asked to implement routing within a large internetwork. Before beginning the planning phase, the organization's administrators present you with a list of some critical requirements:

- Administration of routing tables should be minimal.
- Changes to the network topology should be propagated dynamically.
- Security should be configured between routers.
- To reduce the size of the routing tables, routers should be organized into areas.

You propose the following:

- Configure Windows 2000 RRAS servers with two-way demand-dial connections.
- Configure all interfaces to use RIPv2.

Which of the following are met by the proposed solution? [Choose all that apply.]

❑ A. Administration of routing tables is minimal.

❑ B. Changes to the network topology are propagated dynamically.

❑ C. Security can be implemented between routers.

❑ D. Routers can be organized into areas.

Question 25

Network requirements call for secure dynamic updates. Currently, the network has a Windows 2000 DNS server, Windows 2000 Professional clients, and Windows 95 clients. A single DHCP server will be configured to perform all resource record updates for all clients and a second will be added in the near future. Both will be configured to perform dynamic updates for clients. On which system will you install the DHCP server service?

❍ A. Windows 2000 domain controller

❍ B. Windows 2000 member server

❍ C. Windows 2000 Professional workstation

❍ D. Windows NT 4.0 member server

Question 26

Based on your recommendation, a WINS server was implemented on the local network. One of the managers comes to your office and requests to see some statistics on the total number of name resolutions that the WINS server is performing. How can you provide the manager with this information?

❍ A. Within the WINS management console, right-click the WINS server and select View Server Statistics.

❍ B. Enable event logging.

❍ C. From the Properties window for the WINS server, select the Advanced tab and configure the WINS server to update statistics every five minutes.

❍ D. From the Properties window for the WINS server, select the General tab and configure the WINS server to update statistics every five minutes.

Question 27

You are configuring DNS servers on your network. Four of them will be added to the existing network. You want to provide the highest level of fault tolerance and plan to configure the zones as Active Directory integrated. With this in mind, on which of the following can the DNS Server service be installed?

❍ A. Windows 2000 domain controllers

❍ B. Windows 2000 member servers

❍ C. Windows NT 4.0 domain controllers

❍ D. Windows 2000 standalone servers

Question 28

Which layer of the TCP/IP DoD model is responsible for addressing and routing?

❍ A. Application

❍ B. Transport

❍ C. Network

❍ D. Internet

Question 29

You are receiving reports that several users are unable to use Web-based certificate enrollment. After some investigation, you determine that the problem is only affecting users running browsers other than Internet Explorer. How can you resolve the problem?

❍ A. Upgrade all browsers to Internet Explorer.

❍ B. Nothing. Web-based enrollment can only be used with Internet Explorer.

❍ C. Change the authentication type to Basic on the **CertSrv** virtual directory.

❍ D. Install the Certificate Services client on the workstations.

Question 30

You are configuring the elements of a remote access policy. In what order are the policy elements evaluated?

❍ A. Permissions, conditions, profile

❍ B. Profile, conditions, permissions

❍ C. Conditions, profile, permissions

❍ D. Conditions, permissions, profile

Question 31

You are working as part of a team that has been asked to implement routing within a large internetwork. Before beginning the planning phase, the organization's administrators present you with a list of some critical requirements:

- Administration of routing tables should be minimal.
- Changes to the network topology should be propagated automatically.
- Password authentication should exist between routers.
- To reduce the size of the routing tables, routers should be organized into areas.

You propose the following:

- Configure Windows 2000 RRAS servers with two-way demand-dial connections.
- Configure all interfaces to use RIPv1.

Which of the following are met by the proposed solution? [Choose all that apply.]

- ❑ A. Administration of routing tables is minimal.
- ❑ B. Changes to the network topology are propagated immediately.
- ❑ C. Password authentication exists between routers.
- ❑ D. Routers can be organized into areas.

Question 32

A DHCP server is used to assign IP addresses to clients and member servers on the network. Three of the member servers host print devices. How can you ensure that these print servers lease the same IP address from the DHCP server? [Choose all that apply.]

- ❑ A. Exclude the IP addresses from the scope.
- ❑ B. Create a separate scope for each of the print servers.
- ❑ C. Create a client reservation for each print server.
- ❑ D. Configure the DHCP options for the scope.

Question 33

Due to budget constraints, you can only implement a single WINS server on a network that consists of two subnets. You place the WINS server on the subnet with the most users. A computer on the other subnet will be configured as a WINS proxy. How should you proceed?

❍ A. Install the WINS proxy component using the Add/Remove programs applet.

❍ B. Install the WINS service and select the WINS proxy component during the installation.

❍ C. Edit the HKEY_LOCAL_MACHINE\System\CurrentControlSet\Services\Netbt\Paramters Registry key on the local computer and change the value of the **EnableProxy** parameter to **1**.

❍ D. Edit the local computer Registry and change the value of the **WINSProxy** parameter to **1**.

Question 34

John has been informed by his senior network administrator that he needs to be able to control which users and groups can perform dynamic updates to the DNS database. How should John proceed?

❍ A. Convert all zones to Active Directory integrated. Using the Dynamic Update tab from the properties window for the DNS server, select Only secure updates.

❍ B. Convert all zones to Active Directory integrated. Using the General tab from the properties window for the DNS server, select Only secure updates.

❍ C. Convert all zones to Active Directory integrated. Using the Dynamic Update tab from the properties window for the zone, select Only secure updates.

❍ D. Convert all zones to Active Directory integrated. Using the General tab from the properties window for the zone, select Only secure updates.

Question 35

Which of the following statements are true regarding enterprise CAs?

❍ A. Enterprise CAs do not require Active Directory.

❍ B. Enterprise CAs require WINS.

❍ C. An enterprise CA should be installed to issue certificates to users outside the domain.

❍ D. Enterprise CAs require DNS.

Question 36

You have been put in charge of securing a Web server. Your senior administrator has asked you to configure TCP/IP filtering to permit only FTP and HTTP access on all adapters. How should you proceed?

❍ A. From the TCP/IP Properties window for the adapter, select Enable TCP/IP Filtering. Configure traffic to be permitted for TCP ports **80** and **81**.

❍ B. From the TCP/IP Properties window for the adapter, select Enable TCP/IP Filtering. Configure traffic to be permitted for TCP ports **21** and **80**.

❍ C. From the TCP/IP Properties window for the adapter, select Enable TCP/IP Filtering. Configure traffic to be permitted for UDP ports **80** and **81**.

❍ D. From the TCP/IP Properties window for the adapter, select Enable TCP/IP Filtering. Configure traffic to be permitted for UDP ports **21** and **80**.

Question 37

The NAT protocol is installed and the public and private interfaces have been added. From the properties window for the public connection, you enable DNS name resolution. What else must you do to ensure that internal clients can resolve DNS names?

❍ A. Install a DNS server on the internal network.

❍ B. Configure the internal clients with the IP address of the ISP's DNS servers.

❍ C. Configure the private interface with the IP address of the ISP's DNS servers.

❍ D. Configure the DHCP Allocator to assign internal clients the IP address of the ISP's DNS server.

Question 38

You are working as part of a team that has been asked to implement routing within a large internetwork. Five of the remote offices are being configured with demand-dial connections to the head office. Before beginning the planning phase, the organization's administrators present you with a list of some critical requirements:

- Administration of routing tables should be minimal.
- Changes to the network topology should be propagated immediately.
- The link should be used only when required to reduce costs.
- To reduce the size of the routing tables, routers should be organized into areas.

You propose the following:

- Configure Windows 2000 RRAS servers with one-way nonpersistent demand-dial connections.
- Configure the interfaces to use OSPF.

Which of the following are met by the proposed solution? [Choose all that apply.]

- ❑ A. Administration of routing tables is minimal.
- ❑ B. Changes to the network topology are propagated immediately.
- ❑ C. The link is used only when required to reduce costs.
- ❑ D. Routers can be organized into areas.
- ❑ E. None of the requirements is met.

Question 39

Due to security needs and the different needs of dial-in clients, three remote access policies have been configured. When a remote access client attempts to connect to a remote access server, which of the following statements is true regarding policy evaluation?

- ❍ A. All policies in the list are evaluated.
- ❍ B. The first policy to match the conditions of the connection attempt is evaluated.
- ❍ C. Only the first policy in the list is evaluated.
- ❍ D. The first policy that allows the user remote access is evaluated.

Question 40

Your primary DNS server is located in the corporate head office. The five branch offices are all configured with secondary DNS servers. The WAN links between offices are extremely slow. You want to increase the interval at which secondary servers poll the primary server for updates to the zone file. Which of the following settings should be changed?

❍ A. Retry Interval

❍ B. Polling Interval

❍ C. Refresh Interval

❍ D. Time to Live

Question 41

Your WIN2K server has a dial-up connection to the Internet with ICS enabled. Another administrator recently made some configuration changes to the server. Users now report that there are times when they cannot access Internet resources. What could be causing the problem?

❍ A. ICS has been disabled.

❍ B. The range of IP addresses assigned by the DHCP Allocator has been changed.

❍ C. Demand dialing has been disabled.

❍ D. Name resolution has been disabled on the server.

Question 42

RRAS has been configured on **Win2k01**. **Win2k01** is configured to obtain IP addresses from the DHCP server. The default policy has been configured to allow access, and account properties are configured to control access through the remote access policy. When testing the configuration, you can successfully connect but are unable to access file shares on the internal network by computername. How can you resolve this problem?

❍ A. Configure the DHCP server to assign the IP address of the internal WINS server.

❍ B. Configure **Win2k01** as a WINS proxy agent.

❍ C. Manually configure the IP settings on the client.

❍ D. Configure **Win2k01** as a DHCP relay agent.

Question 43

You create a static mapping for one of the workstations on the network. The workstation obtains its IP address from a DHCP server. Yesterday, clients were able to resolve the NetBIOS name to an IP address. Today, clients report that they are unsuccessful. What must you do?

❍ A. The static mapping must be configured for dynamic updates.

❍ B. Create a client reservation on the DHCP server for the client.

❍ C. Create a client reservation on the WINS server for the client.

❍ D. Delete and re-create the static mapping.

Question 44

You have configured NAT on a Windows 2000 Server. The external interface has been assigned the IP address of **200.205.10.55**. The internal network uses the IP address range of **192.168.0.1–192.168.0.254**. There is a Web server on the internal network that you want Internet users to access. It is configured with the IP address of **192.168.0.24**. How should you proceed?

❍ A. From the properties for the public interface, create a special port mapping port **80** on **200.205.10.55** to port **80** on **192.168.0.24**.

❍ B. From the properties for the private interface, create a special port mapping port **80** on **200.205.10.55** to port **80** on **192.168.0.24**.

❍ C. From the properties for the public interface, create a special port mapping port **21** on **200.205.10.55** to port **21** on **192.168.0.24**.

❍ D. From the properties for the public interface, create a special port mapping port **8080** on **200.205.10.55** to port **8080** on **192.168.0.24**.

Question 45

You have recently deployed a DHCP server to centralize the administration of all IP addresses on the network. Prior to this, they were all statically configured. All users are successfully leasing IP addresses but now report that they can no longer print to the network interface printers. Upon examining the printers' properties, you notice they have been assigned incorrect IP addresses. What should you have done?

❍ A. Defined separate scopes for each of the print devices.

❍ B. Created client reservations for the print devices.

❍ C. Excluded the IP addresses of the print devices from the scope.

❍ D. Created client exclusions for the print devices.

Question 46

A long-term employee is leaving the company. You revoke the user's certificate within the Certificate Authority snap-in. When you check the certificate revocation list, the revoked certificate does not appear. What is the problem?

❍ A. The revoked certificate must be manually copied to the CRL.

❍ B. You must choose the Add to CRL option when revoking the certificate.

❍ C. The publishing interval has not expired.

❍ D. Once the certificate is revoked, the CRL must be manually updated.

Question 47

One of the servers on your network is being reconfigured to optimize performance. Over time, several protocols and services have been installed on the server, some of which are no longer necessary or are used infrequently. When configuring the binding order, which of the following should you do?

❍ A. Bind all protocols to all services for fault tolerance.

❍ B. Place the most commonly used protocols first in the binding order.

❍ C. Place the protocols used least often first in the binding order.

❍ D. Bind all protocols to all network adapters.

Question 48

You have recently made changes to the topology of your internetwork. You now have to change the routes configured in the routing tables. Which of the following will delete an existing route and add a new persistent route?

❍ A.

route delete 192.168.126.0
route -p 192.168.126.0 mask 255.255.255.0 192.168.125.1 metric 2

❍ B.

route delete 192.168.126.0
route add 192.168.126.0 mask 255.255.255.0 192.168.125.1 metric 2

❍ C.

route delete 192.168.126.0
Route -p add 192.168.126.0 mask 255.255.255.0 192.168.125.1 metric 2

❍ D.

route delete 192.168.126.0
route add 192.168.126.0 mask 255.255.255.0 gateway 192.168.125.1
➥metric 2

Question 49

Your primary DNS server is located in the corporate head office. The five branch offices are all configured with secondary DNS servers. The WAN links between offices are extremely slow with no plans to upgrade them. You are now adding a second DNS server to each office to increase fault tolerance should the secondary server within the office or the primary server become unavailable. However, you do not want any more traffic generated across the WAN links from zone transfers. How should you configure the new DNS servers?

❍ A. Configure them as secondary servers. Configure the existing secondary servers as the master name servers.

❍ B. Configure them as caching-only servers. Configure the existing secondary servers as the master name servers.

❍ C. Configure them as secondary servers. Configure the primary name server as the master name server.

❍ D. Configure them as caching-only servers. Configure the primary server as the master name server.

Question 50

Clients on the network are configured to use H-node for NetBIOS name resolution. In what order will they resolve NetBIOS names?

❍ A. NetBIOS name cache, broadcast, WINS, LMHOSTS, HOSTS, DNS

❍ B. NetBIOS name cache, HOSTS, DNS, LMHOSTS, WINS, broadcast

❍ C. NetBIOS name cache, WINS, LMHOSTS, broadcast, Hosts, DNS

❍ D. NetBIOS name cache, WINS, broadcast, LMHOSTS, HOSTS, DNS

Question 51

ICS is enabled on a computer in your home office. You want to be able to play Internet games from one of the other three home office computers. What must you do?

❍ A. Nothing. Once ICS is enabled, all traffic will pass through the shared connection.

❍ B. Install the game on the computer running ICS.

❍ C. Add the TCP or UDP port numbers to the ICS computer that the application uses.

❍ D. Nothing. ICS does not support Internet games over the shared connection.

Question 52

Which of the following are required to install an enterprise root certificate authority? [Choose all that apply.]

❑ A. WINS

❑ B. Commercial CA

❑ C. Active Directory

❑ D. DNS

❑ E. Enterprise subordinate CA

Question 53

Seaside is deploying a DHCP server that will assign IP addresses to clients on four logical subnets. The IP address ranges are as follows:

192.168.0.1–192.168.0.254

192.168.1.1–192.168.1.254

192.168.2.1–192.168.2.254

192.168.3.1–192.168.3.254

When configuring the DHCP server, what should you do first?

❍ A. Create a separate superscope for each range of IP addresses.

❍ B. Create a single superscope, including all four IP address ranges.

❍ C. Create a single scope, including all four IP address ranges.

❍ D. Create a separate scope for each IP address range.

Question 54

If a remote user's connection attempt does not meet the conditions of the first remote access policy, what occurs next?

❍ A. The connection attempt is denied.

❍ B. The properties of the user's account are evaluated.

❍ C. The next policy in the list is evaluated.

❍ D. The profile settings are evaluated.

Question 55

Some of the existing routers on the network are being upgraded to Windows 2000 RRAS servers. You really want to take advantage of security features included with RIPv2 so the interfaces on the new servers are configured to use this routing protocol. You notice that the existing servers using RIPv1 are not communicating with the new network routers. What is the source of the problem?

❍ A. The RIPv1 routers are configured to use broadcasts.

❍ B. The RIPv2 routers are configured to use multicasting.

❍ C. The RIPv1 routers are configured to use multicasting.

❍ D. The RIPv2 routers are configured to use broadcasts.

Question 56

You are receiving a number of calls from users that they are receiving error messages when they try to connect to a secure Web page on your company's Web server. They have no problem connecting to the server with FTP. What should you do?

❍ A. Verify that TCP port **443** is permitted.

❍ B. Verify that TCP port **80** is permitted.

❍ C. Verify that UDP port **443** in permitted.

❍ D. Verify that UDP port **80** is permitted

Question 57

There is currently a single DNS server on the network that is heavily used by clients for name resolution. To improve response time for users, you decide to add a secondary server to the network. How can you ensure that requests are load-balanced between the two servers?

❍ A. You do not need to do anything. Name resolution requests are automatically distributed among servers.

❍ B. Select the Load Balance Requests option on the General tab of the DNS server's properties window.

❍ C. Configure the order of use so half of the clients use the secondary server first and the remaining use the primary server first when resolving hostnames.

❍ D. Select the Load Balance Requests option on the General tab of the zone's properties window.

Question 58

What is the default location of the WINS database?

❍ A. **%systemroot%\System32\WINS**

❍ B. **%systemroot%\WINS\Drivers\Etc**

❍ C. **%systemroot%\Wins\Database\Etc**

❍ D. **%systemroot%\System32\WINS\Etc**

Question 59

NAT has been configured on a Windows 2000 Server. You do not want the DHCP Allocator to assign IP addresses because there is already an existing DHCP server on the network. How should you proceed?

❍ A. Within the Registry on the NAT server, disable the DHCP Allocator.

❍ B. Using the Address Assignment tab, select the option to automatically assign IP addresses by using DHCP.

❍ C. Using the Address Assignment tab, deselect the option to automatically assign IP addresses by using DHCP.

❍ D. Configure internal clients to use the existing DHCP server.

Question 60

Your organization has recently acquired a new company that is being integrated into the existing infrastructure. A new child domain is added to the forest. The existing infrastructure has an enterprise root CA and two subordinate CAs. The subordinate CAs are unable to publish certificates within the new child domain. How can you resolve this problem?

❍ A. Add the subordinate CAs to the Cert Update group within the new domain.

❍ B. Add the subordinate CAs to the Cert Publishers group within the new domain.

❍ C. Add the subordinate CAs to the Cert Users group within the new domain.

❍ D. Create accounts for the new users in the domain where the subordinate CAs reside.

Answer Key for Practice Test 1

1. C	**16.** C	**31.** A, B	**46.** C
2. C	**17.** C	**32.** A, C	**47.** B
3. A, D	**18.** A	**33.** C	**48.** C
4. C	**19.** C	**34.** D	**49.** A
5. A, C	**20.** B, C	**35.** D	**50.** D
6. D	**21.** B	**36.** B	**51.** C
7. A, C, D, F	**22.** A	**37.** C	**52.** C, D
8. A, C, D	**23.** C	**38.** E	**53.** D
9. B	**24.** A, B, C	**39.** B	**54.** C
10. B	**25.** B	**40.** C	**55.** B
11. A	**26.** A	**41.** C	**56.** A
12. D	**27.** A	**42.** D	**57.** C
13. B	**28.** D	**43.** B	**58.** A
14. A	**29.** C	**44.** A	**59.** C
15. A, B	**30.** D	**45.** B	**60.** B

Question 1

Answer C is correct. When clients are configured to use H-node, they contact a NetBIOS name server first. If the server does not respond, a local broadcast will be used to resolve the name. Answer A is incorrect because clients using P-node use only a NetBIOS name server to resolve names.

Answer B is incorrect because clients using B-node perform broadcasts. Answer D is incorrect because clients using M-node perform a broadcast, and then use a NetBIOS name server.

Question 2

Answer C is correct. To use the callback feature, you must select Link Control Protocol (LCP) Extensions from the RRAS server's properties window. Therefore, answers A, B, and D are incorrect.

Question 3

Answers A and D are correct. Both Windows 2000 and BIND 8.1.3 DNS servers support dynamic updates. Therefore, answers B and C are incorrect.

Question 4

Answer C is correct. For a two-way demand-dial connection to work, the user account names used for authentication must be identical to the name assigned to the demand-dial interface name on the calling routers. Therefore, answers A, B, and D are incorrect.

Question 5

Answers A and C are correct. Windows 2000 supports the detection of rogue DHCP servers. For a DHCP server to assign IP addresses to clients, they must first be authorized in Active Directory and DHCP must be installed on a member server or domain controller. Answer B is incorrect because the DHCP server service cannot be installed on a Windows 2000 Professional workstation. Answer D is incorrect because the server must be a member of the domain to be authorized in Active Directory.

Question 6

Answer D is correct. Because the certificate infrastructure should be implemented outside the domain, a standalone CA should be configured. The CA should be configured as a subordinate to a commercial CA so Internet clients are assured of your Web server's identity. Therefore, answers A, B, and C are incorrect.

Question 7

Answers A, C, D, and F are correct. Windows 2000 provides NAT editors for the following protocols: FTP, PPTP, ICMP, and NetBIOS over TCP/IP. Therefore, answers B, E, and G are incorrect.

Question 8

Answers A, C, and D are correct. When configuring TCP/IP filtering, IP traffic can be filtered based on the IP protocol, a UDP port, or a TCP port. Traffic cannot be filtered based on IP addresses; therefore, answer B is incorrect.

Question 9

Answer B is correct. Because Routing and Remote Access is installed by default, the first thing you need to do is enable it within the Routing and Remote Access snap-in; therefore, answer A is incorrect. A remote access policy and profile settings cannot be configured until the service is enabled; therefore, answers C and D are incorrect.

Question 10

Answer B is correct. The first thing that should be verified is that the a shorter lease duration has not been configured. Once that has been verified, you can begin using the other tools to troubleshoot the problem if it continues. Therefore, answers A, C, and D are incorrect.

Question 11

Answer A is correct. Using the `#Pre` option within the LMHOSTS file specifies that a specific record be preloaded into the local cache. Answer B is incorrect because there is no such option. Answer C is incorrect because the `#MH` option indicates a multihomed computer. Answer D is incorrect because the `#Include` option indicates a LMHOSTS file other than the default should be used.

Question 12

Answer D is correct. By configuring caching-only servers within each location, you can decrease the name resolution response time for users. Because the caching-only servers do not maintain any zone information, no traffic is generated from zone transfers. Therefore, answers A, B, and C are incorrect.

Question 13

Answer B is correct. The IP address of `131.107.2.10` is a class B address. Answer A is incorrect because class A addresses are in the range of 1–126. Answer C is incorrect because class C addresses are in the range of 192–223. Answer D is incorrect because class D addresses are in the range of 224–247.

Question 14

Answer A is correct. Because the CA must integrate within Active Directory, an enterprise CA must be configured. An enterprise root CA must be installed because no other CA exists on the network. Answer B is incorrect because a parent CA is required to install an enterprise subordinate CA. Answers C and D are incorrect because standalone CAs do not use Active Directory.

Question 15

Answers A and B are correct. For nonpersistent demand-dial connections, either RIPv1 or RIPv2 can be used. Answer C is incorrect because OSPF is not supported for non-persistent connections. Answer D is incorrect because ICMP is not a routing protocol.

Question 16

Answer C is correct. ICS can be enabled using the Sharing tab within the Properties window for the Internet connection. You can access the properties window through the network and Dial-up Connections applet. Answer A is incorrect because the Networking tab is used to install and configure network services and protocols. Answers B and D are incorrect because ICS is not enabled using the Routing and Remote Access snap-in.

Question 17

Answer C is correct. The WINS database can be backed up automatically by specifying the backup path on the General tab within the WINS server's properties window. Once the backup path is specified, the database is backed up every three hours. Therefore, answers A, B, and D are incorrect.

Question 18

Answer A is correct. If the hostname cannot be resolved using the `nslookup` command, adding a host record to the zone file will allow you to resolve the name to an IP address. Answer B is incorrect because `Wrk02` is not the hostname being resolved. Answers C and D are incorrect because `PTR` records are used to map IP addresses to their associated hostnames.

Question 19

Answer C is correct. If clients have not been configured with the IP address of the default gateway, they cannot access resources outside of their local subnet. Answer A is incorrect because the clients are already successfully leasing IP addresses from the server. Answer B would solve the problem but it would not be the easiest solution; therefore, it is also incorrect. Answer D is incorrect because configuring the DNS server option allows clients to resolve hostnames but does not give them access outside of the local subnet.

Question 20

Answers B and C are correct. Certificate Services can be installed using the Add/Remove Programs applet or during the installation of Windows 2000. Therefore, answers A and D are incorrect.

Question 21

Answer B is correct. ISAKMP/OAKLEY is responsible for negotiating security associations before any IP data is transferred. This includes authentication, hashing, and encryption methods. Answer A is incorrect because this is a management tool used for creating and managing IP Security policies. Answer C is incorrect because the IPSec driver is responsible for securing the data before it is transferred. Answer D is incorrect because the IPSec policy agent is responsible for retrieving policy information.

Question 22

Answer A is correct. When using the Routing and Remote Access Server setup wizard to configure NAT, you select the option to configure an Internet connection server. Therefore, answers B and C are incorrect. Answer D is incorrect because there is no such option.

Question 23

Answer C is correct. The Bandwidth Allocation Protocol (BAP) is used to enhance the functionality of multilink and allow lines to be dynamically added and dropped. Answer A is incorrect because LCP is used by the callback feature. Answer B is incorrect because PPP is used to establish dial-up connections. Answer D is incorrect because EAP is an authentication protocol.

Question 24

Answers A, B, and C are correct. Implementing RIPv2 means the routing tables do not need to be manually updated and changes to the routing table will occur dynamically. RIPv2 also supports security features such as password authentication and RIP route filters. Answer D is incorrect because RIPv2 broadcasts updates to all routers; routers cannot be logically grouped into areas.

Question 25

Answer B is correct. The DHCP service should be installed on a Windows 2000 member server. Because more than one DHCP server will be performing updates, the DHCP servers must be placed in the `DNSUpdateProxy` group. Because domain controllers running DHCP should not be placed in this group, the DHCP server service should be installed on a Windows 2000 member server. Therefore, answers A, C, and D are incorrect.

Question 26

Answer A is correct. To view the statistics for your WINS server, right-click the WINS server within the management console and select Display Server Statistics. Answer B is incorrect because enabling event logging logs errors and warnings to the System log. Answer C is incorrect because there is no such option on the Advanced tab. Answer D is incorrect because configuring the update interval only specifies how often server statistics should be updated.

Question 27

Answer A is correct. Active Directory integrated zones can only be configured on Windows 2000 domain controllers with the DNS server service installed. Therefore, answers B, C, and D are incorrect.

Question 28

Answer D is correct. The Internet layer is responsible for addressing and routing IP packets. Answer A is incorrect because the Application layer is used by applications to access the network. Answer B is incorrect because the Transport layer is responsible for session establishment. Answer C is incorrect because the Network layer is responsible for sending and receiving frames over the physical medium.

Question 29

Answer C is correct. To support browsers other than Internet Explorer, the authentication method for the `CertSrv` virtual directory must be set to Basic. Answer A is incorrect because clients may not support Internet Explorer. Answer B is incorrect because Web-based enrollment can be used with browsers other than Internet Explorer. Answer D is incorrect because there is no client software that needs to be installed.

Question 30

Answer D is correct. Elements of a remote access policy are evaluated in the following order: conditions, permissions, and then profile settings. Therefore, answers A, B, and C are incorrect.

Question 31

Answers A and B are correct. RIPv1 uses broadcasts to dynamically update changes as they occur. Answer C is incorrect because RIPv1 does not support password authentication. Answer D is incorrect because RIPv1 does not support the logical grouping of routers into areas.

Question 32

Answers A and C are correct. By creating a client reservation for each of the print servers, you ensure that they will always lease the same IP address. The IP addresses must also be excluded from the scope to avoid any IP address conflicts. Therefore, answers B and D are incorrect.

Question 33

Answer C is correct. To enable a computer as a WINS proxy, change the `EnableProxy` value to `1` within the local Registry. Answers A and B are incorrect because you do not have to install additional software to enable a WINS proxy. Answer D is incorrect because there is no option called `WINSProxy` within the Registry.

Question 34

Answer D is correct. To use secure updates, the zones must be changed to Active Directory integrated. Secure updates can be enabled using the General tab from the zone's properties window and selecting Only secure updates. Therefore, answers A, B, and C are incorrect.

Question 35

Answer D is correct. Before an enterprise CA can be installed, a DNS server must be available. Answer A is incorrect because enterprise CAs require Active Directory. Answer B is incorrect because WINS is not required. Answer C is incorrect because enterprise CAs are installed to issue certificates to domain users.

Question 36

Answer B is correct. To permit HTTP and FTP traffic, you would have to permit traffic to TCP ports `80` and `21`. Therefore, answers A, C, and D are incorrect.

Question 37

Answer C is correct. For DNS name resolution to occur, the internal interface of the NAT server must be configured with the IP address of the ISP's DNS server. Therefore, answers A, B, and D are incorrect.

Question 38

Answer E is correct. Because OSPF cannot be used with nonpersistent demand-dial connections, none of the requirements would be met by the proposed solution. Therefore, answers A, B, C, and D are incorrect.

Question 39

Answer B is correct. The first elements in a remote access policy to be evaluated are the conditions. The first policy to match the conditions of the connection attempt is evaluated for permissions. If the permissions of that policy deny the user access, the connection attempt is denied. Therefore, answers A, C, and D are incorrect.

Question 40

Answer C is correct. The `refresh` interval determines how often the secondary servers poll the primary server for updates to the zone database file. Answer A is incorrect because the `retry` interval determines how often a secondary server will continue to contact the primary server if it does not respond. Answer B is incorrect because there is no such configurable setting as the `polling` interval. Answer D is incorrect because TTL specifies how long records from that zone should remain in the cache.

Question 41

Answer C is correct. If demand dialing has been enabled, clients will only be able to access the Internet when the ICS server has an Internet connection established. Once disconnected, the server will not auto-dial the connection for internal clients. Answer A is incorrect because if ICS was disabled, clients would never be able to access the Internet. Answer B is incorrect because the IP address range assigned out with ICS is not configurable. Answer D is incorrect because name resolution with ICS is in the form of the DNS proxy, which cannot be disabled.

Question 42

Answer D is correct. To have optional parameters assigned to remote access clients, the DHCP relay agent must be configured on the RAS server. Answer A is incorrect because the relay agent needs to be configured to pass the messages between the remote client and the DHCP server. Answer B is incorrect because the WINS proxy agent is used to forward name resolution requests and updates to the WINS database between subnets connected by routers. The IP settings can be manually configured but it's simpler from an administrative perspective to use the relay agent.

Question 43

Answer B is correct. If a static mapping has been configured for a DHCP client, a client reservation must be configured on the DHCP server so the client always leases the same IP address. Answer A is incorrect because static mappings cannot be enabled for dynamic updates. Answer C is incorrect because client reservations are not configured on the WINS server. Answer D is incorrect because, although the record could be deleted and re-created, it would have to be done each time the client leased a new IP address.

Question 44

Answer A is correct. For the Web server to be accessible to Internet users, a special port must be created that maps port `80` and the public IP address of the NAT server to port `80` and the private IP address of the internal Web server. Therefore, answers B, C, and D are incorrect.

Question 45

Answer B is correct. To ensure the IP address of the network interface printers did not change when the DHCP server was placed on the network, client reservation should have been defined. Therefore, answers A and C are incorrect. Answer D is incorrect because there is no such option in DHCP called a client exclusion.

Question 46

Answer C is correct. Revoked certificates do not appear on the CRL until the publishing interval has expired. This is not the next time that the CRL will be updated. Answers A and D are incorrect because the revoked certificates will automatically appear on the CRL. How long it takes for them to appear depends on the publishing interval. Although the CA can be manually published, it is not necessary. Answer B is incorrect because there is no such option.

Question 47

Answer B is correct. When configuring the binding order, the most frequently used protocols should be listed first to optimize network communication and traffic. Therefore, answers A, C, and D are incorrect.

Question 48

Answer C is correct. The correct syntax when adding a persistent route adding the `route` command is `route -p add` *`<network> mask <subnetmask> <gateway> metric`*. Therefore, answers A, B, and D are incorrect.

Question 49

Answer A is correct. You can increase fault tolerance by configuring the servers as secondary servers. The existing secondary servers can be configured as the master name servers so no extra traffic will be generated across the WAN link from zone transfers. Answers B and D are incorrect because caching-only servers would not provide fault tolerance for the existing zone. Answer C is incorrect because configuring the primary server as the master name server means the new secondary servers would get their zone information from this server, generating more traffic across the WAN links.

Question 50

Answer D is correct. When a client is configured for H-node, it resolves NetBIOS names using the following method: NetBIOS name cache, WINS, broadcast, LMHOSTS, HOSTS, DNS. Therefore, answers A, B, and C are incorrect.

Question 51

Answer C is correct. For applications to function through the ICS computer, you must configure the TCP and/or UDP port numbers used by the application on the ICS computer. Therefore, answers A, B, and D are incorrect.

Question 52

Answers C and D are correct. To install an enterprise CA, Active Directory and DNS must be present. Answer A is incorrect because WINS is not required. Answers B and E are incorrect because a root CA is not made a child CA. There can be only one root CA in a hierarchy and a root CA cannot be made subordinate to another CA.

Question 53

Answer D is correct. Before you can create the superscope, you must define a separate scope for each range of IP addresses. Answers A and B are incorrect because the scopes must be defined first. Answer C is incorrect because a single scope can include only IP addresses from a single network ID.

Question 54

Answer C is correct. If the connection attempt does not match the conditions of the first policy in the list, the conditions of the next policy are evaluated. The permissions and profile settings of a policy are not evaluated until the connection attempt meets the conditions of a policy. Therefore, answers A, B, and D are incorrect.

Question 55

Answer B is correct. RIPv2 supports using multicasting for routing table updates. Because RIPv1 supports only broadcasts, RIPv1 routers cannot communicate with any RIPv2 routers configured to use multicasting. Answer A is incorrect because RIPv1 routers only support broadcasts. Answer C is incorrect because RIPv1 routers cannot use multicasting for routing table updates. Answer D is incorrect because the RIPv2 routers must be configured to use broadcasts to communicate with the RIPv1 routers.

Question 56

Answer A is correct. If users are unable to access secure Web pages, verify that TCP traffic is permitted for port `443`. This is the port used by secure

HTTP (HTTPS). Answers B and D are incorrect because HTTPS uses port 443. Answer C is incorrect because HTTPS uses TCP, not UDP.

Question 57

Answer C is correct. By configuring the order of use (either manually or using DHCP options), you can specify which DNS server clients will contact first when resolving hostnames. To load balance requests, configure half the clients to use the primary server first and the other half to use the secondary server first. Answer A is incorrect because requests are not automatically load balanced between DNS servers. Answers B and D are incorrect because there is no Load Balance Requests option available from either property window.

Question 58

Answer A is correct. The default location for the WINS database is `%systemroot%\System32\Wins`. Therefore, answers B, C, and D are incorrect.

Question 59

Answer C is correct. If you do not want to use the DHCP Allocator included with NAT to assign IP addresses to internal clients, you must use the Address Assignment tab within the properties of Network Address Translator and deselect the option to automatically assign IP address by using DHCP. Answer A is incorrect because this is configured within Routing and Remote Access. Answer B is incorrect because selecting this option enables the DHCP Allocator. Answer D is incorrect because clients cannot be configured to use a particular DHCP server.

Question 60

Answer B is correct. For the subordinate CAs to publish certificates within the new domain, they must be added to the Cert publishers group within the new child domain. Therefore, answers A, C, and D are incorrect.

Practice Test 2

Question 1

You create a one-way demand-dial interface between a branch office and corporate office. The connection is used by clients for Web access. You only want HTTP traffic to initiate the connection. How should you proceed?

❍ A. Create a RIP route filter for port **80**.

❍ B. Configure an IP demand-dial filter for port **80**.

❍ C. Create a RIP route filter for port **21**.

❍ D. Configure a connection filter for port **80**.

Question 2

How can you prevent the reuse of previously generated session keys?

❍ A. Unassign and assign the IP Security Policy.

❍ B. From the rules Properties window, select the Do Not Use Previous Keys option.

❍ C. From the rules Properties window, select the Master Key Perfect Forward Secrecy option.

❍ D. Restart the IPSec-enabled client workstation.

Question 3

Your network consists of three subnets: Subnet A, Subnet B, and Subnet C. There is an RRAS server on Subnet C configured with a range of IP addresses to assign to remote access clients. There are two DNS servers on the network: **DNS01** and **DNS02**. You would like remote access clients to use **DNS02**. What should you do?

❍ A. Configure the RRAS server to use DHCP. Install a DHCP server on Subnet C. Configure a scope on the DHCP server for the remote access clients. Configure the DHCP relay agent on the DNS server.

❍ B. Install a DHCP server on the network and configure the RRAS server to use DHCP for IP address assignment. Configure a scope on the DHCP server for the remote access clients.

❍ C. Install a DHCP server on the network. Configure a scope on the DHCP server for remote access clients. Configure RRAS to use DHCP. Configure the relay agent on the DHCP server.

❍ D. Install a DHCP server on the network. Configure a scope on the DHCP server for remote access clients. Configure RRAS to use DHCP. Configure the relay agent on the RRAS server.

Question 4

Several DHCP servers are being deployed in different domains throughout the forest. Of which group must you be a member to authorize the DHCP servers?

❍ A. DNSUpdateProxy

❍ B. Enterprise Admins

❍ C. Domain Admins

❍ D. Administrators

Question 5

For security purposes, your senior administrator does not want users to be able to encrypt any of their files. He asks you to remove this capability for all users within the domain. How should you proceed?

❍ A. Edit the domain group policy. Delete the Encrypted Data Recovery Agents container. Initialize the empty policy.

❍ B. Disable the Encrypted Data Recovery Agents container within Active Directory Users and Computers.

❍ C. Delete the Encrypted Data Recovery Agents container within the Certificate Authority snap-in.

❍ D. Delete the Encrypted Data Recovery Agents container within the Certificates snap-in.

Question 6

A routed IP network has a mixture of WINS and non-WINS clients. Three of the seven subnets contain WINS servers. Several users report that they are unable to browse hosts on other subnets. Upon investigating the reports, you discover that the problem is affecting only non-WINS clients. How can the B-node broadcasts be resolved across the network?

❍ A. Configure static mappings for the non-WINS clients.

❍ B. Install a WINS proxy on each subnet that does not have a local WINS server.

❍ C. Configure replication between the three WINS servers.

❍ D. Configure a DHCP relay agent on each subnet.

Question 7

Seaside is planning its DNS implementation. The network currently consists of 250 workstations running Windows 2000 Professional and five Windows 2000 servers. Three of the servers are domain controllers and the remaining two are member servers. The workstations and servers are spread out between two office locations. The following requirements must be met:

- Fault tolerance must be provided for the zone.
- Hostnames should be cached on the DNS servers.
- Users should be able to resolve hostnames locally.
- Dynamic updates should only be performed by specific users.

You propose the following:

- Install DNS on the two member servers.
- Configure one as the primary server and the other as the secondary server.
- Place a DNS server in each of the offices.
- Enable dynamic updates for the zone.

Which of the following are met by your proposal? [Choose all that apply.]

- ❑ A. Fault tolerance is provided for the zone.
- ❑ B. Hostnames are cached on the DNS server.
- ❑ C. Users can resolve hostnames locally.
- ❑ D. Dynamic updates can be performed only by specific users and groups.

Question 8

You have recently added two new Windows 2000 Professional workstations to the network. Existing computers access the Internet through a NAT server. How can you configure the new computers to use the NAT server?

- ❍ A. Install the NAT client on both workstations.
- ❍ B. Configure Internet Explorer to use a proxy server.
- ❍ C. Configure the gateway on each client to point to the internal IP address of the NAT server.
- ❍ D. Configure the clients to use DHCP.

Question 9

You have a Windows NT 4.0 member server configured as a RAS server and a Windows 2000 RRAS server running on your Windows 2000 domain. The domain is running in native mode. Remote access users can successfully authenticate with the Windows 2000 server but not with the Windows NT 4.0 server. What requirement must be met for users to authenticate with the Windows NT RAS server?

❍ A. Permissions must be compatible with pre-Windows 2000 servers.

❍ B. The domain must be running in mixed mode.

❍ C. All user accounts must be re-created on the Windows NT system.

❍ D. The Windows NT system must be upgraded to a BDC.

Question 10

During certain times of the day, your WINS server is overburdened with name registration requests. How can you increase the number of name registration requests that a WINS server can handle so clients do not receive negative responses?

❍ A. Use persistent connections.

❍ B. Use burst handling.

❍ C. Add another WINS server.

❍ D. Configure the refresh interval.

Question 11

You notice that the CRL is published only on a weekly basis. You need to change the interval to once a day. How should you proceed?

❍ A. Edit the Registry on the CA.

❍ B. Open the Certificates snap-in. Edit the Properties of the Issued Certificates container.

❍ C. Open the Certificates Authority snap-in. Edit the Properties of the Revoked Certificates container.

❍ D. Open the Certificates snap-in. Edit the Properties of the Revoked Certificates container.

❍ E. Open the Certificates Authority snap-in. Edit the Properties of the Issued Certificates container.

Question 12

You configured a demand-dial interface. You have been asked to reduce the cost associated with using the link. Upon examining the settings of the interface, you notice that it is a persistent connection. You change it to a demand-dial. You want the connection terminated after five minutes of inactivity. How should you proceed?

- ❍ A. Configure the dial-out hours for the connection.
- ❍ B. Configure the redial attempts to five minutes.
- ❍ C. Configure the idle time before disconnect to five minutes.
- ❍ D. Configure the maximum session time to five minutes.

Question 13

Your network consists of two subnets: subnet A and subnet B. Subnet A has a WINS server that is used by all clients on the network to resolve NetBIOS names to IP addresses. A Windows 2000 DHCP server assigns IP addresses to clients. The DHCP option **044** WINS/NBNS Servers option is configured at the scope level to assign clients the IP address of **WINSRVA**. You move the WINS server from subnet A to subnet B and configure the **044** WINS/NBNS option at the server level to assign clients the new IP address of the WINS server. You discover that clients are still being assigned the old IP address. What is causing the problem?

- ❍ A. Clients must use the **ipconfig /renew** command to obtain the new WINS IP address.
- ❍ B. The IP address of the WINS server must be statically configured on client workstations.
- ❍ C. You must configure the **046** WINS/NBT node type.
- ❍ D. The new **044** WINS/NBNS option has to be configured at the scope level.

Question 14

You have been asked to ensure that the IP Security policy put into place secures all communications while still allowing non-IPSec aware clients to authenticate. Which of the following policies should you use?

- ❍ A. Client (respond only)
- ❍ B. Server (request security)
- ❍ C. Secure server (require security)
- ❍ D. Secure client (respond only)

Question 15

You want to clear the contents of the cache on your DNS server. How can you most easily accomplish this?

❍ A. Uninstall the DNS Server Service.

❍ B. Delete the **cache.dns** file.

❍ C. Use the Clear Cache option from the DNS server's property window.

❍ D. Use the Clear Cache option from the Action menu.

Question 16

Which of the following statements are true of Network Address Translation? [Choose all that apply.]

❑ A. NAT only uses a fixed range of IP addresses to assign to clients.

❑ B. NAT supports multiple public IP addresses.

❑ C. NAT supports a configurable range of IP addresses for internal clients.

❑ D. Internal services cannot be made available to Internet users with NAT.

Question 17

Your network consists of three UNIX servers that provide name resolution services. The servers are all configured with static IP addresses. How can you ensure that the DHCP server does not assign these three IP addresses to any DHCP clients on the network?

❍ A. Configure client reservations for the three UNIX servers.

❍ B. Exclude the three IP addresses from the scope.

❍ C. Place the UNIX servers on a separate subnet.

❍ D. Create a superscope for the three IP addresses.

Question 18

You want to give a specific user on the network the capability to view the WINS database. However, you are concerned about the user making configuration changes. How can you limit the user's permissions so they can only view the database contents?

❍ A. Add the user account to the Administrators group.

❍ B. Add the user account to the Domain Admins groups.

❍ C. Add the user account to WINS Administrators.

❍ D. Add the user account to WINS Users.

Question 19

RRAS is installed on **Server1**. All remote access clients are running Windows 2000 Professional. You want to configure the most secure authentication protocol. Which of the following should you enable?

❍ A. PAP

❍ B. CHAP

❍ C. MS-CHAP version1

❍ D. MS-CHAP version2

Question 20

You have recently moved your small home office to a new location. The network now consists of five computers with no plans for expansion. You perform all network administrative tasks, although your experience and knowledge is very limited. There is currently one Internet connection. Which of the following would be the best solution for Internet connectivity without incurring additional costs?

❍ A. Dedicated Internet connections

❍ B. ICS

❍ C. RIP

❍ D. NAT

Question 21

Which of the following options ensures that routes learned from a network are not announced on that network?

❍ A. Triggered updates

❍ B. Split horizon

❍ C. Periodic announcement interval

❍ D. Clean-up updates

Question 22

A group of servers has been placed in an OU. An IPSec policy is created and configured. What is your next step in applying the policy to the OU?

❍ A. Use the **secedit /refreshpolicy machine_policy** command.

❍ B. Restart the servers.

❍ C. Enable the IP security policy.

❍ D. Assign the IP security policy.

Question 23

You have finished upgrading the workstations on your network to Windows 2000 Professional. The primary and secondary DNS servers are running on Windows NT 4.0 domain controllers. There is also a Windows 2000 DHCP server. Upon examining the zone database, you notice that the records are not being dynamically updated. What must you do?

❍ A. Upgrade the Windows NT 4.0 DNS servers to Windows 2000 DNS.

❍ B. Install service pack 4 or higher on the Windows NT 4.0 DNS servers.

❍ C. Configure the clients to perform dynamic updates through the properties of TCP/IP.

❍ D. Configure the DHCP server to perform the updates on behalf of clients.

Question 24

You have recently configured an Enterprise CA on your company's network. You want to see the certificates that have currently been issued. Where can you go to view such information?

❍ A. Under Issued Certificates within the Certificates console.

❍ B. Under Issued Certificates within Active Directory Users and Computers.

❍ C. Under Issued Certificates within Computer Management.

❍ D. Under Issued Certificates within the Certificate Authority snap-in.

Question 25

You have a Windows 2000 DNS server and a Windows 2000 DHCP server on the network. Both are configured as member servers in the domain. The DHCP server is configured to update all records with the DNS server because clients are running Windows NT 4.0. After the workstations are upgraded to Windows 2000 Professional, the DHCP server is configured to no longer update the DNS server. However, some of the Windows 200 clients are unable to update their records. What has caused this to occur?

❍ A. The DHCP server was not a member of the **DNSUpdateProxy** group.

❍ B. The workstations have not been configured to perform dynamic updates.

❍ C. The DNS server is no longer configured to accept dynamic updates.

❍ D. The clients are not configured with the IP address of the DNS server.

Question 26

The WINS server on the local subnet is configured as a replication partner with other WINS servers on the network and you are now concerned about the integrity of the WINS database. How can you verify the entries within the local WINS servers database?

❍ A. Back up and restore the WINS database.

❍ B. Use the Verify Database Consistency option.

❍ C. Use the Verify WINS Entries options.

❍ D. Force replication between the WINS servers.

Question 27

Which of the following DNS servers support SRV records? [Choose all that apply.]

❑ A. Windows 2000

❑ B. BIND 4.9.6

❑ C. BIND 8.1.3

❑ D. Windows NT 4.0

Question 28

Which of the following protocols can be used to establish a VPN tunnel with a Windows 2000 VPN server? [Choose all that apply.]

❑ A. PPP

❑ B. PPTP

❑ C. SLIP

❑ D. L2TP

Question 29

You are configuring a user account on the answering router that will be used to authenticate the calling router. Which of the following tasks should be done when configuring the password options? [Choose all that apply.]

❑ A. Enable User Must Change Password at Next Logon

❑ B. Disable Password Never Expires

❑ C. Enable Password Never Expires

❑ D. Disable User Must Change Password at Next Logon

Question 30

You've just revoked a certificate for an employee who has been terminated from the organization. You'd like to publish the CRL immediately instead of waiting for the publishing interval to expire. How should you proceed?

❍ A. Right-click the revoked certificate and choose Publish Now.

❍ B. Right-click the Revoked Certificates container and choose Publish.

❍ C. Right-click the CRL container and choose Update.

❍ D. Right-click the CRL container and choose Publish.

Question 31

Your network hosts a single NetWare server and multiple Windows 2000 servers. The NetWare server is running version 3.12. How should you configure the frame type?

❍ A. The frame type must be manually configured for **802.3**.

❍ B. The frame type must be manually configured for **802.2**.

- ❍ C. Leave the frame type to autodetect.
- ❍ D. Leave the frame type to autoselect.

Question 32

Which of the following statements are true regarding Internet Connection Sharing?

- ❍ A. ICS can only be enabled on computers running Windows 2000 Server.
- ❍ B. ICS supports a fixed range of IP addresses with the DHCP Allocator.
- ❍ C. Additional software must be installed on client workstations to use ICS.
- ❍ D. ICS is enabled through Routing and Remote Access.

Question 33

You have just finished installing DNS. You need to add a record into the zone file for the mail server on the domain. Which type of resource record should be created?

- ❍ A. **A**
- ❍ B. **MX**
- ❍ C. **PTR**
- ❍ D. **CNAME**

Question 34

Users on the network require remote access. All users should have the same remote access security requirements except the Administrators group. How should you configure RRAS?

- ❍ A. Create two groups within RRAS, one for Users and one for Administrators. Create two remote access policies and use the Windows Groups condition to apply each policy to the appropriate set of users.
- ❍ B. Create two groups within Active Directory User and Computers, one for Users and one for Administrators. Create two remote access policies and use the Windows Groups condition to apply each policy to the appropriate set of users.

❍ C. Create two groups within RRAS. Configure different settings within a single policy for each group.

❍ D. Create two access policies. Using the Dial-in tab for each user account, specify which remote access policy should be applied.

Question 35

Your internetwork consists of 10 subnets. All subnets are connected using Windows 2000 RRAS servers. Persistent demand-dial connections have been created between all routes. You do not want an increase in broadcast traffic from routing table updates. Changes should be propagated immediately. Which of the following should you implement?

❍ A. Static routes

❍ B. ICMP

❍ C. OSPF

❍ D. RIPv1

Question 36

Which of the following URLs can be used to access the Web-based enrollment page?

❍ A. **http://<servername>/CertEnroll/default.asp**

❍ B. **http://<servername>/CertSrv/default.asp**

❍ C. **http://<servername>/CertWeb/default.asp**

❍ D. **http://<servername>/CertIssue/default.asp**

Question 37

In which order are DHCP options applied?

❍ A. Scope, Class, Client, Server

❍ B. Client, Class, Scope, Server

❍ C. Server, Scope, Class, Client

❍ D. Class, Server, Scope, Client

Question 38

Which of the following name-resolution methods is used by a client configured to use M-node?

❍ A. Broadcast and then NetBIOS name server

❍ B. Broadcast only

❍ C. NetBIOS name server only

❍ D. NetBIOS name server and then broadcast

Question 39

Workstations on the internal network will access the Internet through a Windows 2000 Server configured for NAT. You have been assigned multiple public IP addresses. How should you configure the public interface of the NAT server?

❍ A. Configure multiple IP addresses through the properties of TCP/IP.

❍ B. Using the Address Assignment tab within the Network Address Translation properties window.

❍ C. Using the Address Pool tab within the Network Address Translation properties window.

❍ D. Using the Address Pool tab within the properties window of the public connection.

Question 40

You have recently placed a Windows 2000 server that was running in a NetWare environment on your Windows 2000 network. TCP/IP needed to be installed and NWLink was removed. Which of the following commands can you use to verify that the new server can communicate with hosts on the network using TCP/IP?

❍ A. **ipconfig**

❍ B. **ping**

❍ C. **arp**

❍ D. **icmp**

Question 41

Which of the following commands allows you to clear the cache on a Windows 2000 Professional workstation?

❍ A. **ipconfig /clearcache**

❍ B. **ipconfig /all**

❍ C. **ipconfig /flushdns**

❍ D. **ipconfig /cleardns**

Question 42

You want to increase the amount of time that must lapse before a client is required to renew its NetBIOS name with the WINS server. Which of the following parameters should you configure?

❍ A. Update Interval

❍ B. Renew Interval

❍ C. Refresh Interval

❍ D. Registration Interval

Question 43

You install the DHCP server service on a Windows 2000 member server. The server has been authorized and a scope has been configured. When you use the **ipconfig** command on the Windows 2000 Professional workstations, you find that they are all assigned an IP address in the range of **169.254.x.x**. What is causing the problem?

❍ A. The clients are not DHCP-enabled.

❍ B. The DHCP scope has not been activated.

❍ C. The DHCP server has not been activated.

❍ D. The DHCP server service must be installed on a domain controller.

Question 44

Your senior network administrator has informed you that an employee is leaving the company for unspecified reasons. You have been asked to revoke the user's certificate immediately. How should you proceed?

❍ A. Revoke the certificate through the properties of the user account.

❍ B. Revoke the certificate within the Certificate snap-in.

❍ C. Revoke the certificate within the Certificate Manager console.

❍ D. Revoke the certificate within the Certificate Authority snap-in.

Question 45

You have 20 clients that will be accessing your VPN server. You need to increase the number of available PPTP ports. How can you accomplish this?

❍ A. Within the Routing and Remote Access console, open the Properties window for the server and select the Ports tab.

❍ B. Within the Routing and Remote Access console, open the Properties window for the remote access policy and select the Ports tab.

❍ C. Within the Routing and Remote Access console, open the Properties window for the Ports option.

❍ D. Within the Routing and Remote Access console, open the Properties window for the Ports option and select the PPTP tab.

Question 46

A single Internet connection will be shared among 10 workstations. You want to be able to continue using the existing DHCP server and the existing IP address scheme while not incurring additional costs. Which of the following solutions should you choose?

❍ A. NAT

❍ B. RIP

❍ C. ICS

❍ D. CIS

Question 47

You are implementing an IP security policy for your network. It's a low security environment, so secure communications are not required. The policy you enable should allow IPSec-aware clients to use secure communications when they request it. Which of the following policies should you use?

❍ A. Server (request security)

❍ B. Secure server (require security)

❍ C. Client (respond only)

❍ D. Secure client (request security)

Question 48

Your internetwork consists of 10 subnets. All subnets are connected using Windows 2000 RRAS servers. Non-persistent demand-dial connections have been configured. You do not want to manually update routing tables. You want to configure password authentication between routers. Which of the following should you implement?

❍ A. Static routes

❍ B. ICMP

❍ C. OSPF

❍ D. RIPv2

Question 49

Two DHCP servers are configured on a network with two subnets. How can you configure the scopes so the DHCP servers can provide fault tolerance for one another?

❍ A. Configure replication to occur between the two DHCP servers.

❍ B. Nothing needs to be done because DHCP servers on the same network share scope information to provide fault tolerance.

❍ C. Configure each server with a range of IP addresses for both subnets.

❍ D. Configure all clients with the IP address of both DHCP servers.

Question 50

You are trying to configure secure updates on your DNS server. When you open the property window for the zone you do not see the Only Secure Updates option. What is causing this to occur?

❍ A. You are not logged on as the administrator.

❍ B. You do not have permission to dynamically update the zone database.

❍ C. The zone is configured as an Active Directory integrated zone.

❍ D. The zone is configured as a standard primary zone.

Question 51

Which of the following statements is true in regards to two-way demand-dial connections?

❍ A. The user account name on the answering router must match the demand-dial interface name on the calling router.

❍ B. The demand-dial interface names must be identical.

❍ C. The user account names on both routers must be identical.

❍ D. The user account name on the answering router must be different than the interface name on the calling router.

Question 52

You are installing a RAS server on the network to provide business managers with remote access. You need to meet the following requirements:

- Only business managers should be permitted access.
- Users in this group should have access any time of the day except weekends.
- Remote clients should be automatically assigned an IP address.
- Remote clients should be assigned optional parameters needed to communicate on the internal network.

You perform the following tasks:

- Enable routing and remote access.
- Configure the RAS server with a range of IP addresses.

- Configure the user account properties to control access through a remote access policy.
- Delete the default remote access policy and create a new one.
- Edit the conditions of the profile to only allow access to the remote users group and allow use from Monday through Friday with no restrictions on time.
- Set the permissions of the policy to allow access.

Which of the following requirements are met? [Choose all that apply.]

❑ A. Only business managers are permitted access.

❑ B. Users can dial in anytime between Monday and Friday.

❑ C. All remote users are assigned an IP address.

❑ D. All remote users are assigned any required optional parameters.

Question 53

You would like to edit the ACL of existing templates to limit which types of certificates users are permitted to enroll for. How can you change the permissions assigned to certificate templates?

❍ A. Within Active Directory Users and Computers.

❍ B. Within the Certificate Authority snap-in.

❍ C. Within Active Directory Sites and Services.

❍ D. Within the Certificate snap-in.

Question 54

Which of the following components does TCP/IP use to determine whether a destination host is local or remote?

❍ A. IP address

❍ B. Subnet mask

❍ C. Default gateway

❍ D. IP filter

Question 55

You are in charge of implementing DHCP on the local subnet. The subnet consists of 150 Windows 2000 Professional workstations, 20 Windows 95 workstations, three Windows 2000 domain controllers, and two Windows 2000 DNS servers. The domain controllers are all configured with static IP addresses. With your implementation, the following requirements must be met:

- All hosts must be assigned a unique IP address.
- There should be no IP address conflicts on the network.
- Host and PTR records for all clients should be updated by the DHCP server.
- All clients should be configured with the IP address of the default gateway.

You perform the following tasks:

- Install DHCP on a member server.
- Authorize the server.
- Configure and activate a scope.
- Configure the `003` router option at the scope level.
- Configure the DHCP server to Always Update DNS and Enable updates for DNS clients that do not support dynamic updates.

Which of the following requirements are met by your implementation? [Choose all that apply.]

- ❑ A. All hosts are assigned an IP address.
- ❑ B. IP address conflicts are eliminated.
- ❑ C. All host and PTR records are updated by the DHCP server.
- ❑ D. Clients are configured with the IP address of the default gateway.

Question 56

If a client is configured to use P-node for name resolution, which of the following methods are used to resolve NetBIOS names to IP addresses?

- ❍ A. NetBIOS name server
- ❍ B. Broadcast
- ❍ C. NetBIOS name server and then broadcast
- ❍ D. Broadcast and then NetBIOS name server

Question 57

An IP address of **192.168.0.1** belongs to which of the following address classes?

❍ A. Class A

❍ B. Class B

❍ C. Class C

❍ D. Class D

Question 58

Which of the following parameters can be used with the **route** command to ensure a static route is not deleted from the routing table upon restart?

❍ A. **/f**

❍ B. **/s**

❍ C. **/r**

❍ D. **/p**

Question 59

You are installing a RAS server on the network to provide business managers with remote access. The following requirements must be met:

- Only business managers should be permitted access.
- Users in this group should have access any time of the day except weekends.
- Remote clients should be automatically assigned an IP address.
- Remote clients should be assigned optional parameters needed to communicate on the internal network.

You perform the following tasks:

- Enable Routing and Remote Access.
- Configure the RAS server to use DHCP and configure the relay agent component.
- Configure the user account properties to control access through a remote access policy.

- Delete the default remote access policy and create a new one.
- Create a new group called `remoteusers` within the Active Directory Users and Computers snap-in and add the business managers.
- Edit the conditions of the profile to allow access to only the remote users group and allow use from Monday through Friday with no restrictions on time.
- Set the permissions of the policy to allow access.

Which of the following requirements are met? [Choose all that apply.]

- ❑ A. Only business managers are permitted access.
- ❑ B. Users can dial in anytime between Monday and Friday.
- ❑ C. All remote users are assigned an IP address.
- ❑ D. All remote users are assigned any required optional parameters.

Question 60

You are configuring a LMHOSTS file for use by clients to resolve NetBIOS names to IP addresses. To facilitate the logon process, you want to place entries in the file for domain controllers on the network. Which of the following directives should be included when creating the entries for the domain controllers?

- ❍ A. **#pre**
- ❍ B. **#MH**
- ❍ C. **#Include**
- ❍ D. **#DOM:domain_name**

Answer Key for Practice Test 2

1. B	**16.** B, C	**31.** C	**46.** A
2. C	**17.** B	**32.** B	**47.** C
3. D	**18.** C	**33.** B	**48.** D
4. B	**19.** D	**34.** B	**49.** C
5. A	**20.** B	**35.** C	**50.** D
6. B	**21.** B	**36.** B	**51.** A
7. A, B, C	**22.** D	**37.** C	**52.** B, C
8. C	**23.** A	**38.** A	**53.** C
9. A	**24.** D	**39.** D	**54.** B
10. B	**25.** A	**40.** B	**55.** A, C, D
11. C	**26.** B	**41.** C	**56.** A
12. C	**27.** A, B, C	**42.** B	**57.** C
13. D	**28.** B, D	**43.** B	**58.** D
14. B	**29.** C, D	**44.** D	**59.** A, B, C, D
15. D	**30.** B	**45.** C	**60.** D

Question 1

Answer B is correct. By configuring an IP demand-dial filter, you can specify which types of IP traffic can initiate the connection. The IP demand-dial filter must be configured for port `80`. Answers A and C are incorrect because RIP route filters are used to control routing table updates. Answer D is incorrect because there is no such option as a connection filter.

Question 2

Answer C is correct. By selecting the Master Key Perfect Forward Secrecy option, session key information will not be reused. Therefore, answers B and D are incorrect. Answer A is incorrect because there is no such option available.

Question 3

Answer D is correct. Install a DHCP server on Subnet C and configure it with a scope for remote access clients. The scope should assign the clients the IP address of the DHCP server. Configure RRAS to use DHCP and configure it as a relay agent. This ensures remote users are assigned the IP address of the DNS server. Therefore, answers A, B, and C are incorrect.

Question 4

Answer B is correct. To authorize DHCP servers throughout the forest, the user account you log on with must be a member of the Enterprise Admins group. Therefore, answers A, C, and D are incorrect.

Question 5

Answer A is correct. The capability for users to encrypt files can be removed by deleting the Encrypted Data Recovery Agents container within the Active Directory Users and Computers snap-in and initializing the empty policy. Therefore, answers B, C, and D are incorrect.

Question 6

Answer B is correct. To allow B-node broadcasts to be resolved across the network, a WINS proxy agent must be configured on each subnet. The WINS proxy agent listens for B-node broadcasts and passes the requests to a WINS server on another subnet, resolving the name on behalf of the client. Therefore, answers A, C, and D are incorrect.

Question 7

Answers A, B, and C are correct. Fault tolerance is provided for the zone because a secondary server is configured with a copy of the zone information. Name resolutions are cached because this is the default behavior of DNS servers. Clients can resolve names locally because each location has a DNS server providing name resolution services. Answer D is incorrect because secure updates must be enabled to specify which users and groups are permitted to perform dynamic updates.

Question 8

Answer C is correct. To configure a client to use a NAT server, configure the properties of TCP/IP on the workstation so the IP address of the default gateway is pointing to the internal IP address of the NAT server. Therefore, answers B and D are incorrect. Answer A is incorrect because additional software is not required.

Question 9

Answer A is correct. For users to authenticate with the Windows NT remote access server in a native mode domain, permissions must be compatible with pre–Windows 2000 servers. This grants the Everyone group read access to Active Directory objects. Therefore, answers B, C, and D are incorrect.

Question 10

Answer B is correct. Burst handling allows an administrator to increase the number of registration requests that a WINS server can accept without actually registering them in the WINS database. Answer A is incorrect because persistent connections are used for replication. Answer C is incorrect because although a second WINS server can be configured, it is less costly to configure burst handling. Answer D is incorrect because there is no such refresh interval in WINS.

Question 11

Answer C is correct. The default publishing interval for the CRL is once a week. To change the value, you edit the properties of the Revoked Certificates container within the Certificate Authorities snap-in. This makes answers A, B, and D incorrect.

Question 12

Answer C is correct. By configuring the Idle time before hanging up option, you can specify how long the connection must be idle before the connection is terminated. Answer A is incorrect because the dial-out hours determine when the connection can be used. Answer B is incorrect because the redial attempts option specifies the number of times the number should be automatically redialed. Answer D is incorrect because the maximum session time determines how long a client can remain connected to a server. If a client exceeds that time, it will be disconnected automatically, which could cause data loss.

Question 13

Answer D is correct. Because there is an existing `004` WINS/NBNS option configured at the scope level with the old IP address of the WINS server, it is overwriting the new one configured at the server level. DHCP options configured at the scope level override those configured at the server level. Therefore, answers A and B are incorrect. Answer C is incorrect because configuring this option defines how the client will resolve NetBIOS names.

Question 14

Answer B is correct. By assigning the Server (Request Security) policy, the server will attempt secure communications with clients. If the client is non-IPSec aware, they will still be able to authenticate. Answer A is incorrect because the server will respond only to client requests for secure communications. Answer C is incorrect because the server will require secure communications and not allow sessions for non-IPSec aware clients. Answer D is incorrect because there is no such default policy.

Question 15

Answer D is correct. Using the Clear Cache option from the Action menu within the DNS management console allows you to delete the contents of the cache file. Although uninstalling the service would clear the contents of the cache, it's not the easiest way to perform the task; therefore, answer A is incorrect. Answer C is incorrect because there is no Clear Cache option available from the server's property window.

Question 16

Answers B and C are correct. NAT supports multiple public IP addresses. The range of IP addresses that can be assigned to internal clients through the DHCP Allocator is configurable. Therefore, answer A is incorrect. Answer D is incorrect because public IP addresses and ports can be mapped to internal computers, making services available to Internet users.

Question 17

Answer B is correct. To ensure that the IP addresses of the UNIX servers are not leased to any DHCP clients, you must exclude the three IP addresses from the scope. Answer A is incorrect because client reservations are configured for those DHCP clients who need to lease the same IP address. Answer C is incorrect because placing the UNIX servers on a different subnet will have no impact on the IP addresses leased out by the DHCP server. Answer D is incorrect because superscopes are created to support multinetted environments.

Question 18

Answer C is correct. To give a user the capability to view database entries, add the user account to the WINS Users group. Answers A and B are incorrect. Although adding a user account to either of these groups would give the user the capability to view database entries, it would also allow the user to make configuration changes. Answer D is incorrect because there is no such group called WINS Administrators.

Question 19

Answer D is correct. Because all the remote access users are running Windows 2000 Professional, the authentication protocol to use is MS-CHAP version 2. Therefore, answers B and C are incorrect. Answer A is incorrect because PAP sends credentials in cleartext and should only be used for non-Windows clients.

Question 20

Answer B is correct. Because ICS is the simplest to configure, it would be the best choice for the scenario. Answer A is incorrect because this solution would result in an increase in cost. Answer C is incorrect because RIP does not enable a single connection to be shared. Answer D is incorrect because NAT requires more configuration.

Question 21

Answer B is correct. The split horizon feature ensures that any routes learned from a network are not sent as RIP announcements on that network. Answer A is incorrect because triggered updates ensure that any changes made to the routing table trigger immediate updates. Answer C is incorrect because the periodic update announcement specifies the number of seconds between RIP announcements. Answer D is incorrect because clean-up updates enables a router to send an announcement when it is stopping in order to notify other routers that the routes it was servicing are no longer available.

Question 22

Answer D is correct. Once a policy has been created and configured, the next step is to assign it to the group policy or the local computer by right-clicking the policy and choosing the Assign option. Answer A is incorrect because this command is used to refresh machine policy settings. Answer B is incorrect because restarting the server does not force an IPSec policy to be applied. Answer C is incorrect because policies are assigned, not enabled.

Question 23

Answer A is correct. Windows NT 4.0 DNS servers do not support dynamic updates regardless of the service pack installed. The DNS servers need to be upgraded to Windows 2000 DNS. Therefore, answers B, C, and D are incorrect.

Question 24

Answer D is correct. To view the certificates that have been issued by a CA, open the Certificate Authority snap-in and click the Issued Certificates container. Answers A, B, and C are incorrect because issued certificates cannot be viewed within these snap-ins.

Question 25

Answer A is correct. Because the DHCP server was not a member of the `DNSUpdateproxy` group, it owns the resource records in the DNS database, causing the updates to fail. Therefore, answers C and D are incorrect. Answer B is incorrect because Windows 2000 Professional clients are configured by default to perform dynamic updates.

Question 26

Answer B is correct. To verify the database entries for consistency, use the Verify Database Consistency option. Answers A and D are incorrect because performing these actions will not verify the integrity of existing database entries. Answer C is incorrect because there is no such option.

Question 27

Answers A, B, and C are correct. Windows 2000 DNS, BIND 4.9.6, and BIND 8.1.3 all support SRV records. (SRV records are used to map the name of a specific service to the IP address of the server offering this service.) Answer D is incorrect because Windows NT 4.0 DNS supports SRV records only if service pack 4 or later is installed.

Question 28

Answers B and D are correct. The two tunneling protocols supported by Windows 2000 are the point-to-point tunneling protocol (PPTP) and the Layer 2 tunneling protocol (L2TP). PPP and SLIP are used to establish dial-up connections. Therefore, answers A and C are incorrect.

Question 29

Answers C and D are correct. When configuring the password options for the user account, enable the Password Never Expires option and disable the User Must Change Password at Next Logon Option. Therefore, answers A and B are incorrect.

Question 30

Answer B is correct. The CRL can be manually published by right-clicking the Revoked Certificates container within the Certificate Authority snap-in and choosing the Publish option. Answer A is incorrect because there is no such option. Answers C and D are incorrect because there is no CRL container within the Certificate Authorities snap-in.

Question 31

Answer C is correct. Because there is only a single NetWare server on the network, the frame type can be left to autodetect. Answers A and B are incorrect because the frame type does not need to be manually configured if there is only a single NetWare server on the network. Answer D is incorrect because there is no such option as autoselect.

Question 32

Answer B is correct. ICS includes the DHCP Allocator service but can only assign clients IP addresses from the range of `192.168.0.1` to `192.168.0.254`. Answer A is incorrect because ICS can be enabled on Windows 2000 Professional, Windows 98, and Windows Me. Answer C is incorrect because no additional software is required on the client. Answer D is incorrect because ICS is enabled through the properties window of the connection.

Question 33

Answer B is correct. A Mail Exchanger (MX) record is used to identify mail servers. Answer A is incorrect because A records are used to map hostnames to IP addresses. Answer C is incorrect because PTR records map IP addresses to their associated hostnames. Answer D is incorrect because CNAME records are used to assign an alias to a host already referenced in another record.

Question 34

Answer B is correct. To use the Windows Groups condition, the groups must first be created within Active Directory Users and Computers. Two policies should be created and configured with the appropriate settings. Use the Windows Groups condition to specify the group of users to which the policy should be applied. Therefore, answers A, C, and D are incorrect.

Question 35

Answer C is correct. Implementing OSPF will not result in a large amount of broadcast traffic from routing table updates and changes will be propagated immediately. Answer A is incorrect because static routing would require manual changes to be made on every router. Answer B is incorrect because ICMP is not a routing protocol. Answer D is incorrect because RIPv1 only supports broadcasts for propagating routing table updates.

Question 36

Answer B is correct. The default URL that can be used for Web-based enrollment is `http://<servername>/CertSrv/default.asp`. Therefore, answers A, C, and D are incorrect.

Question 37

Answer C is correct. When configuring DHCP options at different levels, they are applied in the following order: Server, Scope, Class, and Client. Therefore, answers A, B, and D are incorrect.

Question 38

Answer A is correct. Clients that are configured for M-node perform a local broadcast, and then attempt to resolve the name using a NetBIOS name server. Therefore, answers B, C, and D are incorrect.

Question 39

Answer D is correct. If you have been assigned multiple public IP addresses, they must be added to the public interface. This can be done using the Address Pool tab from the public interface's properties window within the RRAS console. Therefore, answers A, B, and C are incorrect.

Question 40

Answer B is correct. The `ping` command can be used to verify TCP/IP connectivity between two IP hosts. Answer A is incorrect because `ipconfig` is used to view IP parameters configured on a computer. Answer C is incorrect because ARP is a protocol used to map IP addresses to MAC addresses. Answer D is incorrect because ICMP is a protocol used by the `ping` command to test for connectivity.

Question 41

Answer C is correct. To clear the contents of the client resolver cache, use the `ipconfig` command with the `flushdns` parameter. Answers A and D are incorrect because there are no such parameters available with the `ipconfig` command. Answer B is incorrect because this displays the current TCP/IP parameters configured on the client.

Question 42

Answer B is correct. The Renew Interval determines how long a client can continue to use a NetBIOS name before it must be registered. Therefore, answers A, C, and D are incorrect.

Question 43

Answer B is correct. Before a DHCP server can lease IP addresses to clients, the scope must be activated within the DHCP management console. Answer A is incorrect because Windows 2000 Professional clients are DHCP-enabled by default. Answer C is incorrect because DHCP servers are not activated. Answer D is incorrect because the DHCP server service can be installed on a member server, domain controller, or standalone server.

Question 44

Answer D is correct. Certificates can only be revoked through the Certificate Authority snap-in. To do so, right-click the certificate within the Issued Certificates container and choose the Revoke Certificate option. Answers A and B are incorrect because certificates cannot be revoked through either snap-in. Answer C is incorrect. There is no such administrative tool called Certificate Manager. All management tasks are performed through the Certificate Authority snap-in.

Question 45

Answer C is correct. To increase the number of available PPTP ports, open the properties window from within the Routing and Remote Access management console. Select PPTP and click Configure. Therefore, answers A, B, and D are incorrect.

Question 46

Answer A is correct. Because NAT supports a configurable range of IP addresses to assign to internal clients, this would be the correct choice. Therefore, answer C is incorrect. Answer B is incorrect because RIP is a routing protocol. Answer D is incorrect because there is no such solution called CIS.

Question 47

Answer C is correct. If you do not want the server to require secure communications but still be able to respond to any client requests to use secure communications, select the Client (Respond only) policy. Therefore, answers A and B are incorrect. Answer D is incorrect because there is no such default policy.

Question 48

Answer D is correct. RIPv2 is a routing protocol that can be used with nonpersistent connections and supports password authentication between routers. Answer A is incorrect because implementing static routes means the routing tables must be manually updated. Answer B is incorrect because ICMP is not a routing protocol. Answer C is incorrect because OSPF is not supported by nonpersistent demand-dial connections.

Question 49

Answer C is correct. By configuring each DHCP server with a range of IP addresses from the remote subnet you can provide some level of fault tolerance. Each server should be configured with 80% of the IP addresses for their local subnet and 20% of the IP addresses for the remote subnet to avoid IP address conflicts. Answers A and B are incorrect because DHCP servers do not replicate nor share scope information. Answer D is incorrect because clients are not configured with the IP address of DHCP servers.

Question 50

Answer D is correct. To configure secure updates for a zone, the zone type must be Active Directory integrated. If the zone is a standard primary, the Only Secure Updates option is not available. Therefore, answers A, B, and C are incorrect.

Question 51

Answer A is correct. When configuring a two-way demand-dial connection, the user account names on the answering routers must be identical to the demand-dial interface names on the calling routers. Therefore, answers B, C, and D are incorrect.

Question 52

Answers B and C are correct. By configuring the day and time restrictions, users can dial in during the weekdays. Because the RRAS server is configured with a range of IP addresses, all clients will lease an IP address when they establish a connection. Answer A is incorrect because you must configure the Windows Groups condition to limit access to a specific group of users. Answer D is incorrect. The RRAS server must be configured to use DHCP and the relay agent must be configured on the RRAS for clients to be assigned optional parameters.

Question 53

Answer C is correct. The permissions for a certificate template can be edited through the Active Directory Sites and Services snap-in. This makes answers A, B, and D incorrect.

Question 54

Answer B is correct. The subnet mask is used to determine whether a destination host is on the local subnet or a remote subnet. Answer A is incorrect because the IP address uniquely identifies a host on a given subnet. Answer C is incorrect because the default gateway is used to access other subnets. Answer D is incorrect because TCP/IP filters are used to control the type of IP traffic allowed to enter a computer or network.

Question 55

Answers A, C, and D are correct. By creating and activating a scope, all clients can lease an IP address. Configuring the DHCP server to update records for all clients, including those that do not support dynamic updates, ensures that the DHCP server performs all updates. Configuring the `003` Router option configures the clients with the IP address of the default gateway. Answer B is incorrect because the static IP addresses assigned to the domain controllers are not excluded from the range of IP addresses configured in the scope.

Question 56

Answer A is correct. Clients configured for P-node resolve NetBIOS names using a NetBIOS name server only. Answer B is incorrect because this indicates B-node. Answer C is incorrect because this indicates H-node. Answer D is incorrect because this indicates M-node.

Question 57

Answer C is correct. The IP address of `192.168.0.1` is a class C address. Answer A is incorrect because a class A address falls in the range of 1–126. Answer B is incorrect because a class B address falls in the range of 128–191. Answer D is incorrect because a class D address falls in the range of 224–247.

Question 58

Answer D is correct. The `/p` parameter is used to add a persistent route to the routing table. This means the route will not be removed from the routing table when the router is restarted. Therefore, answers A, C, and D are incorrect.

Question 59

Answers A, B, C, and D are correct. The proposed configuration of the RRAS server meets all the necessary requirements.

Question 60

Answer D is correct. The `#DOM:`*`domain_name`* indicates that the record is for a domain controller on the network. Answer A is incorrect because the `#Pre` option is used to preload entries into the local cache. Answer B is incorrect because the `#MH` option is used to identify a multihomed computer. Answer C is incorrect because the `#Include` option specifies an `LMHOSTS` file other than the local one that clients should use.

Additional Resources

There's a lot of information available about the topics covered in exam 70-216 and Microsoft certifications. This appendix distills some of the best resources we've found on those topics.

Web Resources

- Microsoft's Training and Certification home: http://www.microsoft.com/traincert/default.asp
- Windows 2000 Server home from Microsoft: http://www.microsoft.com/windows2000/server/default.asp
- Windows 2000 Resource Kits online at http://www.microsoft.com/windows2000/techinfo/reskit/en-us/default.asp
- Search TechNet on the Web at http://www.microsoft.com/technet
- Windows 2000 Deployment Guide at http://www.microsoft.com/windows2000/techinfo/reskit/dpg/default.asp
- Cramsession's 70-216 Study Guide at http://studyguides.cramsession.com/cramsession/microsoft/win2knet_infra/
- MCSE Guide's 70-216 study guide at http://www.mcseguide.com/2000/2000netinf.htm
- Certguide.com at http://www.certguide.com/2000/70216.asp
- Cram4Exams free exam at http://www.cram4exams.com/exams/w2kinfbig2.shtml
- John Savill's Frequently Asked Questions on Windows 2000 Server at http://www.windows2000faq.com/
- A portal of MCSE information at http://www.hardcoremcse.com/
- CertCities MCSE certification community at http://certcities.com/certs/microsoft/
- TechTarget's Windows 2000 repository at http://searchwin2000.techtarget.com/
- Practice Exams and information on certification at http://www.certtutor.net/
- Paul Thurrott's SuperSite for Windows at http://www.winsupersite.com/

- Active Network's PC and Windows resource at www.activewin.com
- Webopedia's online dictionary and search engine for computer and Internet technologies at http://www.pcwebopedia.com/

Magazine Resources

- *Microsoft Certified Professional Magazine* is directly targeted at those certified by Microsoft: http://www.mcpmag.com
- *Certification Magazine* specializes in information for IT certified individuals: http://www.certmag.com
- *Windows & .NET Magazine* focuses specifically on Microsoft technologies: http://www.winnetmag.com
- *Online Learning* is a resource for professional training and development: http://onlinelearningmag.com
- *Computer* magazine is developed by the IEEE (Institute of Electrical and Electronics Engineers): http://www.computer.org/computer/
- *PC Magazine* is a staple for technology enthusiasts: http://www.pcmag.com

Book Resources

- *Microsoft Windows 2000 Server Resource Kit.* Microsoft Press, January, 2000. ISBN: 1-57231-805-8. This book and CD set include invaluable detailed documentation on Windows 2000. In addition, the CD includes many useful utilities.
- Boswell, William. *Inside Windows 2000 Server.* New Riders, December, 1999. ISBN: 1-56205-929-7. This is an excellent guide for installation and general administration.
- Minasi, Mark, et al. *Mastering Windows 2000 Server*, fourth edition. Sybex, February, 2000. ISBN: 0-78214-043-2. This book is written by *NT Magazine* columnist Mark Minasi and is full of excellent information.

- Russell, Charlie, et al. *Microsoft Windows 2000 Server Administrator's Companion, Second Edition*. Microsoft Press, August, 2002. ISBN: 0-73561-785-6. This book details many of the complex features and capabilities of Windows 2000 Server. It's a great handbook for any network administrator.
- Shilmover, Barry and Stu Sjouwerman. *Windows 2000 Power Toolkit*. New Riders, May, 2001. ISBN: 0-7357-1061-9. This book is a valuable resource for reference material on Windows security and policies.
- Siyan, Karajit. *Windows 2000 Server Professional Reference*. New Riders, January, 2000. ISBN: 0-7357-0952-1. The book has more than 1,800 pages of detailed information on using Windows 2000 Server.
- Stanek, William R. *Windows 2000 Administrator's Pocket Consultant*. Microsoft Press, January, 2000. ISBN: 0-73560-831-8. This book is a detailed hands-on guide for professional Windows 2000 administrators.
- Tittel, Ed, et al. *Windows 2000 Server for Dummies*. Wiley & Sons, April, 2000. ISBN: 0-76450-341-3. This is an excellent beginners resource for Windows 2000 Server.

What's on the CD-ROM

This appendix is a brief rundown of what you'll find on the CD-ROM that comes with this book. For a more detailed description of the *PrepLogic Practice Tests, Preview Edition* exam simulation software, see Appendix D, "Using *PrepLogic, Preview Edition* Software." In addition to the *PrepLogic Practice Tests, Preview Edition*, the CD-ROM includes the electronic version of the book in Portable Document Format (PDF), several utility and application programs, and a complete listing of test objectives and where they are covered in the book. Finally, a pointer list to online pointers and references are added to this CD. You will need a computer with Internet access and a relatively recent browser installed to use this feature.

PrepLogic Practice Tests, Preview Edition

PrepLogic is a leading provider of certification training tools. Trusted by certification students worldwide, we believe PrepLogic is the best practice exam software available. In addition to providing a means of evaluating your knowledge of the Exam Cram material, *PrepLogic Practice Tests, Preview Edition* features several innovations that help you to improve your mastery of the subject matter.

For example, the practice tests allow you to check your score by exam area or domain to determine which topics you need to study more. Another feature allows you to obtain immediate feedback on your responses in the form of explanations for the correct and incorrect answers.

PrepLogic Practice Tests, Preview Edition exhibits most of the full functionality of the *Premium Edition* but offers only a fraction of the total questions. To get the complete set of practice questions and exam functionality, visit `PrepLogic.com` and order the *Premium Edition* for this and other challenging exam titles.

Again, for a more detailed description of the *PrepLogic Practice Tests, Preview Edition* features, see Appendix D.

Exclusive Electronic Version of Text

The CD-ROM also contains the electronic version of this book in Portable Document Format (PDF). The electronic version comes complete with all figures as they appear in the book. You will find that the search capabilities of the reader comes in handy for study and review purposes.

Easy Access to Online Pointers and References

The Suggested Reading section at the end of each chapter in this Exam Cram contains numerous pointers to Web sites, newsgroups, mailing lists, and other online resources. To make this material as easy to use as possible, we include all this information in an HTML document entitled "Online Pointers" on the CD. Open this document in your favorite Web browser to find links you can follow through any Internet connection to access these resources directly.

Using the *PrepLogic Practice Tests, Preview Edition* Software

This Exam Cram includes a special version of PrepLogic Practice Tests—a revolutionary test engine designed to give you the best in certification exam preparation. PrepLogic offers sample and practice exams for many of today's most in-demand and challenging technical certifications. This special *Preview Edition* is included with this book as a tool to use in assessing your knowledge of the Exam Cram material, while also providing you with the experience of taking an electronic exam.

This appendix describes in detail what *PrepLogic Practice Tests, Preview Edition* is, how it works, and what it can do to help you prepare for the exam. Note that although the *Preview Edition* includes all the test simulation functions of the complete, retail version, it contains only a single practice test. The *Premium Edition*, available at `PrepLogic.com`, contains the complete set of challenging practice exams designed to optimize your learning experience.

Exam Simulation

One of the main functions of *PrepLogic Practice Tests, Preview Edition* is exam simulation. To prepare you to take the actual vendor certification exam, PrepLogic is designed to offer the most effective exam simulation available.

Question Quality

The questions provided in the *PrepLogic Practice Tests, Preview Edition* are written to the highest standards of technical accuracy. The questions tap the content of the Exam Cram chapters and help you to review and assess your knowledge before you take the actual exam.

Interface Design

The *PrepLogic Practice Tests, Preview Edition* exam simulation interface provides you with the experience of taking an electronic exam. This enables you to effectively prepare yourself for taking the actual exam by making the test experience a familiar one. Using this test simulation can help to eliminate the sense of surprise or anxiety you might experience in the testing center because you will already be acquainted with computerized testing.

Effective Learning Environment

The *PrepLogic Practice Tests, Preview Edition* interface provides a learning environment that not only tests you through the computer, but also teaches the material you need to know to pass the certification exam. Each question comes with a detailed explanation of the correct answer and often provides reasons the other options are incorrect. This information helps to reinforce the knowledge you already have and also provides practical information you can use on the job.

Software Requirements

PrepLogic Practice Tests requires a computer with the following:

- Microsoft Windows 98, Windows Me, Windows NT 4.0, Windows 2000, or Windows XP
- A 166MHz or faster processor is recommended
- A minimum of 32MB of RAM
- As with any Windows application, the more memory, the better your performance
- 10MB of hard drive space

Installing *PrepLogic Practice Tests, Preview Edition*

Install *PrepLogic Practice Tests, Preview Edition* by running the setup program on the *PrepLogic Practice Tests, Preview Edition* CD. Follow these instructions to install the software on your computer:

1. Insert the CD into your CD-ROM drive. The Autorun feature of Windows should launch the software. If you have Autorun disabled, click the Start button and select Run. Go to the root directory of the CD and select setup.exe. Click Open, and then click OK.
2. The Installation Wizard copies the *PrepLogic Practice Tests, Preview Edition* files to your hard drive; adds *PrepLogic Practice Tests, Preview Edition* to your Desktop and Program menu; and installs test engine components to the appropriate system folders.

Removing *PrepLogic Practice Tests, Preview Edition* from Your Computer

If you elect to remove the *PrepLogic Practice Tests,, Preview Edition* product from your computer, an uninstall process has been included to ensure that it is removed from your system safely and completely. Follow these instructions to remove PrepLogic Practice Tests, Preview Edition from your computer:

1. Select Start, Settings, Control Panel.
2. Double-click the Add/Remove Programs icon.
3. You are presented with a list of software currently installed on your computer. Select the appropriate *PrepLogic Practice Tests, Preview Edition* title you wish to remove. Click the Add/Remove button. The software is then removed from you computer.

Using *PrepLogic Practice Tests, Preview Edition*

PrepLogic is designed to be user friendly and intuitive. Because the software has a smooth learning curve, your time is maximized, as you will start practicing almost immediately. *PrepLogic Practice Tests, Preview Edition* has two major modes of study: Practice Test and Flash Review.

Using Practice Test mode, you can develop your test-taking abilities, as well as your knowledge through the use of the Show Answer option. While you are taking the test, you can reveal the answers along with a detailed explanation of why the given answers are right or wrong. This gives you the ability to better understand the material presented.

Flash Review is designed to reinforce exam topics rather than quiz you. In this mode, you will be shown a series of questions, but no answer choices. Instead, you will be given a button that reveals the correct answer to the question and a full explanation for that answer.

Starting a Practice Test Mode Session

Practice Test mode enables you to control the exam experience in ways that actual certification exams do not allow:

- **Enable Show Answer Button**—Activates the Show Answer button, allowing you to view the correct answer(s) and a full explanation for each question during the exam. When not enabled, you must wait until after your exam has been graded to view the correct answer(s) and explanation(s).
- **Enable Item Review Button**—Activates the Item Review button, allowing you to view your answer choices, marked questions, and facilitating navigation between questions.
- **Randomize Choices**—Randomize answer choices from one exam session to the next; makes memorizing question choices more difficult, therefore keeping questions fresh and challenging longer.

To begin studying in Practice Test mode, click the Practice Test radio button from the main exam customization screen. This will enable the options detailed above.

To your left, you are presented with the options of selecting the pre-configured Practice Test or creating your own Custom Test. The pre-configured test has a fixed time limit and number of questions. Custom Tests allow you to configure the time limit and the number of questions in your exam.

The *Preview Edition* included with this book includes a single pre-configured Practice Test. Get the compete set of challenging PrepLogic Practice Tests at `PrepLogic.com` and make certain you're ready for the big exam.

Click the Begin Exam button to begin your exam.

Starting a Flash Review Mode Session

Flash Review mode provides you with an easy way to reinforce topics covered in the practice questions. To begin studying in Flash Review mode, click the Flash Review radio button from the main exam customization screen. Select either the pre-configured Practice Test or create your own Custom Test.

Click the Best Exam button to begin your Flash Review of the exam questions.

Standard *PrepLogic Practice Tests, Preview Edition* Options

The following list describes the function of each of the buttons you see. Depending on the options, some of the buttons will be grayed out and inaccessible or missing completely. Buttons that are accessible are active. The buttons are as follows:

- **Exhibit**—This button is visible if an exhibit is provided to support the question. An exhibit is an image that provides supplemental information necessary to answer the question.
- **Item Review**—This button leaves the question window and opens the Item Review screen. From this screen you will see all questions, your answers, and your marked items. You will also see correct answers listed here when appropriate.
- **Show Answer**—This option displays the correct answer with an explanation of why it is correct. If you select this option, the current question is not scored.
- **Mark Item**—Check this box to tag a question you need to review further. You can view and navigate your Marked Items by clicking the Item Review button (if enabled). When grading your exam, you will be notified if you have marked items remaining.
- **Previous Item**—This option allows you to view the previous question.
- **Next Item**—This option allows you to view the next question.
- **Grade Exam**—When you have completed your exam, click this button to end your exam and view your detailed score report. If you have unanswered or marked items remaining you will be asked if you would like to continue taking your exam or view your exam report.

Time Remaining

If the test is timed, the time remaining is displayed on the upper right corner of the application screen. It counts down the minutes and seconds remaining to complete the test. If you run out of time, you will be asked if you want to continue taking the test or if you want to end your exam.

Your Examination Score Report

The Examination Score Report screen appears when the Practice Test mode ends—as the result of time expiration, completion of all questions, or your decision to terminate early.

This screen provides you with a graphical display of your test score with a breakdown of scores by topic domain. The graphical display at the top of the screen compares your overall score with the PrepLogic Exam Competency Score.

The PrepLogic Exam Competency Score reflects the level of subject competency required to pass this vendor's exam. While this score does not directly translate to a passing score, consistently matching or exceeding this score does suggest you possess the knowledge to pass the actual vendor exam.

Review Your Exam

From Your Score Report screen, you can review the exam that you just completed by clicking on the View Items button. Navigate through the items viewing the questions, your answers, the correct answers, and the explanations for those answers. You can return to your score report by clicking the View Items button.

Get More Exams

Each *PrepLogic Practice Tests, Preview Edition* that accompanies your Exam Cram contains a single PrepLogic Practice Test. Certification students worldwide trust PrepLogic Practice Tests to help them pass their IT certification exams the first time. Purchase the *Premium Edition* of PrepLogic Practice Tests and get the entire set of all new challenging Practice Tests for this exam. PrepLogic Practice Tests—Because You Want to Pass the First Time.

Contacting PrepLogic

If you would like to contact PrepLogic for any reason, including information about our extensive line of certification practice tests, we invite you to do so. Please contact us online at `http://www.preplogic.com`.

Customer Service

If you have a damaged product and need a replacement or refund, please call the following phone number:

800-858-7674

Product Suggestions and Comments

We value your input! Please email your suggestions and comments to the following address:

`feedback@preplogic.com`

License Agreement

YOU MUST AGREE TO THE TERMS AND CONDITIONS OUTLINED IN THE END USER LICENSE AGREEMENT ("EULA") PRESENTED TO YOU DURING THE INSTALLATION PROCESS. IF YOU DO NOT AGREE TO THESE TERMS DO NOT INSTALL THE SOFTWARE.

Glossary

area border router
A router attached to multiple areas that maintains individual link state databases for each area.

authentication
The process of establishing the identity and/or validity of a sender or message. That is, the determination of whether an entity is who or what it claims to be.

caching-only server
A server that's not responsible for maintaining DNS zone information. It simply resolves name requests to IP addresses on behalf of DNS clients and caches the results.

certificate authority (CA)
A trusted source that issues digital certificates to requestors. A third-party CA or Windows 2000 Certificate Services can be used.

Certificate Revocation List (CRL)
A document published by a Certificate Authority that lists issued certificates that are no longer valid. By default, the CA publishes the CRL on a weekly basis.

delegation
In Windows 2000, this is the ability of an administrator to distribute certain administrative tasks to other individuals or groups. In terms of DNS, delegation involves giving a portion of a domain namespace to another server. That server will then be responsible for resolving name resolution requests.

demand-dial routing
A form of routing that enables on-demand connections over PPP links. On-demand connections can be created over dial-up, persistent, or non-persistent media.

DHCP Allocator
A scaled-down version of DHCP included with NAT (Network Address Translation) and ICS (Internet Connection Sharing). It assigns IP addresses to clients on the local area network in the range of `192.168.0.1–192.168.0.254`. This range is configurable with NAT but not with ICS.

digital certificate
A digital document from a trusted entity (a certificate authority) that binds a public key to a specific identity that has the corresponding private key. Digital certificates are used to authenticate and secure information exchange across networks. They are digitally signed by the certification authority that issued them and can be issued for a user, a computer, or a service.

Domain Name System (DNS)
A name-resolution system used to translate domain names into IP addresses. DNS is included as a service with Windows 2000.

Dynamic Host Configuration Protocol (DHCP)
A protocol used to dynamically assign IP addresses to devices on a network. It can also be used to provide DHCP clients with optional parameters such as the IP address of the default gateway. DHCP in Windows 2000 can also be integrated with DNS.

dynamic routing
The automatic update of routing tables through the use of routing protocols such as RIP (Routing Information Protocol) or OSPF (Open Shortest Path First).

dynamic update (DNS)
Enables a DNS client to automatically register and update its own resource records with a DNS server. It can be used in conjunction with DHCP so clients can update their resource records when IP addresses change.

Encrypting File System (EFS)
Encrypts data that is stored on a Windows 2000/XP hard disk. EFS is public key–based. Contents of an encrypted file cannot be viewed without the corresponding private key.

encryption
The conversion of data into a format that is not readable by an unauthorized individual.

Enterprise Certificate Authority
A certificate authority that is used to assign digital certificates to users within a Windows 2000 domain. An enterprise CA requires Active Directory and DNS. An enterprise root CA is at the top of the hierarchy. A subordinate CA is configured as a child CA to a parent CA. A parent CA can be a root CA or an intermediate (non-root) CA.

frame type

A frame is a packet of information transmitted from one system to another; the type of frame can vary depending on the system in use. To communicate with a NetWare server, for example, the computer running Windows 2000 must be using the same frame type as the computer running NetWare.

Internet Authentication Service (IAS)

A Windows 2000 service that centralizes the administration of multiple remote access servers. IAS provides a centralized means for authentication and storage of auditing and accounting information for RAS clients. This is Microsoft's implementation of a RADIUS server.

Internet Connection Sharing (ICS)

Enables a computer to share a single Internet connection with other computers on the local area network. ICS was introduced in Windows 98 and is included with Windows 2000.

ipconfig

A command that displays the TCP/IP network configuration for a host where the command is run. When used without parameters, it displays the IP address, subnet mask, and default gateway for a host.

IPSec (Internet Protocol Security)

A set of encryption protocols used to support the secure exchange of data at the IP layer. In Transport mode, only the data portion or payload is encrypted. In Tunnel mode, both the header and the payload are encrypted.

lease duration (DHCP)

Determines the amount of time a client can use an IP address assigned from a DHCP server before the address must be renewed.

LMHOSTS

A text file that can be used to resolve NetBIOS names to IP addresses. The file exists in the Windows directory and contains NetBIOS to IP address mappings.

multicast scopes

A range of Internet Protocol (IP) addresses (from `239.0.0.0` to `239.254.255.255`). These are multicast addresses that can be prevented from propagating in either direction (sending or receiving).

Multilink

Multilink is the aggregation of multiple connections to create one connection with combined bandwidth. It can be used with demand-dial connections to automatically add and drop physical links as bandwidth requirements change.

name resolution

This is the resolution of a domain name or a NetBIOS name to an IP address. Names entered by users must be resolved to IP addresses before hosts can communicate. Name resolution can be provided through text files or name servers such as WINS and DNS.

NAT editor

A component of a network address translator that performs additional translation and payload adjustment beyond the IP, TCP, and UDP headers so that information that might not otherwise be translatable can be passed through the translation process. NAT editors were developed by OEMs for different IP protocols that obtain the necessary information for network address translation.

NetBIOS (Network Basic Input/Output System)

An application programming interface (API) used in Windows versions prior to Windows 2000 that provided network naming services for computers, devices, services, and other network resources. With the introduction of Active Directory, NetBIOS naming was replaced with the Domain Name System (DNS).

Network Address Translation (NAT)

Provides a means of connecting multiple computers to the Internet using a single public IP address.

Network Monitor

A tool used to monitor and capture network traffic, which is useful for troubleshooting network problems. It is included with Windows 2000.

NWLink

The Microsoft implementation of the IPX/SPX (Internetwork Packet Exchange/Sequenced Packet Exchange) protocol, which enables a computer to communicate with a NetWare-based computer or another Windows computer running IPX/SPX.

Open Shortest Path First (OSPF)

A routing protocol that uses the shortest path first or link state routing algorithm to calculate the shortest path to each host. It shares that calculated portion of the routing table with other OSPF routers.

packet filter

Limits the type of traffic allowed to pass through a router or Internet gateway.

persistent connections

A network connection that is always active. WINS servers use persistent connections to replicate the WINS database between servers.

ping

A command used to test network connectivity between two TCP/IP hosts. The `ping` command will display whether the destination host is reachable and how long it took to receive a reply.

pull partner
A WINS server that fetches database changes from its replication partners to itself.

push partner
A WINS server that sends update notification messages to its replication partners when changes to its database occur.

Remote Access Dial-In User Service (RADIUS)
An industry standard for providing authorization, authentication, and accounting services for dial-up and remote access services.

Remote Access Service (RAS)
A service that enables remote clients to dial in to a Windows 2000 server and access network resources as though they were physically attached to the network, albeit slower.

root name server
A DNS server that is authoritative for the root of the namespace.

Routing Information Protocol (RIP)
A protocol that allows routers to automatically exchange routing information. Because RIP routers periodically exchange entire routing tables, it is designed for use with small to medium sized networks.

scope
Determines the pool of IP addresses from which a DHCP server can assign IP addresses. Every DHCP server must be configured with at least one scope.

Standalone Certificate Authority
Standalone CAs issue digital certificates to requestors, but don't require an Active Directory domain to operate. A standalone root CA or a standalone subordinate CA can be configured.

static routing
Network routing that uses manually updated routing tables. Routing tables can be updated statically using the `route` command, which is beneficial because there is no traffic generated between routers. The disadvantage of static routing is that the routing tables must be manually updated each time there is a change to the network topology.

subnet mask
The portion of an IP address that indicates the network ID.

superscopes
Enables a DHCP server to assign IP addresses from more than one scope to clients on a single physical network (subnet).

TCP/IP (Transmission Control Protocol/Internet Protocol)
An industry standard suite of protocols that enables two hosts to establish a connection and exchange data.

tombstoning

A process in which records in a WINS database are marked as being extinct. This means they are released by the WINS server for immediate use.

virtual private network (VPN)

A way of using a public infrastructure, such as the Internet, to securely connect to remote offices. The privacy of data transmissions is maintained through a variety of security procedures and tunneling protocols. VPNs can provide the same capabilities as a dedicated leased line while reducing costs.

WINS proxy

A computer that allows non-WINS clients to participate in a WINS environment by listening for name request broadcasts and forwarding them to a WINS server.

WINS replication

The process of duplicating the WINS database on all WINS servers with the most up-to-date naming information.

zones

DNS database files that contain resource records for a single domain or a set of domains. There are two types of zones in DNS: forward lookup zones for mapping names to IP addresses and reverse lookup zones for mapping IP addresses to domain names.

Index

B

C

D

E

F

G

H

I-J

K-L

M

How can we make this index more useful? Email us at indexes@quepublishing.com

N

O

P

How can we make this index more useful? Email us at indexes@quepublishing.com

Q-R

How can we make this index more useful? Email us at indexes@quepublishing.com

S

U

Y-Z